Mixed M
and th

Thanks for
following!

Mixed Martial Arts and the Law

Disputes, Suits and Legal Issues

JASON J. CRUZ

McFarland & Company, Inc., Publishers
Jefferson, North Carolina

ISBN (print) 978-1-4766-7930-3 ∞
ISBN (ebook) 978-1-4766-3728-0

LIBRARY OF CONGRESS CATALOGUING DATA ARE AVAILABLE

BRITISH LIBRARY CATALOGUING DATA ARE AVAILABLE

Front cover images © 2020 Shutterstock

Printed in the United States of America

*McFarland & Company, Inc., Publishers
Box 611, Jefferson, North Carolina 28640
www.mcfarlandpub.com*

Table of Contents

Preface

In October 2010, Dana White, the modern-day architect of the UFC, and arguably mixed martial arts, addressed the Oxford Union Society about his upstart company. The Oxford Union has a tradition of hosting some of the world's most prominent figures, including U.S. Presidents, British Prime Ministers and Mother Theresa. And, here was a street-smart Boston native selling the gathered audience of well-educated people on this new sport of people fighting in a cage. "Fighting is in our DNA," he told the gathered audience about his sport. White has used this talking point when selling combat sports from the beginning. Deconstructing the message, White tells us that despite the common perception that humans avoid conflict, it is instinctive in each one of us. It needs no translation and knows no culture, race or ethnicity. And, whether we know it or not, we are drawn to fighting.

Perhaps White's selling point is true. As early as five years old I recall sneaking into the living room after my bedtime to see what my father was watching. It was boxing. Ray "Boom Boom" Mancini, Alexis Arguello, Thomas "the Hitman" Hearns and "Sugar" Ray Leonard are just a few of the names I recall watching with my dad, who begrudgingly allowed me to stay up with him.

As a child, we were always taught never to fight. And, quite frankly, I think this is a good way to approach life. Resolving issues through physical conflict usually does not provide anyone with a better spot than where they started. Yet, throughout my childhood combat sports were always a certain niche interest for me. Watching two combatants hitting each other in a controlled environment had a certain allure. Although it was uncomfortable to watch a boxer's face begin to spew blood or puff up due to blows to the head, the technical points of defending oneself while inflicting damage presented a constant draw. And, like a fight, it's hard to take your eyes away from it.

Even growing up, I understood what White was conveying. The sport

1

is barbaric and savage but at the same time graceful and beautiful. Those nights past my bedtime were my introduction to combat sports.

Flash forward many decades to a young man living in Orange County, California. In 2002 I came across a documentary, "The Smashing Machine," which featured a mixed martial arts fighter, Mark Kerr. It was a sobering look at the sport and Kerr as he tried to carve out a career fighting in Vale Tudo, the UFC and Pride. The documentary was an amazing look at the world of MMA and the ills of the sport, and it got me interested.

Later that year I went to a sports bar in Costa Mesa, California, and decided to pay a $10 cover charge to watch my first UFC show, Ken Shamrock fighting Tito Ortiz. The draw for me was Shamrock—an MMA fighter who turned to professional wrestling, then returned to being an MMA fighter— stepping in against Ortiz, a bleach-blond Mexican American dubbed "The Huntington Beach Bad Boy." The promotion of the fight was reminiscent of a World Wrestling Entertainment feature. While I didn't understand the rules, I was drawn to the unique skills the athletes possessed. In addition to boxing, wrestling, jiu jitsu and kickboxing were used. In the end, Ortiz earned the victory over Shamrock, and I was sold on this new sport of mixed martial arts.

I have always wanted to be involved in sports and entertainment law but also enjoyed writing. While my day job in law never yielded a steady sports and entertainment law practice, I found writing about sports was cathartic in that I had the chance to remain involved in some form. In 2011, I answered an opening for a job to write for MMA Payout. The website was dedicated to the business side of the sport of mixed martial arts. With just a handful of sports-related clips at the time, I hoped that I'd be able to write about the combat sports world that I became fascinated with as a young boy. Fortunately, the staff at MMA Payout welcomed me. The niche was an interesting dive into the business and legal aspects of sports. From there, I was allowed the freedom to write about legal subjects in mixed martial arts. I took the opportunity and ran with it.

As the sport grew, so did the legal subjects in the industry. Every sport has legal issues but the sport of MMA is unique because of its individuality, business structure and regulation. The characters of the sport also come through in some of the legal filings. Very little has been written about the legal issues in mixed martial arts. Relying on my 20 years of legal experience, court filings and cases, I have written this book as a primer on the legal issues in MMA. Much of the information is evolving, so, while this book attempts to provide the reader with a comprehensive survey of the legal issues of the sport, it is not the last word on the subject.

I want to thank MMA Payout founder Adam Swift for the opportunity to write about the sport of MMA. Swift, also a lawyer, probably thought that a writer with a law degree would be a good fit for the site. I hope it's paid off. I also want to thank Jose Mendoza of the site. His retweets of some of my MMA information has helped me gain followers of my work.

I'd also like to thank my wife, Carol, and my boys, Jacob and Cooper, for their unwavering support. Finally, thank you to my black lab Ricky, who hung out with me at all hours of the night as I read, wrote and researched for the website and for this book.

Introduction

Four Billion Dollars.

This is the approximate amount that WME-IMG paid for the Ultimate Fighting Championships in July 2016. It was the most for a sports league as of that date. Just several years prior, the organization was on the brink of bankruptcy. Instead, the company spearheaded by Frank and Lorenzo Fertitta with long-time friend Dana White as their mouthpiece did well on a property it purchased for $2 million in 1999.

Mixed Martial Arts, or MMA for short, is a full-contact combat sport that is a combination of amateur wrestling, boxing, jiu jitsu and other martial arts disciplines. The sport of MMA can trace its roots back to ancient Greece with a combat sport known as Pankration. The combat sport of vale tudo, which developed in Brazil, was brought to the United States by the famed Gracie family in 1993. The term "Mixed Martial Arts" is thought to have been coined by *Los Angeles Times* columnist Howard Rosenberg. A television reviewer, Rosenberg spent the $14.95 pay-per-view fee to watch UFC 1. Despite the sheer violence that occurred in the Octagon, Rosenberg wrote about the great sportsmanship the fighters displayed towards one another.

The Ultimate Fighting Championships, or UFC for short, was the idea of promoter Rorion Gracie, pay-per-view entrepreneur Bob Meyrowitz and Southern California business executive Art Davie. In its infancy in North America around the time of UFC 1, the sport had few rules and there were questions about how it should be regulated. As told in Davie's book, *Is This Legal?*, the preparation for the event as well as securing the money to invest and finding the fighters for the one-night tournament had its challenges. And while the event was promoted as having no rules, there were some rules (e.g., no eye gouging, no groin shots). The event was the birth of a new sport.

Dubbed "human cockfighting," by Senator John McCain in 1997, the sport has evolved since the days when it was more spectacle than sport. Perceptions of the sport in its infancy drew the ire of those without an understanding of it. Famously, Bernard Hopkins appeared on an episode of the Jim

Rome radio show denouncing the sport. He also has been quoted as comparing the sport of MMA to gay pornography. Ironically, both the late McCain and Hopkins made a 180-degree turn on the sport as each came out in support of MMA.

While McCain and Hopkins warmed to the sport over the years since the first UFC, it took New York until 2015 to pass legislation to legalize professional MMA in the state.

In 2001, Lorenzo and Frank Fertitta purchased the UFC from Semaphore Entertainment. The acquisition was due in part to the Fertittas' old friend, Dana White. The Fertittas' father established the Palace Station casino in Las Vegas, and the brothers worked within the family business. It was White who advised the Fertitta brothers of the purchase opportunity. The Fertittas established Zuffa, LLC and acquired the assets of the UFC for $2 million.

In order to expand the product to build an audience, Zuffa sought to make changes to the old UFC structure. They looked for state regulatory bodies to step in and enforce more rules on a previously unruly sport. Some of the changes included adding weight divisions and outlawing some moves like head butts and kicking a downed opponent for fighter safety. While success was not immediate, Zuffa grew in popularity as more fans began to embrace the sport. Despite the general acceptance of the sport, it still has its adamant detractors. Notably, there was a long-time battle for regulation in the state of New York. We will detail the legal battle later in the book.

Another MMA promotion, Bellator, is run by cable conglomerate Viacom. The promotion does not have the widespread popularity of the UFC, but has experienced legal issues involving its fighters and the organization. It has had contract issues with its fighters who have attempted to break their contract with the company. It also has bumped heads with the UFC when competing for talent.

In most instances, MMA fighters are considered independent contractors by their promotions. This means that they are not afforded some of the perks of an employee of the promotion, which include insurance, reimbursement for expenses, a pension and other benefits. This issue is controversial since most organizations request fighters sign exclusive contracts by which they are not allowed to fight in other organizations while under contract. This inability to work for different promotions at the same time has drawn the consternation of many fighters considering many do not have any input as to their schedule. Several chapters address these issues including Leslie Smith's charging letter to the NLRB, the hearings on the potential for expanding the Muhammad Ali Boxing Reform Act to MMA and the UFC antitrust lawsuit.

MMA lacks a central authority. Similar to boxing, promotions secure talent but sanctioning bodies install and enforce rules and regulations. For

MMA in North America, state athletic commissions or licensing departments are the regulators. Fighters must obtain licenses in each state or province where they fight and must abide by the rules. The UFC has instituted an anti-doping policy in response to a string of failed drug tests. This book will look at how the drug policy and its appeal process have affected the UFC. It will also address the aftermath after a fighter has cleared themselves of wrong-doing after a USADA investigation and sued the supplement distributor and manufacturer.

The landscape of mixed martial arts has grown and with this, the legal issues regarding the sport have increased. Like most stick and ball sports, there are a variety of legal issues from antitrust to contracts to the organization of fighters to the use of performance enhancing drugs and more.

This book will guide you through the emerging legal issues within the sport of MMA.

1

The Fight for New York

Introduction

In the United States, the sport of MMA has slowly gained acceptance. It is regulated by state athletic commissions or a similarly situated regulatory body in 47 states. The states of Alaska and Montana do not have athletic commissions that regulate MMA, although the sport is allowed in the states. The last state to allow the sport of professional mixed martial arts was New York in 2016.

The ban in New York was due to a 1997 law which precluded the sport of professional mixed martial arts in the state. The sport of MMA was much different in 1997. The biggest promotion in the sport of MMA was and still is the Ultimate Fighting Championships ("UFC"). In 1997, the UFC was not the same as it presently is as it had not yet been acquired by Frank and Lorenzo Fertitta (and subsequently purchased by Endeavor in 2015). In 1997 the Fertitta brothers were still involved in their family casino business in Las Vegas. The prior owners sold the sport on the fact it was not regulated which catered to a specific type of demographic. Many individuals that were not steady followers of the sport saw MMA as a glorification of violence. "Barbaric" was an oft-used adjective to describe the events during this period of time. The depiction of the sport was one of the reasons for the ban. A cage, a matchup between two men with small, fingerless gloves and blood. Even though there were rules to these bouts, there were few. The legislative history depicting the concern and fear for the sport reflects the violent perspective of the sport.

While proponents of the ban cited the violence of the sport as a reason for it, supporters of MMA claimed that the law should be repealed. They looked to the many gyms within the state that practiced the sport of mixed martial arts, the variety of martial arts that were allowed to obtain a license to hold events in the state and the variety of ways that the law was interpreted and/or enforced.

Despite aggressive lobbying efforts by the UFC for measures which would make MMA legal in the state, they were consistently turned away in the state's Assembly. The failure to navigate through the Assembly had been the problem as laws which would have legalized professional MMA had several problems attaining passage through the state's Senate. In 2015, pro–MMA supporters believed that a measure to legalize professional MMA in the state would come to a vote before the end of the legislative session. Alas, that did not come to fruition despite the belief that they were close to getting to a vote.

Prior to 2015, the UFC, seeing that it had exhausted all of its options in lobbying lawmakers, decided to go to court.

In November 2011, the UFC, owned by Zuffa, LLC, filed a lawsuit against the state of New York claiming that the state's legislation prohibiting professional MMA was illegal.[1] The lawsuit was filed on behalf of several current UFC fighters including Jon Jones and Frankie Edgar. Jones was born in upstate New York and Edgar is from Long Island. Former MMA stars Gina Carano, Matt Hamill and Brian Stann were also named in the lawsuit.

The lawsuit included seven causes of action directed at New York's combative sport law ban, N.Y. Unconsolidated Laws sec 8905-a ("the Ban"). This included a state law claim related to the restriction of liquor of licensees, N.Y. Alcohol & Beverage Control Law sec 106(6-c)(a)("the Liquor Law").

The causes of action included allegations of violations of the constitution including the First Amendment, Tenth Amendment, Fourteenth Amendment and the Commerce Clause. As for the state claim related to the 2001 Liquor Law, it claimed that the law was unconstitutional as applied to the plaintiffs citing the statute was vague as to whether the 2001 Liquor Law applied to live MMA as the statute makes references to allow certain combat sports to allow alcohol while others are not in the purview of the definition of "combative sport."

The Attorney General of the state of New York, Eric T. Schneiderman, was sued in his official capacity, as was as Dennis Rosen, the Commissioner and Chairman of the New York State Liquor Authority, and Jeanique Green, in her official capacity as Commissioner of the New York State Liquor Authority.

In its lawsuit, the plaintiffs argued that the Ban was unconstitutionally vague and overbroad as the Combat Sports Law Ban did not properly define several key phrases within the law. The effect of the vague language left the law to be enforced in a variety of ways with standard-less discretion.

Here is a brief breakdown of all seven issues:

1. The Live Professional MMA Ban Violates the First Amendment

In this claim, Zuffa argues that the Live Professional MMA Ban ("MMA Ban") is a content-based restriction based on the perceived violent message.[2]

Zuffa points to the legislative history of the MMA Ban as reason to argue that the purpose of the ban was due to the violent content of MMA.[3] Hence, Zuffa concludes that New York misperceives the proper message of MMA.[4]

Here, Zuffa argues that since MMA is public entertainment, it is thereby protected by the First Amendment.

Assuming that the court agrees with Zuffa and that it should be protected under the First Amendment, we look to how a court would analyze the MMA ban. Courts require that governmental regulation of speech protected under the First Amendment be "content neutral." A "content neutral" law is one that applies to all speech regardless of its message.

According to Erwin Chemerinsky's treatise on Constitutional Law, the requirement that the government be content-neutral in its regulation of speech means that the government must be both viewpoint neutral and subject matter neutral.[5] Viewpoint neutral means that the government cannot regulate speech based on the ideology of the message. For instance, a law cannot regulate against one political ideology but not regulate its opposing view. Subject matter neutral means that the government cannot regulate speech based on the topic of the speech. Thus, a law cannot inhibit one particular subject.

In these interpretations, the government is allowed to regulate speech if there is a legitimate state interest. It's plausible that New York argues that the ban was necessary due to the violent nature of the sport and the safety issues related to MMA.

2. The MMA Ban Is Overbroad and Violates the First Amendment

In this claim, Zuffa argues that the MMA Ban is so broad that it regulates certain things that it cannot, by law, regulate. "A law is unconstitutionally overbroad if it regulates substantially more speech than the Constitution allows to be regulated and a person to whom the law constitutionally can be applied can argue that it would be unconstitutional as applied to others."[6]

Zuffa examines the language in the MMA Ban law and indicates how the law was drafted makes things such as attending a "UFC viewing party" or litigating this lawsuit illegal. Zuffa also cites other examples where the law can be construed broadly to make legal conduct and speech illegal.

3. The MMA Ban is Vague on the Face of the Law and Violates the Due Process Clause

"A law is unconstitutionally vague if a reasonable person cannot tell what speech is prohibited and what is permitted. Unduly vague laws violate due process whether or not speech is regulated."[7]

Zuffa points to terms in the MMA Ban which it argues are vague. Zuffa recites relevant portions of the law in its Complaint.

Section 2 of the Ban states that "[n]o combative sport shall be conducted, held or given within the state of New York."[8] Both criminal penalties and civil liability are imposed upon "a person who knowingly advances or profits from a combative sport activity."[9]

Key terms, "combative sport activity" and "professional match or exhibition," which triggered the analysis for the ban, are not defined in a way which would provide definitive guidelines.

Zuffa argues that the practice of martial arts at martial arts schools in New York may or may not be affected by the MMA Ban.[10] Zuffa concludes that there is confusion in the law regarding exemptions for martial arts schools and/or clubs.

In addition, while the triggering provision in the law appears to be whether an MMA match is a "professional match or exhibition," the ban appears to restrict amateur fights.[11]

4. The MMA Ban Is Unconstitutional as It Violates the Equal Protection Rights of the Plaintiffs Under the 14th Amendment

Similar to the first three causes of action, Zuffa argues that New York does not have a rational basis for its blanket ban of professional mixed martial arts in the state. It states that New York does not articulate the reasons for the ban. While safety and messages of violence may be interpreted as the reasons for the law, Zuffa contends that these reasons fall flat since other forms of martial arts are legal in New York and studies show that MMA is a safe sport. In addition, Zuffa argues that there is no rational reason that it bans MMA even though there are other violent forms of speech (i.e., video games, violent movies and music lyrics) that are not regulated.

5. The MMA Ban Is Unconstitutional as It Violates the Due Process Clause

This cause of action relates to the Due Process Clause in the Constitution that prohibits the government from "intruding on liberty without rational reason." Here, Zuffa argues once again that the MMA Ban is vague and overbroad and does not address the purpose for the law.

6. The MMA Ban Unconstitutionally Restricts Interstate Commerce

This cause of action relates to what lawyers term the "dormant commerce clause." State and local laws cannot place an undue burden on interstate commerce. Zuffa argues that the MMA Ban stifles interstate commerce on three fronts.

First, since the MMA Ban is only a ban on professional MMA and not amateur MMA, New York may have MMA training, gyms and exhibitions but New York bars out-of-state businesses from promoting professional events.

Second, the language of the law is so broad that "numerous interstate products and services" required for a live professional MMA event are barred from New York. Here, the argument is that the law does not address the perceived purpose of the law, which is to ban the "violent message of MMA" and improve fighter safety. Zuffa argues that there are no benefits to the ban and states that the ban has forced individuals to turn to "underground" MMA. It also indicates that if the perception of violence was at issue, New York could have found an alternative to a complete ban on MMA. The complaint suggests it could have an age limit for attendance in live events.

Finally, Zuffa argues that the MMA Ban could have an "extraterritorial effect" on interstate commerce as the vagueness of the statute and uncertain enforcement may leave advertisers and merchandisers to limit its exposure in the New York market. As an extension, it could burden advertisers and merchandisers in neighboring states.

7. The 2001 Liquor Law Is Unconstitutional as Applied to the Plaintiffs

This cause of action relates to Zuffa's claims related to the MMA ban as the 2001 Liquor Law prohibits the sale of liquor at both professional and amateur MMA events. It follows that if the MMA ban is unconstitutional, the provision of the 2001 Liquor Law would be unconstitutional as well.

New York Dismisses Zuffa's Original Complaint

New York dismissed two of Zuffa's original claims of due process and equal protection in August 2012.[12] The court held that the 1997 law passed by New York had a rational basis at the time and when the court decided the motion. Even if it didn't, the court stated that the MMA law was still rationally related to its intended purpose.

The plaintiffs argued the theory of "Changed Circumstances" in arguing that the constitutionality of the MMA law was predicated upon the existence of facts which no longer existed. In this case, Zuffa argued that the rules and regulations had changed over time which made it safer for the participants. This meant that the rule was no longer relevant to the current state of professional MMA. In rendering its opinion, the Second Circuit stated that it had not invalidated a statute as irrational based on changed circumstances and had not expressly embraced the viewpoint that changed circumstances may be considered as part of a rational basis review. Emphasizing its point, the court noted that even if it considered the changes made by MMA to promote safety, the ban in New York satisfied the rational basis scrutiny.

In determining a rational basis, one needs a "reasonably conceivable state of facts that could provide a rational basis" for a law. The court identified two primary reasons for the statute, the first being that professional MMA posed a threat to the health and safety of its participants. Secondly, professional MMA was detrimental to public morality and had a negative influence on New York youth. Despite the argument that the two reasons had been addressed over the years since the law was put into place, the court determined that these were viable reasons for a rational basis for the ban. Additionally, the court held that there was sufficient evidence that MMA was detrimental to public morality and painted a bad picture for youth. The court opinion cited evidence that bouts were sold as "blood sport" and "fights to the death" to entice fans seeking this type of violence. It was depicted by lawmakers as "savage" and "barbaric." A portion of the reasoning behind the law was to protect the youth from such events.

In the decision, the court accepted the evidence that the UFC made the sport of MMA safer and the assertion that MMA is "as safe or safer than ... professional boxing." Yet, the court noted the possibility of the long-term effects of head injuries. It also explained that even though there was evidence supplied by Zuffa that the sport was safer, it did not invalidate the law since there was a rational basis for the law.

The opinion seemed to be short-sighted and relied upon the past legislative history as to dismissing Zuffa's claims. For a supporter of MMA in the state, it did not make sense that boxing, which is just as violent as MMA, was legal but MMA was not.

The opportunity to compare it with boxing came up during the opinion. And while one might see the similarities with the violent nature of the sport, the court seemed to reconcile the legalization of boxing with banning professional MMA, because boxing had been regulated for a lengthy duration. In footnotes, the court dismissed the comparisons. "But, even accepting as true that boxing and MMA cannot be distinguished on the basis of safety, the exemption for boxing could have a rational basis on account of its longevity."[13] It further explained that "boxing has been regulated in New York for decades. It would not be unreasonable for New York's legislature to enact legislation restricting activities it considered unduly risky, but to limit those restrictions to activities in which individuals were less likely to suffer economic hardship."[14] In another footnote, they were dismissive of Zuffa's assertion that professional boxing had more deaths than MMA, stating that boxing had compiled statistics over a "significantly longer timeframe and the greater popularity of boxing during much of this period undermined the persuasiveness of this comparison."[15]

In its conclusion to the Order, the court stated that Zuffa should direct its grievance to the state legislature rather than to seek redress with the judiciary.

Zuffa Files First Amended Complaint

As a result of the dismissal, Zuffa filed its First Amended Complaint in September 2012.[16] In this iteration, it included claims of violation of due process and equal protection which it argued was based on additional facts which ballooned the amended complaint to 160 pages. While the trial court dismissed the due process and equal protection claims, Zuffa inserted them into the amended complaint adding more facts which allegedly differed from the original and premised upon New York's shifting nature of its response to the Original Complaint. Once again, New York proceeded to file a Motion to Dismiss. This time, it was to dismiss the entire First Amended Complaint.

Vagueness

Zuffa argued that the terms "professional," "match," and "exhibition" were vague. They argued regulators had adopted "shifting, uncommon, and inconsistent understandings of these terms since the Ban was enacted." It cited the fact that there were several different interpretations of the Ban.

Zuffa claimed that the term "Professional" in the statute was vague. The MMA Ban related to "professional" mixed martial arts matches. According to the plaintiffs the term "professional" was not defined anywhere in the statute and they claimed that state officials used varied definitions of the term.

The complaint brought up the fact that the New York State Athletic Department attempted to shut down an amateur mixed martial arts event despite the fact amateur MMA was considered legal at the time of the legislative ban.[17]

The state's 2001 Liquor Bill states that NY officials understood "professional" as being "one where compensation is received by the contestants for their participation."[18] As argued by Zuffa, there were different ways in which the statute was interpreted.

In addition, the plaintiffs claimed the term "combative sport" was vague. The plaintiffs pointed to a pillow fighting tournament possibly being banned in the state due to the fact that the tournament could be constrained as a combative sport.

Overbroad

Similar to the claims that the New York law was vague, it was also overbroad. Usually, claims of constitutional vagueness are accompanied by claims that a law is overbroad. If a prohibition is expressed in a way that is too unclear for a person to reasonably know whether or not their conduct falls within the law, then to avoid the risk of legal consequences they often stay far away from anything that could possibly fit the uncertain wording of the law.

Sometimes referred to as the overbreadth doctrine, applied to this lawsuit, the claim set forth by the plaintiffs suggested that the New York law banning professional mixed martial arts was unclear as to its application. Due in part to the definitions within the law, it was uncertain as to whether certain conduct broke the law or was in line with it. The doctrine seeks to balance the "harmful effects" of "invalidating a law that in some of its applications is perfectly constitutional" as a possibility that "the threat of enforcement of an overbroad law deters people from engaging in constitutionally protected speech."

Hand in hand with the plaintiffs' vagueness claim, they argued that the New York law was overbroad in its prohibition of MMA and that it prevented those from abiding by the law due to its blanket ban.

First Amendment

Although courts have protected the arts, no court has ever directly confronted the question of whether athletes have a First Amendment right to be seen in action.[19] The Complaint stated, "[l]ive professional MMA is clearly intended and understood as public entertainment and, as such, is an expressive activity protected by the First Amendment."[20]

The Southern District of New York dismissed the plaintiffs' First Amendment claim in its original Complaint as the court was not persuaded by the plaintiffs' argument.

The court held that "live-performance, professional MMA qualifies as expressive conduct only if Plaintiffs establish that MMA is sufficiently imbued with the elements of communication."[21] The court determined that "live-performance MMA does not qualify for First Amendment protection."[22] Essentially, the court concluded that while fighters may have intended to communicate a particularized message, the plaintiffs had not demonstrated a "great likelihood" that viewers will understand the message.[23]

The first hurdle which the court evaluated was whether the plaintiffs sufficiently alleged that live, professional MMA intends to communicate a particularized message. Secondly, there must be a great likelihood that the message will be understood by those viewing it. In evaluating whether the fighters' expressed a "particularized message," it must be determined if the conduct is likely to be understood or perceived as expressing a particular message. The party asserting the First Amendment protection has the burden of demonstrating that there is more than a mere "plausible contention" that its conduct is expressive.

The court opined that the live-performance of MMA does not qualify for First Amendment protection. The pre-fight and post-fight "antics," according to the court, did not dissuade the court opinion as live professional MMA is central to the law at issue. "It is the conduct, not the surrounding fanfare, that must convey the particularized message that the audience is likely to receive."[24] It ruled that there was not a "great likelihood" that viewers would understand the message conveyed by athletes. While the court assumed that athletes were conveying a message, it could not conclude that an audience would understand the message.

Noteworthy in the opinion, the court differentiated public performances to the sporting event. It cited that courts have "generally been unwilling to extend First Amendment protection to sports or athletics." It compared the efforts of athletes in MMA to those reactive moves made in chess or ultimate frisbee, citing if they were to trigger constitutional protection, a line between conduct and speech would be meaningless. While the court conceded that it takes a great deal of skill, training and talent for sports, the First Amendment "does not protect all conduct that involves impressive skill." The court noted that the central question is whether the activity is primarily communicative and expressive.

In addition, the court ruled that the MMA Ban was not unconstitutionally overbroad since the live-performance of MMA does not implicate First Amendment concerns. In determining that a law is unconstitutionally overbroad, the law must punish a substantial amount of protected free speech.

The Court's Motion to Dismiss Zuffa's First Amended Complaint

On March 31, 2015, Judge Kimba Wood issued her opinion in cross-motions for summary judgment by Zuffa and the state of New York. It determined that Zuffa should prevail on its motion. Judge Wood sided with New York's argument that Zuffa had no standing to bring the case as there was no evidence of an injury.

> The concept of an imminent injury warrants further elaboration specific to the claims in this case. In general, the threat of a criminal prosecution based on a plaintiff's prospective conduct may create an injury in fact, where the threat qualifies as "imminent." In such cases, the plaintiff may challenge the constitutionality of the underlying criminal statute immediately, without risking arrest by performing the prospective conduct at issue.[25]

While Judge Wood acknowledges that Zuffa need not expose itself to liability before bringing suit to challenge the basis for the threat, it must have "concrete plans" to perform the conduct that officials would consider illegal.[26] This last point was the reason for Zuffa's dismissal due to lack of standing.

Judge Wood also made two points in her opinion.

First, the plaintiffs must establish an injury in fact, and every other element of standing, "in the same way as any other matter on which [they bear] the burden of proof, i.e., with the manner and degree of evidence required at the successive stages of the litigation."[27]

Judge Wood also noted that "standing is to be determined as of the commencement of the suit."[28] Here, Judge Wood noted that Zuffa could not rely on factual developments after the date of the lawsuit to establish standing.

This statement was in relation to statements made by Zuffa attorneys that indicated that the Ban was interpreted multiple ways by New York officials, rendering the Ban vague as to the law and enforcement. Regardless, Judge Wood determined that Zuffa lacked standing and since it was at the summary judgment stage, it must present evidence of specific facts alleging its claims. It could not and its lawsuit must be dismissed.

Despite the dismissal, Judge Wood left a glimmer of hope for Zuffa as in her conclusion, dicta indicated Zuffa may consider filing new vagueness claims based on events that occurred after this lawsuit commenced. She noted, "The Court advises Plaintiffs to weigh the merits of a new federal suit against those of a state declaratory judgment action, given the latter—unlike a federal decision on vagueness grounds—could decisively settle disputes regarding the Ban's scope."[29]

Implicit in her unofficial directive for Zuffa was the fact that its claims regarding a state law banning MMA in the state should be brought in state court. Did Zuffa take her advice? No.

Zuffa Files Another Lawsuit Against New York, Preliminary Injunction—September 2015

Taking most of the advice from Judge Wood's dicta in its motion to dismiss, the UFC filed a lawsuit against New York once again. In this iteration, Zuffa, operating as the UFC, was the sole plaintiff filing suit against the state. It also requested a preliminary injunction which focused on the Combat Sports Law and Liquor Law and that the ban on professional MMA was unconstitutionally vague as applied to MMA events.

Despite the new lawsuit, it also filed an appeal brief arising from the dismissal of its lawsuit per Judge Wood's Order.

In this lawsuit, which came almost four years later, it claimed that MMA had matured since the Combat Sports Law was implemented. Specifically, it took issue with what an "Exempt Organization" was defined as in the statute.

In addition, it had a second cause of action under the 2001 Liquor Law citing it unconstitutional as applied to professional MMA. Essentially, the UFC claimed that a state liquor law precluded liquor licenses from hosting events related to MMA.[30]

Judge Kimba Wood had dismissed Zuffa's claim for vagueness, citing that the organization lacked standing to sue the state of New York for failure to show that it would suffer injury since it had never attempted to hold an event in the state. The law prevents a party from filing a lawsuit if it cannot show that it would be injured as a result of the law it might be challenging. Judge Wood determined that if there was any harm to affect Zuffa, it occurred after the lawsuit was filed. Thus, Zuffa could not claim to be an aggrieved party with an injury resulting in damages.

Zuffa secured the right to hold an event at Madison Square Garden on April 23, 2016. The strategic move displayed the promotion's ability to work with adversity when its original lawsuit did not work. Highlighting the court's ruling which dismissed its case, Zuffa responded with this move. "Whatever uncertainty may have existed on the matter in the past, it is now crystal clear that the state interprets the law to prohibit Plaintiff [Zuffa] from doing so."[31] With the professional MMA ban, the UFC claimed that it would be harmed.

Utilizing the Combat Law Sports Ban, the UFC stated that it was sanctioned by one of the statutorily exempt organizations to hold its event. While it is clear that the state did not contemplate this result from the professional MMA ban which provided the list of exempt organizations that may sanction events, the UFC used the list to work within the legal ban.

Pointing out a flaw within the CSL, the UFC highlighted that the statute does not define what constitutes permissible "martial arts"; instead it provides only that "'martial arts' shall include any professional match or exhibition sanctioned by" a list of twelve organizations that does not include UFC. It also noted that the New York State Athletic Commission routinely allowed promotions to operate shows in the state. These promotions, according to the UFC, were competitors such as Glory Kickboxing and K1, which touted itself as a mix of several different martial arts.

The UFC argued that during the litigation of the lawsuit it filed against the state, the Attorney General "flip-flopped" over the interpretation of the statute. For instance, the state maintained that the statute allowed only "single discipline" martial arts, but during oral arguments over the state's Motion to Dismiss, it admitted that martial arts do not have to be "single discipline" to be permissible. The admission by the Attorney General could be seen as a misunderstanding of the different martial arts practices or the application of the law.

Notably, despite a Settlement Conference being ordered in the original Jones complaint, the Attorney General abruptly changed his mind, stating that the state would not stipulate to any understanding of the Combat Sports Law that would permit Zuffa to promote an MMA event. Hence, the Attorney General had demonstrated the vagueness of the Combat Sports Law. Yet, as Zuffa asserted, Judge Wood did not reach the substantive issue as she first had to determine whether the plaintiffs had standing.

But in the UFC lawsuit, standing would not be an issue due to its contract to host a live professional MMA event sanction by an Exempt Organization. The UFC committed $25,000 as a non-refundable deposit and claimed it would potentially lose millions of dollars in ticket sales and media revenue if the court did not grant a preliminary injunction.

Clearly, the move forced the hand of New York and the court as it pressed a response either through a grant of the injunction and allowing the event to happen in New York or a denial and actual damages which the UFC would claim in its second lawsuit against New York. With a looming date of April 23, 2016, in a letter to the court on January 19, 2016, attorneys for Zuffa requested that the court decide on the Preliminary Injunction by January 25, 2016. They indicated that the ban on professional MMA was unconstitutional and its inability to hold scheduled events due to the threat of criminal prosecution reflected the real harm the UFC suffered.

The UFC got what it asked for. Except it wasn't what it asked for. The court denied UFC's Preliminary Injunction request. In an order on January 25, 2016, the court cited the "Pullman doctrine" as the reason it would not side with the UFC. The Pullman doctrine is a legal case which dictates that a federal court must abstain from ruling on a state court law until that state court had a chance to adjudicate the matter.

The doctrine was cited by the state of New York in its opposition brief to the UFC's Motion for Preliminary Injunction. Under the Pullman case, where a state law is allegedly vague, a federal court should stay (i.e., hold off on deciding) a decision on state law when the state court has yet to interpret the law. Premised upon the 1941 U.S. Supreme Court case, Railroad Commission v. Pullman Co., there are three factors:

1. The case presents both state grounds and federal constitutional grounds for relief;
2. The proper resolution of the state ground for the decision is unclear; and
3. The disposition of the state ground could obviate the need for adjudication of the federal constitutional ground.

The UFC should have seen this result coming. Judge Wood wrote in her dismissal of the UFC's first lawsuit that the grievance should be addressed in state law court. Yet, the UFC filed the lawsuit and this lawsuit landed once again in Judge Wood's courtroom.

The UFC did appeal this ruling although it did not garner sufficient traction as the case resolved itself prior to the need to file briefing in this appeal.

However, Zuffa's appeal of its First Amended Complaint was filed.

The Appeal

Zuffa filed an appeal to its dismissal of its First Amended Complaint against New York in the Second Circuit Court of Appeals.[32] In its appeal brief, Zuffa argues that it has standing due to the fact the ban addresses the UFC business. Paul Clement, Zuffa's counsel, argued in its brief, "UFC is in the business of promoting and producing professional MMA matches and exhibitions."[33] It stated that the UFC was a licensed promoter for the World Kickboxing Association ("WKA"). The WKA was an exempt organization under the Combat Sports Ban that could promote MMA events within the state. The brief claimed that WKA was "reluctant to take that additional step for fear of the criminal and civil penalties they could face if the event went forward, and the unrecoverable costs they could incur if the event were shut down."[34] Thus, even though the UFC never made a colorable attempt to hold an event in the state, the company had standing to sue.

Additionally, Clement attacked Judge Wood's belief that standing arose only after the lawsuit was filed in November 2011. It cited New York's "mid-litigation waffling" with respect to whether or not an exempt organization could promote an MMA event as evidence that harm existed prior to its filing. Irrespective of the stance by New York, Zuffa claimed that the ban had been ongoing prior to and throughout the litigation. Thus, Judge Wood's ruling that there was no standing since any alleged harm occurred after the lawsuit commenced.

Notwithstanding its arguments that the UFC had standing to sue, it argued the merits of its challenge that the law was vague on its face and in its application. Clement argued that the appeals court should remand to the District Court to reach the merits of the vagueness claim.

> Because the District Court did not reach the merits of Plaintiffs' as-applied vagueness challenges given its erroneous standing holding, at a bare minimum, the Court should remand with instructions to resolve the merits of those challenges. And in doing so, the Court should also reinstate Plaintiffs' facial vagueness claim, which the District Court dismissed only by applying a standard that the Supreme Court has since rejected.

In the alternative, it requested the appeals court to resolve the legal question itself.

The plaintiffs in the first lawsuit argued that live professional MMA was "never permissible." Thus, there was no need to attempt to conduct an event with the result being the threat or actual prosecution for violation of the ban by the state. It also preserved the rights of the first lawsuit.

Another interesting facet of the appeal was Zuffa's argument in favor of live MMA being protected under the First Amendment. Zuffa argued that live entertainment, including MMA is presumptively entitled to First Amendment protection when performed in front of a live audience. This was based on the belief that implicit in the statute prohibiting MMA in New York according to Clement, was that the New York law restricted live MMA but did not prohibit the practice of MMA in gyms and training facilities across the state. Thus, the District Court, as Clement wrote "missed the forest for the trees." Essentially, Judge Wood evaluated the law banning pro MMA in the state from the aspect as to whether MMA is inherently expressive when not part of a live performance. Clement asserted that it was "backwards" rationale. "As the Supreme Court has confirmed time and again, performing before an audience is what brings conduct that might not otherwise be expressive within the scope of the First Amendment," writes Clement. The brief goes on to further argue that "a law that singles out for prohibition public exhibitions of perfectly lawful conduct is plainly problematic...."

Following the rationale that MMA falls within the ambit of free speech Clement argued that the state of New York could not contend that the message MMA live events convey was not entitled to First Amendment protection. He goes on to argue on behalf of the UFC that the district court dismissed the First Amendment claim, in part, due to the fact that even though live MMA conveyed a "particularized message," it must be "understood by those viewing it." Clement negates the belief citing the fact that whether the conduct involves lives performance before an audience, the case law suggests that there is no other need for further inquiry. As stated above, the law specifically addresses live MMA and since the law specifically seeks to regulate live MMA, there should be no further evaluation as to whether the audience will understand the particular message.

New York countered Zuffa's argument with two primary arguments concerning First Amendment and vagueness of the statute.[35]

Violence was the key to the state's argument that the First Amendment did not apply to the law banning MMA in New York. "The First Amendment does not protect violence," it argued in its brief citing the fact that the state has the power to regulate violent or dangerous conduct that can inflict actual physical harm.

Distinguishing fighting from speech, it notes that the combat prohibition restricts physical violence and not what they may or may not say. It argues that the legislative intent of the law was to regulate particular forms of violent conduct rather than speech.

Moreover, it argues that states that allow MMA, or other dangerous contact sports, require strict rules to abide by and fighters must obtain a license. These requirements, according to the argument, would be contrary to First Amendment protection.

Throughout the brief, New York takes jabs at Zuffa's appeal brief. For instance, it states that it misreads the statute in its belief that the regulation prohibiting MMA is limited to just a "live performance" (i.e., fighting in front of an audience). It argues that the interpretation is wrong. In fact, New York argues that the ban prohibits "physical violence regardless of whether anyone watches the fights."[36]

The second major argument in the brief addresses whether the law is vague. First, New York reaffirmed the District Court ruling that Zuffa lacked standing since there was no claim or injury until after the lawsuit commenced. Next, it argued that the correct court to address this issue would be New York state court since it dealt with a New York law. This was the same guidance stated by Judge Kimba Wood in its order dismissing Zuffa's lawsuit.

New York argued that if the court believes Zuffa has standing and a state court is not the appropriate forum for the case, then it should remand (send back) to the District Court to decide whether the "martial-arts sponsorship exemption is vague as applied to ultimate fighting."[37] This was the same thing Zuffa recommended in its brief. It also suggested that the appeals court could decide that the exemption was not unconstitutionally vague.

New York attempts to distance itself from the First Amendment issue contending that the ban relates to the overarching concern of safety. New York focuses on violence rather than describing MMA as sport. Throughout the brief, it offers subtle descriptions and analogies of violence. While New York argues that it has a right to regulate violence and dangerous conduct, the correlations it makes in its brief relate to activities that are mostly criminal. Thus, the argument here seemed to fall flat as laws that regulate animal fighting or use of weapons are criminal law. Is MMA on the level of these activities?

As for the vagueness claim, this issue seems to be one that might be the point of contention. While New York offers the "lack of standing" argument, it also identifies a potential key mistake by Zuffa. It notes that the case may be best decided by a state court. Finally, it focuses on legislative history and intent in arguing that the law was always about banning MMA.

The inevitable oral argument which would pit Zuffa and New York in front of appellate court judges never came to fruition. The good news for MMA fans in the state of New York was that the legislative efforts looked better than ever in 2016.

Professional MMA Becomes Legal in New York

After several failed attempts by Zuffa to lobby the state of New York to legalize professional mixed martial arts, the state Assembly finally passed a bill and it was signed into law by Governor Andrew Cuomo on April 14, 2016. The sport became legal and regulated in New York on September 1, 2016.

In its first fight under the new law, the UFC had to pay $1,675 per fighter to cover its insurance premium based on a $1 million traumatic brain injury insurance provision. The amounts per fighter did not include the typical $50,000 medical and $50,000 accidental death insurance policies. The provision was one of the concessions supporters of the MMA bill had with legislators that were concerned with the health and safety of fighters.

The UFC debut in Madison Square Garden on November 12, 2016, did not disappoint as it brought in the largest gate in UFC history at the time with $17.7 million for the 20,427 attending the event.

Certainly, one of the arguments made by supporters of the bill to legalize professional MMA was the revenue that it could bring to the state. With its debut, it showed that it could produce. Still, there were some remaining questions after the initial support for the sport.

Fallout from the Lawsuit

The lawsuits highlighted the need for the legalization of mixed martial arts in New York. Making MMA legal in New York was one of the factors that paved a way for the acquisition of the company by WME-IMG for $4.2 billion as financial documents note that the legalization of the sport in New York was one of the reasons it became a valuable sports property.

Fortunate in legal cost savings, but unfortunate for those that may have sought resolution of a First Amendment issue, MMA became legal in New York. One of the pending issues that was left hanging by the appellate court was whether MMA could be considered protected under the First Amendment.

With Paul Clement in charge of the appellate review for the UFC, the argument for First Amendment protection of live MMA was compelling. In general, sports are not considered an art and are therefore not subject to the same First Amendment protections as theatre plays or an opera. The lawsuit and subsequent appeal argued that MMA should be considered the same due to a message conveyed by the fighters. In the trial court, the argument was novel and the court agreed with the state of New York in finding that the fighters did not have a claim under the First Amendment. They believed that there was not an articulable message that a viewer would understand. But the appellate brief argued that live entertainment, including live MMA, is presumptively entitled to First Amendment protection. "[T]he very fact that conduct is undertaken before an audience can convert something that might not otherwise be considered First Amendment activity into inherently expressive conduct protected by the Free Speech Clause." Despite opposition from New York, the argument could have served as a precedent for cases in which individuals stream footage through their phones. While there are underlying copyright issues involved with this issue, the argument that First Amendment protection attaches to these issues could have been a big factor in determining the application of law to emerging technologies.

The First Amendment implications are intriguing with the continued advancement of technologies for cell phones. Facebook, Periscope, Twitter and Instagram are some of the more popular platforms where users can upload videos instantaneously. There have been attempts to curb the use of cell phones for commercial purposes. Media must abide by certain rules when afforded the opportunity to cover sporting events. Usually, these are written and outlined for them and media run the risk of having their credentials taken if they do not follow the rules. But, what about citizen journalism? Blogs and online news sources are prevalent and have usurped the popularity of the newspaper. Yet, some outlets are not credentialed.

The U.S. Supreme Court decided whether a news organization could broadcast an individual's entire performance without prior consent. In *Zacchini v. Scripps-Howard Broadcasting Co.*, the U.S. Supreme Court held that the First and Fourteenth Amendments were not a shield to the news media from civil liability.[38] In *Zacchini*, a performer sued the operator of a local Ohio television station for airing a fifteen-second clip of his performance, a circus act at a county fair featuring his human cannonball routine. The case made its way to the U.S. Supreme Court where the Court held that the First Amendment does not privilege the news media to televise a performer's entire act against his express objection. The Supreme Court indicated that state law rights of publicity must be balanced against First Amendment considerations. Perhaps a subtle distinction that a future stakeholder may point out is the fact that the Court evaluated this case as it relates to "a performer's entire act" as opposed to a portion of the act. Whether or not the Court would have been persuaded if only a portion of the performance was shown was not determined here. The dissent suggests that a First Amendment analysis of the case should have taken on a different starting point. It writes that the Court should have looked at the actions of the media and how it used the footage. The dissent asserts that if the footage was used routinely, the First Amendment would protect the station's "right of publicity" or "appropriation" suit, unless the media's use of the footage was a "subterfuge" for private or commercial exploitation.

Since the appeal was filed, there has not been a concrete legal ruling which determines whether live sports could be protected by the First Amendment. In the fall of 2016, the organizers of the World Chess Championship attempted to obtain a preliminary injunction against a website operator from reporting chess moves.[39] U.S. District Judge Victor Marrero denied the preliminary injunction stating that the public interest would be served by "robust reporting." The World Chess Championship sought the exclusive right to disseminate the chess moves in real time.

In the District Court's opinion, it was clear that the Court did not believe First Amendment protection extends to sports. Yet, the District Court believed that performances are protected. One of the reasons is that inherent in theatre, it is conveying a particularized message which could be understood by the audience. The only difference between sport and theatrical perform-ances is that theatre has a predetermined ending whereas sports does not.

The protection of intellectual property is an issue to be discussed in another chapter. But the issue operates in lockstep with the First Amendment claim in this case. The piracy of pay-per-view events is a major impediment to a company's business. Then there is the question of whether First Amend-ment applies to sports. In the time since Zuffa filed this lawsuit, organizations of major sports have worked with media in coming to an understanding over the use of technologies like Periscope.

From a practical viewpoint, the insurance costs of putting on an event in New York are steep and upset small-time promoters as well as established boxing promoters that balked at the additional money they needed to pay up front to hold events in the state. Yet, the additional insurance comes on the heels of the state of New York settling a case with boxer Magomed Abdusalamov and his family for $22 million due to multiple failures by the state athletic commission to aid Abdusalamov after his bout in New York, which left him needing to take a taxi to the hospital.[40] Abdusalamov suffers from permanent brain damage due in part to the lack of help by the state after his fight and will need assistance for the rest of his life. Even with this alarming story, promoters weigh the risks versus the expense.

Regulating professional mixed martial arts in the state was one of the biggest hurdles for the sport. Even with the associated obstacles of its regu-lation, bringing professional MMA to New York was a big win.

2

MMA's Drug Problem—
Enter USADA

Introduction

On July 1, 2015, the Ultimate Fighter Championships implemented its Anti-Doping Policy with all of its contracted fighters. Athletes under contract would have to submit to random drug screening and would be subject to a suspension of two years at a minimum if found to be in violation of the policy. The stiff penalties were applauded at first, but once implemented critics became outspoken about the problems with the policy.

The implementation of the drug testing program came, in part, as a result of some notable fighters failing drug tests. In January 2015, it was discovered that both fighters in the main event for the UFC 183 pay-per-view failed drug tests. Anderson Silva and Nick Diaz were determined to have violated the Nevada Athletic Commission's drug testing policy. Two of the biggest stars at the time testing positive for banned substances was a shock and an embarrassment for the promotion, especially as the main event was ruled a no-contest. Shortly after the finding, a press conference was held where the UFC announced a new anti-doping policy.

The UFC contracted with the United States Anti-Doping Agency (USADA). The organization acts as an independent anti-doping agency for the UFC. USADA conducts in-competition and out-of-competition tests. Out-of-competition testing is conducted with individual athletes at any time or setting with little or no advance notice of the test. In-competition testing is generally conducted immediately before or after an athlete's fight. USADA collects both urine and blood samples as part of its program although in most instances for the UFC Anti-Doping Program, it is the urine sample that is collected.

The UFC Anti-Doping Policy that went into effect in July 2016 required that every athlete be subject to testing year-round. An amendment was put in an athlete's contract which stated that they agreed to the additional condition of their agreement. Information such as dates, times, locations of an athlete's day must be submitted to USADA so that they may be located for out-of-competition testing. Athletes are responsible for keeping USADA informed of their whereabouts. UFC athletes may be subject to penalties if they do not keep USADA apprised of their whereabouts.

Through 2018, Nick Diaz is the only fighter thus far to be subject to discipline for failing to provide USADA with his whereabouts. The UFC middleweight served a one-year suspension as a result of his failure to update his location.

There is a handbook of rules and regulations that the fighters must follow. The aspiration seemed to be providing guidelines for athletes to ensure a clean sport in the UFC. The UFC Anti-Doping Policy sought to provide stability and certainty to drug testing in the UFC.

If a fighter's urine or blood sample comes up positive for a banned substance it is flagged by USADA and the athlete is put on a provisional suspension until it is determined the nature of the substance in his sample. This means that the fighter is immediately suspended and will not be considered for a future fight in the UFC until the test results are confirmed. The fighter can request a test of his "B" sample which is the same sample split from the original. In most cases, the "B" sample confirms the findings in the original test. The "B" sample might differ from the original, which may indicate contamination and would negate the original testing result. The athlete may also request that the case go to arbitration to contest the findings of the test by USADA.

As of 2018, there have been a handful of arbitration hearings. Of those hearings, only one has rendered a decision where the athlete has not received a suspension. In the other cases, USADA prevailed and the athlete served a suspension.

As of this writing in December 2018, there have been two fighters that have been assessed four-year bans and more than two dozen two-year suspensions. While it has been heralded as one of the most comprehensive anti-doping policies in sport, is has its critics. Also, a tangential effect of the UFC anti-doping policy are lawsuits arising after athletes have been punished by USADA.

Jon Jones vs. USADA

The first USADA arbitration taking place involving a UFC fighter occurred in October 2016 when Jon Jones took his case to a three-person arbitration panel.

Jones, who has had a list of out-of-the-octagon problems with the law, is considered one of the top UFC fighters ever. He was scheduled to be the main event at UFC 200 in July 2016. It was billed as the biggest event of the company's to date and would be the last big card under the Zuffa regime of Lorenzo and Frank Fertitta. It was later revealed that weekend that the Fertittas sold the company to media powerhouse WME-IMG for $4 billion dollars.

Jones and Daniel Cormier had several rematches to their UFC 182 fight postponed due to injury and Jones' legal woes. The fight was going to be the anchor to the company's event.

However, USADA flagged a Jones out-of-competition test for what was later determined as hydroxy-clomiphene (or Clomid, a banned anti-estrogenic substance) and "traces of letrozole," an aromatase inhibitor. These substances are banned under the UFC Anti-Doping Policy. Clomid is a suspect substance as it is used after taking steroids in a post-cycle therapy protocol. Letrozole is an anti-cancer drug that lowers levels of estrogen and blocks the conversion of testosterone to estrogen. As was discovered later, the use of these drugs does not conclude that Jones took a performance enhancing drug, but circumstantial evidence would suggest that this appeared to be the case.

The out-of-competition sample Jones provided to USADA on June 16 tested positive for clomiphene and traces of letrozole. His fight with Cormier was set to take place less than a month from the test. Proclaiming his innocence, Jones decided to appeal USADA's decision of a mandatory 2-year suspension from the UFC.

Jones retained renowned sports lawyer Howard Jacobs to represent him at arbitration. Jacobs is well-known for representing cyclist Floyd Landis and track athlete Marion Jones in their respective doping cases.

Under the UFC Anti-Doping Policy, an athlete who appeals his test results must pay $2,500 for an arbitrator.[1] Jones stated that he paid for a three-person arbitration panel, which cost him $55,000.00 in addition to legal fees. Although a fighter seeking an appeal may request a financial waiver of the costs, it does not appear that Jones made such a request.

Under Article 3.1 of the UFC Anti-Doping Policy, USADA had the burden of establishing an Anti-Doping Policy Violation ("ADPV").[2] According to its policy, it must establish an ADPV has occurred to "the comfortable satisfaction of the hearing panel bearing in mind the seriousness of the allegation which is made." The standard of proof is "greater than a mere balance of probability but less than proof beyond a reasonable doubt." The fighter may have a rebuttable presumption or establish specified facts or circumstances if USADA establishes its burden. In that case, the burden would be "by a balance of probability," per article 3.1.

After a one-day arbitration hearing, the panel issued a swift ruling finding Jones not a "drug cheat" but suspending him a year retroactive to July 6,

2016, the date Jones was informed of the out-of-competition doping violation.[3]

It determined that Jones took a sexual enhancement pill which contained the active agent Tadalafil. The testimony revealed that he had used an unauthorized sexual enhancement pill similar to Cialis. The pill was taken from a training partner, Eric Blasich, who Jones had no prior relationship with other than he trained with Jones at the same gym. It was purchased from a web site named, AllAmericanPeptide.com. There was no prior determination as to the whereabouts of the drug.

The arbitration panel found that Jones was reckless in taking the pill without checking on its contents. It noted that the product taken by Jones was not subject to the stringent standards of the Food and Drug Administration.

The Arbitration panel opined in its written opinion:

> Looking at the objective facts, first what is most striking is what the Applicant [Jones] did not do rather than what he did do. Mr. Jacobs relied on the fact that the Applicant believed (mistakenly) that he was taking Cialis, a product which he had previously checked with Mr. Kawa [Jones' agent who testified at the arbitration hearing], was not on the WADA or UFC prohibited list.[4]

The panel placed blame on Jones and Blasich:

> He did not ask Mr. Blasich to purchase the product from a safe environment: he simply asked him for a tablet. In fact, he did not seem to care about where Mr. Blasich got the tablet; but only about what it could do for him in terms of increasing his sexual pleasure. Mr. Blasich himself took no steps to check that the tablet was not, and did not contain, a Prohibited Substance.[5]

The ruling went out of its way to note that Jones did not take the illicit drug as a performance enhancement drug—perhaps as a way to soften the blow with a looming suspension coming. Or, as a way to differentiate one who knowingly used performance enhancing drugs versus someone that did not know. His recklessness in not checking the contents of the drug he was taking was his downfall. In addition, the panel took issue with the fact that Jones enlisted his agent, Malki Kawa to determine the contents of the drug and whether it was banned. The panel wrote that the "imprudent use of what he [Jones] pungently referred to as a 'dick pill' [was] reckless and [will cause him to] lose a year of his career [and] an estimated nine million dollars."[6]

The ruling showed the stringent standards upheld by USADA in enforcing the UFC's drug testing protocol. The panel identified Jones' nonchalant behavior and reckless disregard for what went into his body as part of the reason it ruled for his suspension.

Jones served a 2-year suspension and returned to the UFC Octagon to face Cormier in July 2017. He defeated Cormier to regain the UFC Light

Heavyweight title. But, his recklessness and reliance on others came back to haunt him. Days after his victory it was discovered that he once again failed a USADA drug test. More on this later.

Rivera v. USADA

Francisco Rivera was handed a 4-year suspension from the UFC for "aggravating circumstances" due to a violation of the UFC Anti-Doping Policy.[7] The arbitrator overseeing the matter determined that Rivera knowingly took clenbuterol and attempted to falsify evidence to conceal the wrongdoing. Rivera claimed that he was in Mexico where he ate tainted meat and that was the reason for the failed drug test. However, the case shows that you cannot lie to USADA, as investigators quickly debunked the alibi.

The arbitration was a result of a flagged urine sample taken from Rivera on July 23, 2016. The A and B samples contained clenbuterol, a Prohibited Substance that is not a Specified Substance. At the time, Rivera was preparing for a fight on July 30, 2016.

Notably, at about the same time, UFC welterweight Li Jingliang avoided punishment for a positive test of clenbuterol when it was determined that it was due to consuming contaminated meat in China. Hoping to obtain the same outcome, Rivera claimed that it was possible that the positive finding was due to consuming meat at a family barbecue in Mexico. In order to bolster his alibi, he produced a receipt from a Costco, a falsified bank statement and two falsified witness statements claiming that he was in Mexico visiting family.

As part of the investigation, USADA sent a representative from New York to Los Angeles to accompany Rivera to a local Chase bank branch to obtain a bank statement to confirm the authenticity of the receipt. However, Rivera did not show up and when his attorney attempted to contact him, the fighter did not respond. At that point, his attorney threatened to withdraw from representation due to his failure to show up at an agreed time. USADA informed the arbitrator of what had happened and soon thereafter Rivera emailed USADA stating he was in Mexico. It was later determined that he was actually in San Diego.

In order to save himself, Rivera claimed that his attorney had falsified the information in the Arbitration Brief. But, the Arbitrator did not buy it. Even though there were circumstantial facts, the Arbitrator noted that the short notice of his bout in mid–June, the proximity of time (July 23) that the test was taken to his fight on July 30th and the nature of the finding led to the conclusion that Rivera used clenbuterol to lose weight while maintaining strength and endurance. It was inferred that the Arbitrator saw this as an act of desperation by a fighter that was trying to save his career in the UFC.

Rivera sought to try to find an easy way to lose weight in time for his bout. But, the fighter did not clearly think through the ramifications of his actions or the depth of investigation that would take place.

The overarching lesson from Rivera's case is USADA's vigilance in tracking down and investigating an athlete who may have committed an anti-doping violation. Rivera attempted to misrepresent the truth but was caught by USADA investigators. While the excuse promoted by Rivera may have worked in the past, the new UFC Anti-Doping Policy was different.

Olivieri v. USADA

The second arbitration where a UFC fighter challenged a USADA ruling of a possible ADPV occurred with lightweight Felipe Olivieri.[8] Olivieri lost his first and only UFC contest in January 2016. Remaining in the active pool of fighters after his loss, an out-of-competition drug test revealed substances associated with anabolic steroids. Yet, Olivieri, a Brazilian-born fighter, claimed that the test on March 10, 2016, should be disregarded.

The arbitration took place in January 2017. He argued that the chain of custody of the sample was breached, the laboratory which carried out the analysis of the sample lost its accreditation and it contaminated the sample in the course of its analysis.

The loss of accreditation seemed to be a key argument for Olivieri. The lab which originally took Olivieri's sample, located in Rio de Janeiro, Brazil, had its accreditation suspended "due to a non-conformity with the International Standard for Laboratories." Olivieri's counsel objected to the drug sample, claiming it was mishandled by the Rio laboratory and the chain of custody had been compromised. Seizing on the error, Olivieri's attorney sought dismissal of his client's claim. However, the arbitration panel was not persuaded by the arguments related to the procedural errors.

As a result of proving its burden, Olivieri had to establish that the evidence of the ADPV analytical finding "ought not to be accepted."

Olivieri's arbitration came with less fanfare than Jon Jones. This is due to Jones' success in MMA and overall popularity. Olivieri had just one fight in the UFC, and not at a championship level at the time. It appeared that Olivieri's counsel argued two distinct theories that the arbitrator did not buy. First, the accreditation issue. Despite the fact that the lab that analyzed Olivieri's test sample had its accreditation suspended, it was not during the time that the fighter's sample was examined. This seemed like a losing argument from the origination, even if one might infer that the lab had problems prior to it losing accreditation. Secondly, Olivieri's counsel did not persuade the arbitrator that the chain of custody was compromised. Without being able to prove its burden, the arbitrator denied the appeal.

The arbitration ruling indicated that it would be difficult to argue a technical error in persuading a trier of fact to throw out the test results. While the lab lost its accreditation, the arbitrator was convinced that the actual test was accurate.

The ruling came at a tough time for the lightweight. Around the time of the drug test, Olivieri's brother passed away. Also, Olivieri was injured in a motorcycle accident. Yet, he still was able to give a urine sample. Despite the athlete's willingness to comply, no credit was given in doling out the punishment.

Josh Barnett vs. USADA

Josh Barnett was the youngest fighter to win the UFC Heavyweight Championship, in March 2002. However, the promotion stripped him of his title after a failed drug test. It was the second straight fight in the UFC where Barnett tested positive for a banned substance. The first time happened in November 2001. At the time, the Nevada Athletic Commission just gave him a warning, as it was his first offense.

Barnett took his MMA career to Japan, where he thrived competing in the heavyweight division. A return to the United States had him participate in the startup promotion, Affliction Entertainment. In its third event in Affliction's existence, Barnett, the number two ranked MMA heavyweight fighter in the world, was matched up against the number one fighter in the world, Fedor Emelianenko. It was a much talked about event and a "dream matchup" to take place in Anaheim, California, on August 1, 2009. However, the fight was called off ten days before by the California State Athletic Commission after Barnett tested positive for anabolic steroids for a second time. A test of his B sample revealed the same positive test for steroids. The event was cancelled. The promotion never held another event, and some think that Barnett's drug test failure deterred the company from further promotions.

Barnett re-emerged in the Strikeforce promotion and when it was purchased by the UFC, he returned to the company. With his UFC return in 2013, Barnett added to a Heavyweight division looking for challengers. In his second run in the UFC, Barnett was 3–2 with two Performance of the Night Bonuses.

In December 2016, Barnett was notified of a potential USADA doping violation from an out-of-competition test. From his past history of doping infractions, Barnett had retained a detailed list of his supplements, including portions he ingested. His records assisted USADA in the process of tracing back to the source of his failed drug test.

Barnett tested positive for ostarine in an out-of-competition sample on December 9, 2016. In certain instances, ostarine may be used to assist in increasing physical stamina and fitness.

Barnett noted that he was routinely taking dietary supplements "to maintain his conditioning as an elite athlete." The opinion notes he took 17 supplements prior to providing the sample that came up positive for ostarine. Tributestin 750 was one of the supplements that was supposed to contain only *Tribulus terrestris*. Tribulus is not a Prohibited Substance. "It is claimed to naturally support the production of testosterone among other positive health attributes."

In working with USADA, it was discovered through the process of supplement examination that Barnett's Tributestin was contaminated with ostarine. After testimony at the hearing, USADA conceded that the source of the ostarine found in Barnett's out-of-competition samples were from Tributestin, as the product was contaminated. With this concession which USADA seemed to admit from the outset and confirmed with Barnett's testimony, the case "became one of the Applicant being the victim of a Contaminated Product with a Prohibited Substance."

Barnett's prior history of failed drug tests and the matter of whether this was a second infraction of the UFC ADP was discussed. However, the arbitrator determined that a drug sample taken by the California State Athletic Commission during his stint with the Affliction promotion should not be considered in punishment for Barnett.

Barnett gave the UFC notice that he was taking a "leave of absence" on December 14, 2016. Two weeks later, his A sample came up positive for ostarine. There's no indication that the leave had anything to do with his positive sample or that USADA claimed that the time away inferred wrongdoing.

The arbitration hearing took place on March 6, 2018, 14 months after his sample was taken. The Arbitrator seemed to be persuaded by Barnett's testimony as he described in detail his trying to make sure that he was compliant with USADA rules. Notably, after his dealings with the California State Athletic Commission he devised a practice of "keeping each original container of any supplement he used and ensuring that a small portion of its content remained and could be analyzed." This seemed to sway the trier of fact.

"I find this Applicant to be a very meticulous and careful person," wrote the Arbitrator in his decision. "In my experience as an arbitrator of hundreds of doping cases I have never heard testimony from an individual who has taken so much care to record his supplement regime in order to avoid the very problem he is now experiencing."[9]

Clearly, Barnett's past history in anti-doping cases helped him with avoiding further suspension. But, Barnett's skepticism of the USADA likely pushed the heavyweight to be much more meticulous about the records he kept, knowing the perils if he were to be flagged for a positive drug test. As a result of his time away from the Octagon, and in order to clear his name, Barnett sued the supplement maker.

Barnett's outcome at arbitration was the first where a UFC fighter was not issued a suspension. Despite the finding that Barnett was not "at fault," he was issued a public reprimand. Barnett's arbitration came over a year after he was flagged by USADA however. Put on a "provisional suspension" by USADA, Barnett's career was in limbo until USADA could determine the substance Barnett tested positive for.

Barnett decided to leave the UFC, citing concerns about USADA. During the process, he refused to accept any settlements offered by USADA. "I would be willing to do anything else but work with USADA at this point," Barnett said in an interview prior to the arbitration.[10] Barnett is not alone. There have been several athletes that have been outspoken about USADA and the testing protocol. Barnett's positive outcome at arbitration may prove to help others in the future.

Jon Jones Fails Another Drug Test

Jon Jones returned to the UFC in July 2017 to face Daniel Cormier for the UFC Light Heavyweight Championship. It was just his second fight after returning from the suspension that kept him out of the main event of UFC 200. In an emotional rematch between the two fighters, Jones defeated Cormier. After the fight, Jones reflected on his rivalry with Cormier and stated that he aspired to be a better person and praised his once-hated opponent for helping him become better.

While this may have been a great redemption story, three weeks later news surfaced that Jones had tested positive for a steroid in an in-competition USADA drug test. It was the second straight year Jones had failed a USADA drug test. This time it was the steroid turinabol that was found in his urine sample. Despite claiming that he and his lawyers had gone through an extensive audit of all of the supplements he had ingested, none revealed the source for the drug. Turinabol results in lean muscle gain without any significant accompanying water retention or rise in estrogen levels. This would give the athlete an unfair advantage.

Jones appeared before the California State Athletic Commission with his attorney, Howard Jacobs. Known as the "athlete's lawyer," Jacobs has represented Brock Lesnar, track star Marion Jones and cyclist Floyd Landis. Even with Jacobs' expertise, the strategy to proclaim Jones' innocence was muddled. Jacobs attempted to link Jones' drug test for turinabol with an unintentional use. But there was no scientific evidence which would explain the reason why turinabol was in Jones' system. Jones' expert testifying on his behalf stated that the turinabol metabolites would have been higher if the use was intentional. Thus, it may have been a contaminated supplement that may have had the turinabol. However, Jones' expert indicated that he had worked just four hours on the matter, based on a request from Jacobs. He also could not draw any definitive conclusions on how the drug got into Jones' system.

The commission's witness stated that one could not be conclusive as to whether Jones took a contaminated supplement. But, one thing was for certain with the testing: Jones had turinabol in his system. According to the rules, he was guilty regardless of whether the ingestion was intentional or not.

Jones did not help his cause during his testimony. He admitted that he had his management team complete the required online educational classes provided from USADA. These classes are mandatory and provide information on the UFC Anti-Doping Policy. Jones allowed his management team to forge his signature on the USADA tutorial forms proving that he completed the classes. Thus, Jones admitted he did not make an attempt to learn about the rules, while putting his management team in a bad light as enablers for Jones and being guilty of falsifying documents.

The California State Athletic Commission chastised Jones for his indifference to his second drug test failure in as many years. There was no evidence presented which would overturn the drug test finding and it appeared as though the former light heavyweight champion was throwing himself at the mercy of the commission in hopes that they would give him a break.

But Jones' appearance came across as a spoiled athlete that was enabled by his management team looking to get away with another problem. During the hearing, commissioners brought up his past indiscretions which likely came into consideration when thinking about his punishment. The notification by Jones' lawyer to his expert seemed a concern. With Jones' career possibly on the line, as a second infraction of the UFC Anti-Doping Policy would command at least a four-year suspension, Jones' retained expert spent only four hours studying the case. With little time to come up with a theory, it appeared to be a hasty strategy meant to provide a scientific component to their defense. The effort may have been futile regardless of how much time they spent on the case, but admitting that the expert had limited time to evaluate the matter might indicate the lack of a competent theory of the case.

The Commission fined Jones $205,000 which was 40 percent of his $500,000 purse from his fight against Cormier, and revoked his license to fight in the state of California. It was a strong rebuke compared to the hope that Jones would just receive a public reprimand. "I don't believe we should end Mr. Jones' career, but I do believe he should sit out for a while," stated CSAC Executive Director Andy Foster to the commission while it deliberated the anti-doping case. The statement seemed to reflect disappointment in Jones' actions, as well as imply that Jones could re-apply for a CSAC license at the conclusion of his pending case with USADA.

USADA Issues 15-month Suspension
for Jones' Second Offense

After defeating Daniel Cormier for the UFC Light Heavyweight title, Jon Jones failed another USADA urine sample test on July 28, 2017. The test result found turinabol in Jones' system. It was the second infraction under the UFC Anti-Doping Policy.

Facing the possibility of a 4-year suspension based upon the policy guidelines, Richard McLaren, an arbitrator for McLaren Global Sport Solutions, gave Jones a lighter sentence. McLaren reduced the suspension by 30 months, allowing just a 15-month suspension.[11]

Unlike other arbitrations heard under the UFC Anti-Doping Policy, the parties stipulated and agreed to a "Joint Stipulated Partial Factual Resolution and Arbitration Agreement." Notably, the 30-month reduction in the sanction would not be contested.

The ruling issued on September 13, 2018, once again declared Jones innocent of attempting to purposely be a "drug cheat." The banned substance found in his system was not traced back to any of the supplements Jones had shared with USADA in their joint attempts to determine the source of the positive drug test. Jones' cooperation with USADA was a factor in the reduction of the penalty. Notably, McLaren believed that he could have reduced the suspension down to 12 months but determined that Jones could have done other things to mitigate his risk. In the decision, McLaren states that Jones could have used third party "certified dietary supplements which may have further reduced his risk of testing positive from a contaminated supplement."[12]

Based on the UFC Anti-Doping Violation rules, McLaren believed that he did not have to determine the source of the banned substance to determine fault and reduce the penalty. He concluded that the level of liability for Jones was minimal and believed that the banned substance found in his system would not have helped his performance. "There was absolutely no intention to use Prohibited Substances on the part of the Athlete [Jones]," wrote the arbitrator.

The arbitrator determined that the UFC Anti-Doping Rules were drafted in a way in which the finder of fact need not determine the source of the banned substance. The arbitration decision cited cases in which an athlete is discharged of his burden of proving lack of intent without establishing the source of the banned substance. In prior cases, the athlete's testimony, evidence/testimony supporting athlete's contention and no evidence undermining athlete's theory have satisfied the burden that the use of a banned substance was not intentional.

The second Jones arbitration decision reflects a level of leniency based on the fact that the parties could not determine the source of the banned substance found in the fighter's drug test. Without finding the source, it's hard to explain why and how Jones tested positive for a banned substance. Thus, the reduction of the sanction would have been harder to justify. But McLaren, citing similar cases and the ambiguity in the UFC Anti-Doping Policy Rules, determined that despite the inability to pinpoint the source of the banned substance, it would reduce the sanctions. McLaren determined that Jones had no intention of using a prohibited substance. But, according to the arbitrator decision, Jones' mistaken intention was his belief that he was using USADA-approved supplements.

The arbitrator seemed to sympathize with Jones despite the circumstantial evidence that this was his second failed test and arbitration. There was also his admission at the California State Athletic Commission hearing that he did not do the educational component of the USADA training which he was supposed to do. Yet, the arbitrator wrote, "Jones has gone through a great deal of difficulties. He gave me the very distinct impression that he has learned a lot from the loss of the image of himself that he had as a champion MMA fighter. He has been humbled and humiliated by the experience but has learned from his misfortune." The arbitrator added, "[he] needs the opportunity to regain his dignity and self-esteem."[13]

The California State Athletic Commission instituted another three months of community service in addition to USADA's 15-month penalty. This would make the overall time away from the Octagon 18 months. As a result, Jones was scheduled to return to the UFC in December 2018.

Based upon the Jones decision, it's clear that an athlete's level of transparency with USADA in determining a suspension is one of the objective factors used by the organization. Although he's had a checkered past and a previous UFC Anti-Doping Violation, Jones was a credible witness for the arbitrator which seemed to assist in reducing his penalty. In comparison, Francisco Rivera's story of eating tainted meat in Mexico was not readily accepted by USADA and when it came to verify the story, Rivera was nowhere to be found. Josh Barnett's success in his arbitration was based on the level of detail he kept about his supplements which allowed USADA to pinpoint the contaminated supplement. Jones' situation differed due to the minimal level of the banned substance found in his sample which was likely a reason why the arbitrator determined that finding the source was not a necessity in reducing the suspension.

The Jones decision has been criticized due to a portion of the decision which indicates that Jones would actively assist in providing USADA with information on other athletes that may have committed violations of the UFC Anti-Doping Policy. While Jones disputes this characterization, the instruction was the first of its kind under the UFC Anti-Doping Policy and provides

Jones with an affirmative action to report others he may know or suspect of violating the rules.

In December 2018, Jon Jones returned to the California State Athletic Commission seeking to obtain a temporary license in order to fight later in the month in his return to the UFC. During the hearing which granted him his license, it was suggested by the commissioners that Jones enroll himself into additional drug testing with the Voluntary Anti-Doping Association (VADA). Similar to USADA, VADA conducts athletic drug testing although it sends results directly to athletic commissions. Jones, his attorney Howard Jacobs and UFC executive Marc Ratner did not formally agree to the proposal as they wanted to explore the option. A couple days after the hearing, Jones decided to decline the invitation to take additional drug testing along with his obligation with USADA. While it was in his right to decline the suggestion, the gesture would clear up any belief of wrongdoing on the part of Jones. The commission even offered to pay for the additional testing so that Jones would not be paying out of pocket. The move seemed to be an offer to restore Jones' image.

CSAC Executive Director Andy Foster criticized USADA's handling of Jones' case identifying the length of time and the cost of the investigation which eventually led to the 15-month suspension. Foster's comments made at Jones' hearing providing him a temporary license to fight highlight one of the issues with drug testing of MMA athletes especially in the UFC—the dual jurisdiction of the UFC and its anti-doping program versus the state regulators that also have authority. In this instance, the CSAC deferred to USADA after Jones' drug test failure but there are rumblings that the commissions should have more authority.

Another Drug Test, Another Issue for Jon Jones

One week before Jon Jones' return to the Octagon on December 29, 2018, the event was moved from Las Vegas, Nevada, to Inglewood, California, due to an issue with an out-of-competition test earlier in the month which found traces of the metabolite turinabol. This was the same anabolic steroid found in Jones' system in 2017. The drug is an anabolic steroid which is used to maintain muscle mass while losing weight. It helps with cutting weight while not losing any strength by fighters. Yet, without classifying Jones' test as being "flagged" or failing the drug test, USADA looked into it more and determined that the December 2018 test had remnants of the same metabolites found in Jones' system a year-and-a-half earlier.[14] USADA pointed out that Jones had passed several drug tests prior to his December 2018 test.

Despite USADA's proclamation that Jones would have no benefits of the banned substance in his system, the state of Nevada had concerns and would not issue Jones a license. Rather, they wanted more time to decide what caused the negative result. Since California had issued Jones a temporary license, the UFC made the hasty decision to move the entire event from Nevada to California. As a condition of moving the event to the state with just six days' notice, the California State Athletic Commission required Jones to register with the VADA.

It was once again another debacle for an athlete perceived to be the greatest in the sport of MMA. Jones' drug test revealed a banned substance; however, USADA and the UFC defended the move to California from Nevada because of the low level of turinabol in Jones' test. While the UFC and USADA praised the move to California, fans and other athletes on the event card protested the late move due to the money spent to go to Las Vegas.

The presence of turinabol in Jones' system over a year after it was discovered is baffling to many, since Jones stated that he's never taken steroids, and in July 2017, the source of the banned substance was not found. Yet, unlike Jones' 15-month suspension, this finding did not yield a suspension or cause Jones to be pulled from the main event of UFC 232.

The move of the entire card to California with less than a week was unprecedented and disrupting for the rest of the fighters scheduled to appear on the card. It brings into question the veracity of the UFC and USADA in touting that its anti-doping policy was created to ensure fighter health, safety and a level playing field for all. But, the perception from this decision was preferential treatment for Jones. The California State Athletic Commission also seemed to turn their head with the USADA ruling on Jones and issued him a temporary license without a concern. This brings up the question of the regulators and how independent they appear for the promotion's that operate in their jurisdiction.

USADA's Effect on UFC Athletes

The implementation of the UFC Anti-Doping Policy was embraced at first by athletes due to the number of failed drug tests for performance enhancing drugs prior to the program. There was belief that drug testing would cure the issue of having to fight athletes with an unfair and illegal advantage. However, as the policy was implemented and athletes began to be tested and flagged for drug failures, the feelings changed. Many athletes believe that the drug policy is burdensome and still leaves room for those wanting to use performance enhancing drugs to do so. Moreover, the appeal process takes time and some, like Barnett, do not trust USADA or the administration of the program. The December 2018 Jon Jones issue also brought into the question the actual purpose of USADA.

One concern is the perceived intrusiveness of the USADA program. According to its policy, this is an important part of the UFC Anti-Doping Program. "Athletes are subject to testing 365 days a year and do not have 'off-seasons' or cutoff periods in which testing does not occur," reads the Whereabouts protocol. This requires a contracted athlete to provide dates, times and locations as to where they might be to allow the potential for USADA testing. Athletes are required to log in to a dedicated web site. There is also a USADA app that can be downloaded to an athlete's mobile phone. These utilities were provided to make the process of reporting one's whereabouts more accessible and easier for the athlete.

However, Nick Diaz became the first UFC athlete to be suspended due to his failure to keep his location current with USADA. According to the rules, three whereabouts failures within 12 months is deemed a violation and is treated similar to that of failing a drug test. Diaz did not keep the UFC apprised of his whereabouts and was suspended one year as a result. Despite the fact that Diaz had not fought since January 2015 and was not tested from April 2017 until the end of that year, he accepted a period of ineligibility for one year. Diaz was a member of the UFC Registered Testing Pool and was not available for three tests at the locations provided in his Whereabouts Filings.[15] According to its announcement of Diaz's sanction, USADA stated that it "conducts in-person and online educational sessions with athletes, sends email reminders about filing dates and obligations, maintains online and app-based filing and updating platforms, and gives athletes the option to receive daily and weekly reminders of their provided Whereabouts information."[16]

There is also the issue of the dual jurisdiction of USADA and the state athletic commissions. The most glaring example would be of UFC women's strawweight Cynthia Calvillo. A USADA drug test after a fight in December 2017 revealed she used marijuana. She accepted a six-month suspension that could be whittled down to three if she participated in a USADA-approved drug awareness and management program. However, the Nevada Athletic Commission, the state where her fight took place, revamped its anti-doping program in 2015 which gave harsher punishments for violators. The commission added three more months to her suspension and fined her 15 percent of her disclosed $41,000 purse plus $436.08 in attorney's fees.[17] Not only does the dual jurisdiction mean multiple concerns over responding to a drug test which includes multiple administrative issues, there is the ability for the commission or USADA to dole out differing penalties.

Most recently, the UFC amended its policy of announcing an athlete's failed drug test until after resolution. The previous policy was to announce a provisional suspension of an athlete testing for a banned substance. The amended policy allows for time for an athlete to resolve the issue with USADA. The policy was changed based on the results from athletes where the failed drug test was the result of an inadvertent use of a banned substance and/or a contaminated supplement.

Outside of the sport, many view the Anti-Doping policy as a success as the promotion was able to shape a policy based on its needs. Yet, the backlash from athletes seems to have stirred concern about USADA and the way the policy has been implemented. As of the end of 2018, there have been no major changes to the Anti-Doping Policy and it does not appear that any changes are coming any time soon.

Without formal input from athletes, the UFC Anti-Doping Policy will have its detractors for its appearance of overreach, substantial penalties and lengthy process to investigate the drug test. Some have lobbied for the UFC to abolish the Anti-Doping Policy and go back to commission-testing. The issue with this testing would be the level of uncertainty from state to state and jurisdiction to jurisdiction. There is also the question of whether commissions would honor another's suspension and not allow an athlete to fight in another jurisdiction while suspended. Then, there is always the question of integrity within a commission. The Jon Jones controversy made USADA and the commissions look as though they were willing to look the other way when a low-level amount of a banned substance was found in Jones' test and yet he was not banned.

The search for a level playing field where all athletes are free of performance enhancing drugs continue. Logistics, cost and administering the rules have been a task for regulators and promoters. While the UFC Anti-Doping Policy has been seen as a success and a move in the right direction, there are still ways for the policy to be enhanced to ensure that only those seeking to gain an unfair and illegal advantage are caught and punished.

3

After Clearing Name
with USADA, Athletes Sue

Introduction

An indirect effect of the UFC Anti-Doping Policy are athletes going after the drug makers, suppliers and distributors due to being flagged by USADA. There have been at least four lawsuits that have been filed by fighters that have been suspended by USADA.

Lyman Good, Carlos Ferreira, Yoel Romero and Josh Barnett have filed lawsuits against the specific supplement makers and distributors as a result of failed drug tests. To date, none of the lawsuits have gone to trial or been settled. The lawsuits allege negligence, breach of warranty and other product liability claims.

The area of product liability refers to a manufacturer or seller being liable for placing a defective product into the hands of a consumer. The law states that when a product has an unexpected defect or danger, the product cannot be said to meet the ordinary expectations of the consumer.

Strict liability applies to this theory of law as the sale of the product must be made in the regular course of the supplier's business. It cannot be passed along through other means. For example, in Jon Jones' first arbitration case, Jones received a pill which likely caused his first positive drug test. The pill was given to him by his training partner. As a result, Jones would not be able to file a lawsuit against the drug manufacturer for failing his USADA test since it was not obtained through the "regular course of the supplier's business."

Similarly, the lawsuits claim that the supplements and/or products used by the athletes did not include all of the contents listed on the label. As a result, the athletes failed their USADA drug test and suffered harm (i.e., put on provisional suspension).

The question arises as to what standard should apply to determine fault in these cases. Foreseeability, a component in tort law relating to consequences of a party's action or inaction could reasonably result in the injury. Would it be foreseeable that MMA fighters in training for a competition would use the supplements and be subject to a suspension for using it?

Here is a look at four of the cases.

Lyman Good

Lyman Good anticipated a homecoming fight in front of friends and family with the UFC's first show in New York at Madison Square Garden in 2016. However, he was removed from the event due to a failed drug test. Good was put on provisional suspension until USADA could determine the source of the failed test.

The target supplements were Anavite and Cordygen-VO2 ULTRA, according to the lawsuit filed in New York by his attorney. Good learned through the provisional suspension process and working with USADA that he tested positive for androstenedione ("andro"). Andro is an anabolic-androgenic steroid and is a banned substance. The drug is used to promote muscle growth.

After his suspension, Good provided unopened bottles to a third-party laboratory for testing. The lab detected andro in both products. Good sued the manufacturers and supplier of the vitamin supplement which he believed was improperly labeled and misleading.[1]

Good requested restitution, damages, injunctive and other equitable relief. Good believed that Gaspari Nutrition misbranded the products as "dietary supplements" to defraud consumers in believing it had superior "dietary supplements."

Vitamin Shoppe, the retail supplier which sold the product, was brought into the lawsuit for breach of warranty for selling the products "despite assurances of product quality and control."

In August 2018, the defendants filed a motion to dismiss Good's claims. The court granted Gaspari Nutrition's motion for claims of fraud, assault and battery and reckless or intentional infliction of emotional distress.

The court indicated that the plaintiff's fraud claim was "threadbare," with conclusory assertions. Similarly, it found only conclusory allegations regarding any intention to inflict personal injury on Good without his consent.[2] It appears that the plaintiff failed to respond to the Gaspari Defendants' arguments regarding the assault claim and as a result Good abandoned it.

In addition, all claims of the individuals named in the lawsuit were dismissed. The court stated, "an officer or director is not personally liable for the torts of a corporation 'merely by reason of his office.'"[3]

One of the more interesting parts of the Court's Motion to Dismiss is its denial for Good to amend his claim to include one for false advertising.

The claim was based on a Vitamin Shoppe employee making a recommendation to Good regarding the supplement. It seemed as though an employee of the Vitamin Shoppe had recommended the supplement which caused Good's failed test. However, the court ruled that one employee's recommendation was not disseminated to the public or would persuade similarly situated consumers. Simply put, Good took bad advice from an employee.

The court did allow for Good to amend his complaint against Gaspari for breach of implied warranty of fitness for a particular purpose. The allegation implies that the seller knows or has reason to know that the product is used for a particular purpose.

Drug Maker Seeks to Dismiss Case for Alleged "Spoliation" of Evidence

In December 2018, defendants Gaspari Nutrition and Hi-Tech Pharmaceuticals filed a motion to dismiss the case against them for spoliation of evidence. Essentially, they claimed that the drug that was tested during the USADA investigation process was gone and Good's explanation of its whereabouts were "suspect at best."[4] The defendants concluded that neither Good nor his attorney had a valid excuse for the disappearance of the supplement that Good took and that was tested by USADA. They claimed that Good played "fast and loose" with the pleading with the inference that the fighter and/or his attorney may have made up some of the information to make up for the lack of evidence. They cite a list of supplements that Good took when he took the USADA drug test which did not include Anavite. The defendants also made the argument that the plaintiff's attorney might have been a witness to the case and would have to be disqualified from representing his client. The reason was due to deposition testimony from Good that he gave the product to his attorney although his attorney stated that he did not have it.

Another factor alleged by the defendants was that the lack of evidence to test to determine the veracity of Good's claim left them at a disadvantage. If there is no evidence, the defendants would be concerned with a presumption that the supplement Good states he took was tainted.

The dismissal is predicated on a potential sanction for "spoliation" of the evidence and would not necessarily be the result given by the court if it determined that the plaintiff destroyed the evidence on purpose to prevent an examination or disposed of it with reckless disregard of its need.

As of this writing the court had yet to make a decision on the motion, but the purported factual assertions about Good's lack of evidence offers circumstantial evidence that the athlete was not telling the truth. Good claimed that he had not changed his regimen of nutrition and supplements since his previous drug test (which came up negative for banned substances) but for the addition of two supplements, one being Anavite.

Will This Lawsuit Be Good for Good?

With a trial pending in 2019, Good's claims have been narrowed with the defendants pressing for a court order to dismiss the lawsuit due to the lack of the alleged tainted supplement. The other claims against the personal executives were dismissed as well as the claims of fraud and/or misrepresentation. It appears that if there is any liability on the part of the manufacturer and/or distributor it is one of negligence rather than a higher level of liability. Even there, Good may not win since it's not clear how foreseeable it may be for a supplement company to know that the products they use may end up on a banned substance list. Then again, the supplement did not list the included ingredient. There is an argument that Good relied upon the label of ingredients when deciding on using the supplement; this is the most logical argument for Good's claims.

If the case does not settle, the issue of whether the supplement maker was at fault for not properly labeling its product must be determined. If it was inadvertent or a knowing omission, it may be an issue as well. Even if most of the supplement's users are not professional athletes that rely on knowing the contents of the product, there is a foreseeability issue in relying on what is included in something consumers will ingest. The question will be the inference posed by the defendants that Good has brought this lawsuit without sound intent and is lashing out to find a scapegoat for his punishment of suspension by the UFC.

Yoel Romero Sues Supplement Maker

As a former Olympian in wrestling for his native Cuba, Yoel Romero won a silver medal at the 2000 Summer Olympics in Sydney, Australia. Romero also represented Cuba at the 2004 Summer Olympics in Athens. Romero turned to the sport of mixed martial arts in 2009 after defecting to Germany. Romero made his debut in the UFC in 2013 at the age of 36. Despite competing in the UFC at an advanced age, the former Olympian fought at a high level and rose through the ranks of the light heavyweight division. His first four UFC fights ended in knockouts and he won his first eight fights in the UFC prior to a loss for the light heavyweight title in 2017.

Whether or not it was warranted, Romero was accused by competitors of using banned substances to gain an advantage. Despite fighting into his late 30s, Romero maintained a perfect physique and superior cardio, as he never tired during fights. This brought suspicion that Romero was gaining an unfair advantage through steroids.

Romero was issued a six-month suspension for testing positive for Ibutamoren following an out-of-competition test in December 2015. According to the USADA press release announcing the sanction, Ibutamoren is a Growth Hormone Secretagogue and a prohibited substance in the class of Peptide Hormones, Growth Factors, Related Substances and Mimetics under the UFC Anti-Doping Policy.[5]

The Cuban fighter worked with USADA to determine the source of the failed drug test. Romero gave USADA a pill from the bottle of a Shred Rx supplement he had been using. It contained Ibutamoren at a concentration of "approximately 5 micrograms per capsule." USADA then purchased an unopened bottle of Shred Rx and found a similar concentration of the banned substance. This led to a lighter sentence for Romero of six months for using a contaminated substance.

Romero alleged that Shred Rx was negligent in maintaining its production facility and knew Shred Rx was contaminated with Ibutamoren. The substance was not listed among its ingredients on the label.

In December 2018, Romero obtained a default judgment against Shred Rx, as the maker of the drug failed to respond to the lawsuit. In these situations, Romero will have the opportunity to have a hearing to determine his damages. Once the court issues an Order for the Judgment, it would be up to Romero to attempt to get the monetary judgment from the company. In certain situations, the reason for the company's failure to respond to the lawsuit is insolvency on the part of a company. Even if a monetary judgment is issued, the plaintiff would not be able to collect. Rarely does a company neglect to respond to a properly served lawsuit due to the possibility of a court order entering a judgment against it. For Romero, the real work will come in attempting to recover the judgment as when a company's not willing to appear in a lawsuit, it will likely be hard to find assets.

Fighter Claims "Spiked" Nutritional Supplement Caused Failed Test

Carlos Diego Ferreira filed a lawsuit against supplement vendors, manufacturers and suppliers for a supplement which resulted in the lightweight being suspended for 17 months. The lawsuit filed in October 2018 in the District Court of Hidalgo County, Texas states that the defendants spiked "360 Lean, a "dietary nutritional supplement" with ostarine while also misleadingly adding a prohibited substance known as 7-Keto DHEA, causing plaintiff to suffer severe injuries after being banned from the UFC."

Ferreira notes that the label of 360Lean did not accurately list 7-Keto DHEA and later changed its description in subsequent batches. The lawsuit states, "[R]epresenting that the supplement contained, 7-Keto®, without indicating the product contained a hormone was wholly deceptive, misleading, and fraudulent."

Both 7-Keto DHEA and ostarine are banned substances and 360Lean was placed on the USADA High Risk List in February 2017 "after testing of Lot Number 9004637 revealed the presence of 7-Keto DHEA and ostarine."[6]

In September 2016, a sealed unopened bottle of 360Lean was sent to a WADA accredited lab when the plaintiff discovered that he had unknowingly and through no fault of his own ingested ostarine from the product 360Lean. Ferreira was charged with a UFC Anti-Doping Violation in November 2016.

Ferreira sued Zinpro and Impact Labs as the developers, manufacturers, marketers and distributors of 360Lean.[7] Vitamin Shack & Shakes sold the 360Lean product.

The lawsuit states a variety of causes of action including negligence, breach of express warranty, breach of implied warrantied and fraud against Zinpro Corporation and Impact Labs.[8] Ferreira also claimed that the defendants are guilty under the theory of strict liability for products liability.

There has been little publicized with this lawsuit although the same legal pattern is present as with others in this chapter. The fighter used a supplement that he believed did not contain a banned substance but a drug test revealed that their ingestion of the supplement included contaminants which included the banned substance.

In August 2018, Ferreira filed a Second Amended Petition to alter his lawsuit against the defendants which was met with a general denial in the answer two weeks later. But in November 2018 the plaintiff abruptly moved for a nonsuit (requesting dismissal) in the matter and the court obliged on November 27, 2018. Although there was no disposition of the case or notice of settlement, the quick dismissal likely meant the parties decided to settle the matter quietly or Ferreira determined it was no longer worth the expense to continue battling in court. As of September 2019, Ferreira continues fighting for the UFC.

Josh Barnett Sues Makers of Supplement

Coming off of a successful arbitration with USADA where he only received a reprimand and not a suspension for allegedly taking a banned substance per the UFC Anti-Doping Policy, Josh Barnett sued the makers of the supplement that was found to have caused the failed test. The lawsuit, filed in Los Angeles Superior Court in Southern California, alleged negligence, strict products liability, breach of implied warranty and breach of express warranty.[9]

Barnett had an out-of-competition test flagged by USADA when it was believed he had a banned substance in his system. It was determined that the banned substance was ostarine, a product that produces muscle growth but its use is prohibited by USADA. Fortunately for Barnett, he kept a detailed accounting of the supplements he ingested and was able to pinpoint which supplement caused the failed test. The product in question was Tributestin. A USADA arbitration found that he should not receive a suspension, but he was publicly reprimanded. Barnett sued the makers of the supplement as a result.

On April 9, 2018, Barnett filed a lawsuit against Biokor, LLC, doing business as Genkor. Barnett claimed that the Tributestin bottle he had kept tested positive for the banned substance. USADA obtained a sealed bottle of the same product for testing and it produced traces of ostarine, according to Barnett's lawsuit. This would indicate that the makers' product was defective as it had a substance not on its label. On October 13, 2018, Barnett filed a First Amended Complaint which added the defendants, all of which claimed responsibility in the manufacture, packaging, distribution, marketing, promotion, and/or sale of the alleged defective Tributestin.

A demurrer was filed on behalf of two individuals with corporate interests of the companies sued stating that as individuals they would not be held liable for anything that may have occurred while working for the corporation. This would be a valid argument considering that individual members sued by a party would be personally liable for any alleged damages. Moreover, if the individual were to have been liable for the alleged contamination of the Tributestin, it would be presumed done on behalf of their companies. From Barnett's perspective, naming individual members of a company would ensure that all parties had been included in the lawsuit. But it would also ensure that if the companies became insolvent, the individuals would be liable.

Assessing the Cases

The lawsuits in this chapter occurred after each fighter was sanctioned by USADA. Each of the lawsuits relate to contaminated supplements which fall into the category of products liability. The commonality in these lawsuits is each athlete's claim that they relied upon the distributor, manufacturer or supplier of the drug to ensure that the supplement did not contain a banned substance. From the defendant's standpoint, product liability cases may come down to the examination of the specific product and whether there was an issue with the process of making the product as it made its way to the store shelf for the athlete to purchase. In certain instances, defendants will file cross-claims against another defendant claiming that it was likely their fault for the athlete's claims. With product liability cases having a strict liability standard, there is a presumption that if the plaintiff can prove the presence of the contaminated substance in the product, the defendant would be held liable. Certain defenses, like those in the Good case, would suggest that they must have an opportunity to examine the product to determine if the supplement was contaminated and if so, who would be at fault.

4

Independent Contractor or Employee

Introduction

Mixed martial arts fighters are considered independent contractors by promoters. As a result, companies need not provide fighters health care, vacation and pension benefits as most employers require. There are no intermediary means to address situations such as what happens if the opponent of a fighter pulls out of a fight at the last minute or does not make the contracted weight per the terms of the fight agreement. In a promotion like the UFC, exclusivity is required of the athlete and they therefore are unable to seek a fight in other promotions. Moreover, there is no way to address grievances against the company except for directly discussing the issue, and if there is no resolution the athlete must either file a lawsuit or accept the situation.

While the UFC is the primary promotion known for an exclusivity requirement, it appears that in others, the promoter is allowed a right of first refusal to accept or deny the athlete the opportunity to fight elsewhere. Although fighters are independent contractors, an exclusivity requirement prevents fighters from participating with other organizations for a certain time period or before a number of fights within the promotion. UFC contracted fighters must agree to submit to the UFC anti-doping policy which requires that they disclose their whereabouts at all times to ensure that they can take a drug test with a moment's notice. Among other obligations of being a contracted fighter is the requirement that athletes adhere to the UFC's clothing policy with Reebok. This requires athletes to wear Reebok clothing during the week prior to the fight and during the fight. This rule negated streams of revenue for fighters, as many received ancillary income from sponsors that paid for fighters to wear their logo on hats, t-shirts and shorts. They were also compensated for having a banner held in front of the cage and behind the fighter during the fight introductions. When the UFC forged a deal with Reebok in which it would pay athletes based on how many fights they had had in the organization, these additional sources of revenue were negated. The money Reebok compensated fighters was less than some fighters made in sponsorships.

In Bellator, the promotion may allow a fighter to work with another promotion, but it must grant the athlete the right to fight elsewhere. Thus, the fighter is not truly "independent" if they must request from their promotion whether they are able to work in another promotion.

The independent contractor has benefits. It allows the freedom to work wherever the contractor may seek. It should give the contractor the flexibility to pick and choose where they want to work and when they would like to do it. It also should give the contractor the opportunity to negotiate their own contracts. As one might see, in the world of mixed martial arts these freedoms are seldom and are likely not afforded to athletes that are in major MMA promotions.

The National Labor Relations Board is an independent U.S. government agency with responsibilities for enforcing U.S. labor law in relation to collective bargaining and unfair labor practices. The NLRB can determine whether workers are employees or independent contractors. However, it is required that at least 30 percent of the employees must sign cards expressing interest in the union. At that point, NLRB agents will then investigate to make sure the Board has jurisdiction and there are no existing labor contracts that would bar an election. If an NLRB election were to take place, a majority of the votes cast will determine whether a union will be certified. If so, it will be deemed the employees' bargaining representative and is entitled to be recognized by the employer as the exclusive bargaining agent for the employees.[1]

Under the National Labor Relations Act, independent contractor status is determined by common law agency criteria, with no factor controlling.

Leslie Smith Attempts to Organize Fighters in UFC

There have been several attempts to organize fighters. One of these attempts occurred when UFC women's bantamweight Leslie Smith launched Project Spearhead in 2017. The goal of the organization was to establish a unified organization that would request better conditions for fighters in the UFC. Smith lobbied fighters to sign authorization cards to allow the NLRB to conduct an election to determine whether a majority of the UFC contracted fighters wanted to become employees.

During the 2017 UFC Athlete Retreat, fighters were treated to a Question and Answer session with retired NBA star Kobe Bryant. Smith asked Bryant about the importance of a players' association. Bryant stated that it was extremely important. It was unlikely that the purpose for Bryant's appearance was to endorse the benefits of a union, yet Smith's question shed some light on the notion of a union and how it may have aided the future NBA Hall of Famer.

Smith also was very active on social media promoting the rights of fighters. According to her Charging Letter with the NRLB, she sent approximately 350 public tweets to different fighters requesting that they sign an authorization card. She indicated that the signing of authorization cards would be confidential. Yet, there was still concern from athletes worried that Zuffa would discover their names. Previously, an organization that attempted to organize athletes disclosed the names of fighters willing to serve as the board despite the fact there was an agreement to keep names confidential. Smith's twitter campaign upset Zuffa officials as they had advocated against a union or association for fighters. But she maintained her right to speak her mind about issues regarding fighters' rights.

The UFC agreed to meet with Smith to address some of her concerns regarding Zuffa's "UFC Promotional Guidelines," which were amended and issued by Zuffa to its athletes in December 2017. She was scheduled to meet with a UFC official the same month but that was rescheduled. Then she was contacted by Zuffa's Chief Legal Officer, Kirk Hendrick, to meet to discuss her concerns. Smith indicated that attempts to coordinate a meeting never came to fruition. So, while there seemed to be a willingness of the two sides to meet, it never happened.

Entering into her last fight of her contract in April 2018, Smith notified the UFC that she would wear a Project Spearhead mouthpiece with the organization's logo. The obvious hope for Smith was that the cameras would show the mouthpiece on television, which could create conversation. But her opponent, Aspen Ladd, was not able to make the requisite weight per the bout agreement. Smith decided not to fight her opponent at a "catchweight," as she was not required to by the commission. Seeing an opportunity to negotiate a furtherance of her fight contract, she engaged in discussions regarding the possibility to extend her Promotional Agreement by two fights with a flat $100,000 per appearance payout. However, the UFC gave Smith her "show" money and her "win" purse for the event in what appeared to be a buyout of her contract. In most instances, fighters that make weight but their opponent does not are awarded their show money (the money they make for showing up for the fight) but are not given their win money. Zuffa informed Smith that the unilateral decision to pay the show and win bonuses "fully satisfied its contractual obligations remaining under her Promotional Agreement." The same day, she received correspondence from Zuffa's legal counsel that they had "decided not to exercise its Right of First Negotiation and Right to Match a Fighter Offers" pursuant to the Promotional Agreement. Smith contends that she did not accept the win and show money as a "quid pro quo." Zuffa contends that it simply chose not to extend Smith's fight contract or provide her a new one. Instead of retaining its right to a match any fight contract that she might find elsewhere, Zuffa decided to waive this right and allow Smith to find fights elsewhere immediately.

Smith was a success in the octagon. Dana White gave her positive feedback after a November 15, 2014 fight against bantamweight Jessica Eye. Smith lost the fight due to doctor stoppage despite wanting to continue to fight. She was prevented from fighting after her right ear separated in half. Even though she risked the chance of losing her ear, she wanted to continue to fight. White was happy about Smith's fighting spirit. She had a winning record in the UFC and as her contract ended, it appeared likely that she wanted to continue to fight for the promotion. At the time of her departure, she was a ranked fighter within the UFC's women's bantamweight division.

According to the Charging Letter submitted by Smith's attorneys, her termination "delivered an unlawful message to the remainder of the fighter employees, which is: dare to form, join or assist a union and you too will accompany Ms. Smith *not* fighting in the UFC."[2]

Smith claimed that Zuffa violated Sections 8(a)(1) and 8(a)(3) of the National Labor Relations Act which protects workers from retaliation for engaging in unionizing activities. There is also the possibility that another complaint may be made against the UFC for misclassifying fighters as independent contractors and not employees.

The NLRB flagged Smith's case and obtained testimony from Smith to determine if there was a need for injunctive relief. Smith would need to show a "permanent effect" in a negative way against a unionization effort. Under Section 10(j) of the National Labor Relations Act, the NLRB could seek a temporary injunction against employers in federal district courts to stop unfair labor practices while the case was being litigated before administrative law judges and the Board.

On June 29, 2018, Smith's attorney announced that NLRB investigators determined that there was sufficient evidence for it to file a complaint against Zuffa. "The determination found meritorious the allegations [Leslie Smith] was a statutory employee & retaliated against for [*sic*] her union activity."[3] The decision came quicker than most and went against the norm in these types of filings. According to statistics provided by the NLRB web site, in 2017 there were 19,280 charging letters filed against employers.[4] Of those, 6,595 were settled and only 1,263 filed complaints.[5]

Politics may be a factor in this case. At the time of the filing, President Donald Trump was in office and appointed the head of the NLRB. President Trump was an early supporter of Dana White and the UFC. If you believe politics may be a factor in the decision-making process, it is hard to believe that the NLRB would rule in favor of Smith. After NLRB Region 4 determined that it would file a Complaint, the case was referred to the NLRB Division of Advice in Washington, D.C. The Regional Advice Branch provides guidance to the General Counsel and to the Regional Offices with respect to difficult or novel legal issues

On September 19, 2018, the NLRB dismissed Smith's complaint against Zuffa. Smith's lawyer exercised his right to appeal the decision.[6] The dismissal came as a surprise considering the initial belief from the region that Smith's Charging Letter had merit. In the dismissal letter, Regional Director Dennis Walsh wrote that Smith's charge lacked merit. "Although there is ample evidence that Smith has publicly engaged in efforts to unionize MMA fighters since 2016, there is insufficient evidence to establish that the UFC's failure to renew her contract in April 2018 was based on any protected activities," opined Walsh.[7] Rather, the NLRB Regional Director believed that the decision for the UFC to decline Smith's request to renegotiate a contract was the grounds for the dismissal rather than for her voicing her opinion about unionizing. Thus, the Regional Director did not have to decide whether Smith was a statutory employee.

Sections 8(a)(3) and (1) of the National Labor Relations Act states that an employee's union or protected concerted activities are "a motivating factor" in an employer's adverse action. Here, the NLRB determined that the failure to renew Smith's contract was not due to her activities in organizing Project Spearhead or speaking out about fighter's rights. Rather, it was based upon Smith attempting to renegotiate her contract and the UFC being unwilling to renew it.

The NLRB decision denying Smith's charges listed three items which refuted the belief that she was removed due to her speaking up for fighter rights. First, the UFC did not dismiss Smith after she had turned down two prior fights. Walsh points out that the UFC could have terminated Smith's fight contract in 2017 but extended her contract twice. He points out that the extensions occurred after she had been vocal about unionization. Second, the UFC would have allowed Smith to wear the mouth guard with the Project Spearhead logo despite its policy of not allowing athletes to use third-party logos in light of their Reebok uniform deal which demand exclusivity of its brand during fight week and during the event. Finally, it had reimbursed Smith for travel expenses in the amount of $500 which was above the usual amount it provides to its athletes.

Walsh concluded that the investigation found Smith attempted to broker a new contract deal when her scheduled opponent did not make the contracted weight per her signed bout agreement. The denial letter claimed that Smith attempted to receive a 222 percent increase over her then-current contract. Based on the NLRB's investigation that Smith was negotiating with the

UFC, it stated that it was not the proper role of the NLRB to "second-guess UFC's business decisions not continue or negotiate or renew Smith's contract...."[8]

The Division of Advice may have thought differently from the regional office. However, Smith's lawyer believes that the dismissal may have been politically motivated. Again, Smith's lawyer inferred that White's relationship with the Trump Administration may have caused the dismissal. In October 2018, the UFC announced a special program that focused on President Trump's relationship with MMA. Granted, the NLRB administrators make certain decisions based on the appointees made by the current administration. One may infer that there may have been influence to shuttle the charges to the D.C. office for a further look which would end in a dismissal. But, there has been no specific citation of evidence related to this inference from Smith's attorney.

In his appeal letter, Smith's attorney requested that certain investigators recuse themselves from the appeal.[9] Smith's attorney claimed that they could not serve as impartial decision-makers as they were directly involved with the decision to dismiss this matter which occurred only after Region 4 had first issued a merit determination in favor of Smith. In addition to the appeal, Smith's attorney requested that an investigation occur regarding why her case was transferred after it was decided from the Regional office that her claim had merit.

Smith filed a declaration in support of her appeal which addressed some of the issues in the NLRB dismissal letter. She indicated that she was precluded from attending her own appeal hearing. Smith pointed out that the characterization in the letter dismissing her claim was incorrect on several factual points. She clarified that she was willing to fight but her opponent had not made the contracted weight. She also claimed that she never demanded to be paid 222 percent more than her current contract. According to the UFC, they believed she wanted to be compensated $100,000 per fight and another $100,000 if she won her fight.

Even if Smith didn't fight, she pointed out that in New Jersey, the promoter had to compensate her "in the event the contest fails to materialize." Smith had passed the requisite requirements to fight including making the weight, getting licensed in the state and passing her medical exams.[10]

Smith outlined her UFC contract related to Bout Agreements. She states that the UFC had an "obligation in the event of a bout postponement, cancellation or termination ... to reschedule the bout or to terminate the existing UFC Bout Agreement."[11] Smith argues that due to her bout cancellation, her UFC Promotional Agreement required the UFC to provide her with one more fight.

This contradicts the NLRB finding that Smith's contract "expired by its terms" which makes the conclusion that the UFC simply decided not to negotiate a new deal with Smith erroneous. According to Smith, regardless of her attempt to negotiate a new contract with the UFC, she should have been afforded one more fight per the terms of her existing Promotional Agreement and the terms of the Bout Agreement.

She clarified the Dismissal Letter's explanation which cited that the UFC's action did not reflect a suppression of protected activities. In response to the NLRB stating that Smith turned down fights in 2017, Smith clarified that she would accept a fight if certain conditions were met and it was not a complete denial of a request to fight. Secondly, her union efforts began in August 2016 when she was active with the Professional Fighters' Association. But, unlike the Dismissal Letter suggests, she was not active in union organizing in 2017.

Smith described a time after a media day in 2016 when she spoke out about fighter issues. She was told by a UFC-employed commentator, Brian Stann, that she said her peace "and can be proud of that," but shouldn't talk further about unionizing.

She also highlighted her record and ranking. At the time of her release by the UFC, she was ranked 9th in the world and had won three of her last four fights. Her only loss was one she took in a higher weight division against women's Featherweight Champion Cristiane "Cyborg" Justino. She had an entertaining fight style and White personally endorsed her heart, as exemplified by her November 2014 bout in which she almost lost her ear.

Based on the contrary facts of the Dismissal Letter and Smith's Declaration, it would appear that Smith would at least have a modicum of chances on an appeal due to the mischaracterization of facts.

NLRB Findings May Have Favored Smith

Although an appeal was not successful, there are still some NLRB decisions that might help her case.

The NLRB noted that the cases challenging contractor status are fact-intensive as there is an assessment based on the 11-part factor test.

The NLRB utilizes an exhaustive 11-part test. However, there is no factor that is weighed heavily than another and no one factor may be decisive.

The NLRB 11 factors are:

1. Extent of control by the employer;
2. Whether or not the individual is engaged in a distinct occupation or business;
3. Whether the work is usually done under the direction of the employer or by a specialist without supervision;

4. Skill required in the occupation;
5. Whether the employer or individual supplies instrumentalities, tools, and place of work;
6. Length of time for which individual is employed;
7. Method of payment;
8. Whether or not work is part of the regular business of the employer;
9. Whether or not the parties believe they are creating an independent contractor relationship;
10. Whether the principal is or is not in the business;
11. (New:) Whether the evidence tends to show that the individual is, in fact, rendering services as an independent business.

In addition to these factors, the Board considers the extent to which a putative independent contractor is, in fact, rendering services as part of an independent business with an actual entrepreneurial gain or loss.

There are several cases which may have supported Smith's argument but for not meeting the initial threshold question.

Junior high and high school lacrosse referees in Pennsylvania were determined to be statutory employees of the Pennsylvania Interscholastic Athletic Association (PIAA) despite being assigned to a game at a time.[12] Rather, the NLRB determined that the referees were employees because they had to follow specific rules to follow lacrosse games. The outcome was controversial considering the argument that the referees had the freedom to apply and interpret the rules during the game without supervision and they had their fees paid by the schools and not the PIAA.

In *Velox Express, Inc.*, medical couriers were deemed as employees after one of the company's couriers challenged the independent contractor status.[13] Her termination came after she questioned detailed rules for its drivers and a new requirement that the drivers provide their driver's license and social security number for background checks. The "independent contractor" questioning the organization called out the need to sign the new driver's background check information and told the employer that she would sign it after speaking with an attorney. According to the facts of the case, her contract was terminated three days later. The dismissal and surrounding facts related to it gave rise to her claim. While the employer cited an incident made by the "independent contractor" as cause to terminate her contract, the NLRB investigation determined that this was a pretext for the dismissal and the underlying reason she was terminated was due to her questioning the additional workplace background check. In going through the test to determine whether the independent contractors were in fact employees the administrative judge noted that random drug testing and exclusive contracts were two indicators that the couriers were employees. The UFC utilizes USADA to conduct random drug tests of its contracted fighters. The fighters must comply with the program which includes listing their whereabouts 24 hours a day. Exclusivity in the UFC contracts are a constant. This prevents athletes from participating in fights in other promotions. In *Velox*, the administrative judge found that the courier drivers were statutory employees.

In *FedEx Home Delivery v. NLRB*, post truck drivers claimed that FedEx should engage in collective bargaining with them and by not doing so committed an unfair labor practice.[14] FedEx maintained that drivers were independent contractors because they took on "entrepreneurial opportunity." Applying the multi-factor totality test, the court determined that the drivers were independent contractors. This was based on whether the person's position "presents the opportunities and risks inherent in entrepreneurialism."

In a sports-related case, operators of the scoreboard for the National Basketball Association's Minnesota Timberwolves were deemed employees.[15] Originally, the Regional Director went through the 11-part test to conclude that the test sided in favor of the operators to be independent contractors. But on appeal in applying the 11-factor test, the NLRB found that more of the factors favored employee status rather than independent contractor. Notably, the employer maintained multiyear relationships with its crewmembers, enlisted their services to accomplish a core part of its business as a professional athletics company, dictated when and where they worked, provided all the key instrumentalities of the crew members' work, and exerted much more significant control than originally determined by the Regional Director. Additionally, the opinion determined that crewmembers enjoyed neither a proprietary interest in their work nor a voice in any important business decisions, outweighing the evidence that favored independent contractor status.

The interesting ending to this case was that the scoreboard operators were allowed the chance to vote on whether they wanted to be employees or independent contractors. In an overwhelming vote, the operators decided to remain independent contractors. Yet, this case revealed the subjective nature of the 11-part test. While one authority might interpret the test to side with employees, another judge of the facts could determine them to be independent contractors.

With this information, if the NLRB reconsidered its ruling in light of the facts and the history of cases such as these, Smith would have a chance at reversing the decision on appeal.

NLRB Appeal Is Denied

On November 27, 2018, the NLRB denied the administrative appeal from Smith citing back to the Regional Director's denial letter. The letter stated that evidence failed to establish Zuffa took adverse action against Smith for her work attempting to obtain signatures for Project Spearhead. The letter stated,

> To determine whether an employer's adverse action against an employee was discriminatorily motivated, the General Counsel must demonstrate by preponderance of the evidence that the employee's protected activity was a motivating factor for the adverse decision; only after such showing is established, the inquiry turns into whether the employer would have taken the action in the absence of the protected conduct.[16]

The NLRB determined that Smith's assertions that the re-evaluation of her claim was due to politically charged motives was false. It stated that the investigation and resulting ruling was in accordance with the Board's practice and procedures. The NLRB believed that the claims by Smith did not give rise for a hearing on the issue and the claim was decided by letter ruling only.

The grievance with the NLRB, which appeared to have some promise, will be decided by another legal proceeding or end without a resolution for Smith. It could be that Zuffa could have been motivated to terminate Smith's contract, but from the face of the proceedings, it was plausible that the reasons for letting Smith go was that it no longer wanted her on the UFC roster. While one might be able to see the claims, here, it was hard to prove without further means. It still remained unclear as to a ruling on the remaining fight on her contract when interpreting her bout agreement under the rules of the state of New Jersey. What is clear is that barring an appeal, there would be no lawsuit against Zuffa.

The denial affirmed the decision that Zuffa did not infringe upon Smith's right to engage in protected activities such as she did with Project Spearhead. However, the NLRB also believed that the facts and events that took place surrounding her leaving Zuffa were not against the rules cited by Smith or her attorney.

Smith made a valid argument that she should have been afforded her last fight on her contract as she met all her obligations per the New Jersey State Athletic Commission Bout Agreement and her UFC Promotional Agreement. There was not an affirmative measure for her to fight at a "catchweight" to accommodate her opponent who could not make the contracted weight.

There is also Smith's affidavit where she was told by an employed commentator of the UFC that she should not make any more comments about unionizing if she wanted to keep fighting for the company. This would seem to be an issue related to the company preventing her from doing a protected activity. Either the NLRB investigated the issue and determined that the incident was not indicative of preventing Smith from participating in a protected activity or it did not investigate the issue and determined that the incident was negligible.

There are several indicators that Zuffa controls its independent contractor athletes. First, there is a mandatory "athlete outfitting policy" which all contracted fighters must adhere to in order to avoid punishment. The policy requires that fighters wear mandatory Reebok fight kits which negated the possibility of athletes obtaining ancillary sponsorships which helps earnings. There is also the UFC Anti-Doping Policy to which each athlete must agree in order to compete in the UFC. Active fighters must agree to allow USADA to know of their whereabouts at all times in order to be tested if called upon. If an athlete were to go on a trip or leave town unexpectedly, they must let USADA know. Finally, Zuffa is in control of making matches despite a rankings system. In the event that a fighter declines a fight without a viable excuse such as injury, they are subject to punitive measures. This occurred in the case of up-and-coming featherweight contender Yair Rodriguez. The 25-year-old turned down two fights in the UFC. In declining the second time, he was released by the organization.[17] Rodriguez, ranked the number 11 fighter in his division in the UFC, sought a fighter in the top 10 to face to improve his position. The matchup offered by the UFC was not with a fighter in the top 10. He was released without an official reason by the UFC.

Rodriguez changed course after speaking with the UFC matchmakers and accepted the fight. While Rodriguez returned to the UFC, the power that the company has over fighters to coerce them into fights or else be released from their contract is real. The practical issue is that there is not much the fighter can do when called upon to fight despite being "independent."

Conclusion

Leslie Smith's NLRB challenge could have been the tipping point for athletes and Zuffa. Unless another legal challenge is successful, it would only be a minor blip that was summarily denied. Unfortunately, the NLRB decisions are dependent on the current Administration which makes the board decisions sway from pro-union to pro-employer based on the philosophy of the current Administration. Smith's attorney suggested that since UFC head Dana White is personal friends with President Donald Trump, Smith's case was reassigned to the Washington, D.C. office so that it would be ensured to be denied instead of the original ruling that found merit in her claims. One could only wonder if Smith's case would have been different if the NLRB was under a president in favor of worker's rights. The inference that Smith's dismissal was based on a political favor is mere speculation and was denied in the letter denying Smith's appeal. Based on the position of the NLRB, it has accepted Zuffa's argument that this was merely a contractual negotiation in which the sides failed to come to a consensus.

Even if this case were to be found in favor of Smith, Zuffa would have appealed the decision. The 11-part test to determine independent contractor or employee appears to be too subjective and without a deciding factor within the test; the exercise to go through each part would lead to many conclusions by the trier of fact. Going through each component of the tests yields one to conclude that each part themselves is vague enough to be interpreted several ways.

The determination on whether mixed martial artists are independent contractors or employees of the companies they fight for is a difficult question that may never be addressed unless an athlete were to successfully challenge a promotion's contractual status. If it is ever determined that fighters are employees, this would heap additional costs on a promoter including health insurance, disability, workers compensation and additional benefit issues. The added overhead would sink many small-time organizations as many could not finance the additional costs. Moreover, with fighters getting injured on a regular basis, the costs to cover insurance premiums would be exorbitant and constantly rise. This additional financial exposure might actually hurt fighters since it would be easy to fathom the demise of several promotions if they were forced to sign on athletes as employees. This would narrow the options for athletes to find promotions that would be able to hire them. Yet, this foreshadowing should not be a concern when it comes to the interpretation of whether an MMA fighter is an independent contractor or employee.

5

Injunctions and Matches— Trying to Leave a Promotion

Introduction

There are times when fight promotions deem it necessary to sue contracted fighters. In the cases discussed, money is the prime reason for the dispute between athletes and their promoters. But, the root of these issues relates to the contract. As discussed in this book, the contracts in mixed martial arts bind the athlete to exclusivity and allow the company an opportunity to retain the athlete even in instances where their contract runs out. This chapter will take a look at Rampage Jackson as he attempted to leave Bellator. Jackson, a seasoned veteran with a built-in fan base, attempted to break his contract with Bellator. The facts of the case are interesting and the perks he had were unique to Rampage. Eddie Alvarez was an up and coming fighter looking to make good on his career he established in Bellator. Wanting to take advantage of his "free agency," Alvarez hoped that he would be able to negotiate a good contract with his next company. All signs pointed to the UFC as they had the money and competition for a budding star.

Bellator Sues Rampage Jackson

Quentin "Rampage" Jackson was sued by Bellator MMA in March 2015 for an alleged breach of contract for signing with rival organization, the UFC.[1] Bellator, the Viacom-owned company that owns the MMA organization, requested that the court file an injunction which would prevent Jackson from fighting in the UFC.

Jackson, an aging MMA veteran who made a name for himself in Japan, was coming off a successful stint in the UFC where he won the UFC Light Heavyweight title. But Jackson lost three fights in a row to end his contract with the company which included losing his title to Jon Jones in September 2011. In November 2013, Jackson made his debut with Bellator and won three in a row with the organization before he declared that Bellator was not upholding its end of the bargain.

Jackson proclaimed that due to a breach on the part of Bellator, he rejoined the UFC. An announcement was made in December 2015. The lawsuit was filed in New Jersey despite the fact that both Jackson and Bellator resided in Irvine, California. Jackson's management claimed that Jackson had a right to terminate his existing contract with Bellator as they had given the company time to "cure" the deficiencies it saw in his contract but were not able to do so. Jackson's management team viewed his contract as an entertainment contract versus a pure sports contract. Although the issue between entertainment and sports never came to a head in the litigation its curious to note that there are differences in the interpretation. Jackson was only in his third fight of a six-fight contract with Bellator when he attempted to sever ties.

According to Bellator's lawsuit, it had an Exclusive Right of First Refusal. The contract with Jackson allowed Bellator the right to match any offer made to Jackson at the end of the term of the contract or prior to its end.[2] The lawsuit also claimed to have "rebuilt" Jackson's image. The complaint states, Bellator put him in competitive fights, put huge marketing dollars into his events, aired a reality series on his life, hired a writer to create a movie treatment for a vehicle in which he could star, paid him and made him "relevant again in the MMA industry."[3] Bellator argues that this investment in Jackson made people forget about his previous losses.

The contract in dispute was signed by Jackson with Bjorn Rebney, the former executive in charge of Bellator MMA. Rebney was ousted as the company's head as it sought to go in a new direction. But, the promotion still upheld the contract with Jackson. Details of Jackson's contact with Bellator revealed some interesting tidbits which saw a contract that favored the athlete. Several incentives that were reported from Jackson's contract included:

- 30 percent of Bellator's net gate receipts over $400,000 at events where he fought;
- $35,000 per episode for the SpikeTV Reality Series "Rampage 4 Real";
- A screenwriter for a feature film project and access to Paramount Pictures to develop film projects;
- A red carpet appearance at the 2013 MTV Video Music Awards;
- $4 for every Bellator 120 PPV buy over 190,000;
- $250,000 to advertise Bellator 120 during the NBA Playoffs;

- $200,000 to secure rights to a Rolling Stones song for an advertisement featuring Rampage.

Some of these incentives seemed unattainable. For instance, Jackson receiving $4 for every PPV buy over 190,000 seems more like a lottery ticket than anything. Up to this point, there had been only one Bellator PPV event which scraped to 100,000 PPV buys. Asking the company to double that amount for a PPV bonus appeared to be more of an aspiration than anything. Also, requesting 30 percent of Bellator's net gate receipts over $400,000 where Rampage appeared seemed to be predicated on ticket prices and demand. Both of the above requests appear to appeal to both Spike TV and Rampage, as they would motivate Jackson to promote an event so that it would draw PPV buys and ticket sales. The reality series seemed to be a vehicle to help Rampage with his career after combat sports. Also, the possibility of developing film projects was another avenue outside of the cage for Rampage.

In addition, Jackson received a $200,000 bonus for Bellator's May 2014 PPV despite the company not meeting the PPV threshold bonuses indicated in his contract. This was in part due to Jackson's disappointment in how the PPV was promoted. There were other sweeteners for Jackson. His contract also included a 2013 Tesla Sport worth $129,603, a $100,000 signing bonus and guaranteed fight purses between $200,000 and $300,000 for non–PPV fights. He would receive between $200,000 and $450,000 for a PPV fight. Jackson also received a $50,000 guarantee if the event did not receive a certain revenue amount from sponsors. The contract was negotiated between Jackson's representatives and then–Bellator CEO Bjorn Rebney.

Jackson claimed that Bellator breached its contract when it failed to provide him with the appropriate pay-per-view data from his May 2013 fight in a timely manner. In addition, he claimed that Bellator did not properly promote Jackson's fights and that the entertainment opportunities included in his contract were not given to him in good faith.

Even without an official release from the promotion, Jackson determined that he was done with the company. Jackson had negotiated a deal to come back to the UFC and appear on its card in April 2015. He would be one of the main attractions for the card. Hence, the reason for the injunction was to prevent Jackson from jumping straight into a competitor's main card. Bellator argued that it made attempts to placate Jackson, but he remained unsatisfied.

On April 7, 2015, Judge Karen Suter granted Bellator MMA its injunction in its lawsuit against Jackson.[4] The trial court made it clear that the merits of the case were not at issue and that it would not be determining whether or not there was a breach of contract.

The four factors in determining a preliminary injunction are as follows:

1. A substantial likelihood of success on the merits of the case;
2. A substantial threat of irreparable damage or injury if the injunction is not granted;
3. The "balance of harms" (threatened injury) weighs in favor of the party seeking the preliminary injunction;
4. Granting an injunction would serve the public interest.

The court found "clear and convincing" evidence that Bellator would be harmed if Jackson were to appear at a UFC event.

The 25-page ruling included some interesting points:

- The court emphasized the exclusivity of the contract between Bellator and Jackson. It also stressed the fame and notoriety of Jackson as evidence that Bellator would suffer injury if Jackson were allowed to participate at UFC 186.
- The court did not buy the argument that Bellator breached its contract since it did not provide Rampage or his management with a PPV summary report. The court indicated Bellator had substantially complied and that not providing the PPV summary was not a material breach of the contract.
- Rampage's claim that his fights were not adequately promoted by Bellator, and the need to obtain the PPV summary was necessary, fell flat. The court ruled that there was no marketing provision setting a certain amount of money that was required to promote his fights. Even without producing the summary report for PPV, there would be no breach since the actual compensation Rampage received was not in dispute. Furthermore, the court opined that Rampage offered no rationale for why Bellator would not want to market and promote one of the company's top stars.
- The court sided with Bellator with its argument that if Rampage were allowed to fight at UFC 186, it would harm Bellator more than just monetarily, but from a reputation and brand standpoint. Bellator argued that the "MMA community" would denigrate Bellator if Rampage were allowed to leave for the UFC. Moreover, Bellator argued that denying the injunction would be a sign to other fighters and their managers that they could just "ignore their contracts" and leave for perceived better opportunities. Bellator also argued that if Rampage were to leave, Bellator would have lost out on the time and money it had invested in promoting him.
- The opinion also notes that on December 4, 2014, Scott Coker

claims to have notified the UFC that Rampage was still under contract while negotiations by Rampage to the UFC were ongoing. This seems to call into question how much the UFC knew about the Bellator-Rampage contract dispute. It also highlights the UFC's decision to sign him and then put him on a card prior to a legal determination.

The UFC issued a statement on the state court's decision and indicated it was "surprised about the ruling because Mr. Jackson represented to the UFC on multiple occasions that he was free to negotiate and contract with UFC. The UFC organization is also surprised that Bellator sat on its alleged rights for months before taking action." The statement also indicated that it was "considering action to protect its rights and minimize damages."[5] The statement distances itself from Jackson as it indicates that it was Jackson who told the UFC he was "free to negotiate." The official UFC statement appears to be plausible deniability on the part of the UFC. Even if Jackson claimed he was "free" and could negotiate a contract with the UFC, one would think that the UFC would do its due diligence in making sure that Jackson was really free of his Bellator contract.

Not satisfied with the trial court decision, Bellator requested an emergency appeal from the decision to enjoin Jackson from participating in the April 2015 UFC event. A New Jersey appellate court overturned the portion of the Preliminary Injunction preventing Rampage Jackson from fighting at a UFC event. The assertion by the trial court that there was "irreparable harm" was overturned by the appellate court calling Bellator's claims of harm "vague speculation." Bellator claimed that Jackson's leaving for the UFC would cause harm because "other fighters" would be encouraged to "ignore their contracts" and because the "social networking sphere is filled with negative chatter" about them. But, the appeals court did not believe this to be reliable. "Given plaintiff's [Bellator] failure to adduce evidence other than speculation to support the Chancery Division's conclusion that the harm Plaintiff alleges 'cannot be rectified by money damages alone.'"[6]

Essentially, the appeals court believed that the issue could have been addressed with monetary compensation rather than having to go through the process of an injunction preventing Jackson from fighting on the UFC card.

The appellate court remanded the rest of the case to the trial court for "adjudication of the merits of the parties' respective claims and defenses" that require "a factual determination." Bellator allowed Jackson to fight on the UFC card in April 2015 where he won a lackluster fight and subsequently returned to Bellator after just his one appearance. The UFC fight was apparently a part of the settlement agreement between Bellator, Jackson and its rival promotion. After the April 2015 fight, Jackson returned to Bellator in June 2016.

Rampage ... the Aftermath

The lawsuit reveals that contracts favor the drafter in MMA. It was Jackson that attempted to cite a breach of the contract and sought to be removed from his contract. There had to be some semblance of a legal argument by Jackson for the UFC to decide to sign him. At the time, the UFC needed a big name for its April 2015 PPV event and Jackson was an athlete who carried name recognition and could still attract viewers. In an effort to avoid the lawsuit, Bellator contacted UFC's attorneys to state that Jackson was under contract, and since he was, the promotion should not attempt to sign him. Although the legal counsel for the UFC indicated it would look into the situation when it spoke with Bellator, the next event was the announcement that Jackson signed with the UFC.

One of the possible outcomes of this lawsuit, if not for the emergency appeal, would be for Bellator to have sued the UFC for Interference with Contractual Relations. There was no doubt that the UFC knew of the contract for Jackson. Apparently, the UFC made an independent legal determination that Jackson's claim that Bellator breached his contract was valid. But, the official statement from the UFC indicated that it was Jackson who represented he was free to contract with the UFC, which infers he was no longer under contract with Bellator. It's unlikely that the UFC would have tried to sign Jackson if it had known that he was still under a valid contract with Bellator. Fortunately for the parties, they came up with a resolution short of an all-out legal battle. The UFC got Jackson for one event and then he returned to Bellator.

The opinion of the Emergency Appeal is a far departure from the initial trial court ruling granting the injunction. The Appellate Court determined that there was no irreparable harm because the alleged harms claimed by Bellator were "vague speculation." Bellator claimed that there would be a lasting "stigma" on Bellator if it allowed Jackson to breach his contract. It claimed that other fighters would attempt to do this and that online and social media would skewer Bellator, which would paint its business and retention in a bad light. While one might argue that Bellator's business practice would be irreparably harmed, the appellate court did not believe that its situation gave rise to the "extraordinary remedy" of a preliminary injunction.

Indeed, the appellate court took into consideration the type of remedy it considered versus the evidence submitted by Bellator. The appellate court decision made a point that the trial court did not consider the severity of granting a preliminary injunction. Rather, it focused on the unique skills of the fighter in making its ruling. It sought to determine whether there was another way that this dispute could be rectified. The appellate court did state that the promotion substantially complied with the requirement that Jackson be given a PPV report to verify the buys. Although the buy rate was relayed to Jackson from a network executive, it still does not bode well for future use. With fighters requesting better pay and an amendment to the Ali Act to include MMA fighters, the ruling does not adhere to a strict interpretation of the rule. Here, they believed that monetary compensation could have rectified the situation of harm on Bellator.

It depends on whether one is a Rampage Jackson fan or not to determine if he was at fault in this case. Few MMA athletes would receive as lucrative a deal with its perks as Jackson did in his contract to join the promotion. Yet, Jackson attributed falling short of numbers to make his contractual bonuses the fault of Bellator. Whether or not the entertainment-side of the contract was fulfilled was a question of fact that Jackson could have stressed more in its pleadings.

The tale of Rampage seems to be one of an athlete attempting to maximize his earnings and not being afraid to file a lawsuit as a result. It is questionable to determine whether Jackson was disenchanted with Bellator or really thought that the company breached its contract or perhaps both. He was able to return to Bellator through a settlement agreement with Bellator and was scheduled to fight in one of the company's biggest events in the fall of 2018.

Alvarez v. Bellator: The Match Game

Don't ever say copying and pasting documents works. At least, don't tell Bellator MMA. Eddie Alvarez, an MMA lightweight, fell out of favor with Bellator. As its lightweight champion, Alvarez was nearing the end of his contract with the company. In his contract, there was a clause which allowed the company to match any offer made to the fighter. The contract indicated that if Bellator matched the rights, it would extend the existing contract. This is where the fun began.

In a letter to Alvarez dated November 1, 2012, Bellator's attorney allowed the fighter to negotiate with Zuffa, LLC, provided that it gave Bellator the full agreement so that it might have the opportunity to match the material terms of the offer. If Bellator agreed to match, it would obligate Alvarez to return to Bellator based on the matched terms.

Alvarez obtained an offer from the UFC which included more money, in addition to a portion of the pay-per-view revenue of events in which he fought. It also offered non-monetary opportunities with the company. After reviewing the UFC contract, Bellator MMA copied and pasted the contract to ensure that the contract was "matched" by the UFC. The contract offered by Zuffa, LLC offered Alvarez a $250,000 signing bonus upon the completion of his first four bouts in the UFC.

Bellator decided to counter the offer, as well as offer additional incentives, including a cable television special to feature Alvarez, and payment to him of $25,000; a feature on a Bellator reality show, and $100,000 for his participating; and a guest host spot on a Spike TV broadcast on an upcoming season of Bellator MMA. Although not a condition of the matching agreement, it appeared that the additional compensation was meant as a "sweetener" to lure Alvarez back to Bellator.

However, Alvarez decided that he wanted to head to the UFC. One of the things that the UFC offered, which Bellator could not, was the PPV compensation. Similar to earning a commission, the PPV "upside," as many refer to it, pays out bonus money if the event exceeds a certain number of PPV buys. In this case, Alvarez would receive $2 per buy for every buy over 200,000. This might mean a massive windfall for a fighter with such a deal— or no money at all if the event does not sell.

Bellator argued that it had matched the material terms of the contract with the UFC. Alvarez claimed that it had not and believed that there was no "match" of terms by the UFC. As a result of this impasse, the dispute was destined for litigation.

In January 2013, Bellator filed a lawsuit against Eddie Alvarez in the U.S. District Court of New Jersey.[7] The exhibits revealed the negotiations between the parties, and, provided without redactions, the UFC and Bellator contracts offered to Alvarez. These exhibits are notable because after this reveal, Zuffa has been extremely protective of its contracts, and in any subsequent litigation it has brought motions to seal this information from public view.

The Complaint pleads two causes of action: Breach of Contract and Tortious Interference. The Breach of Contract claim is based on Bellator's claim that Alvarez did not honor the "matching rights" provision in his contract as Bellator literally copied the exact words of the UFC contract Alvarez was offered. A copy of the UFC Bellator contract (with use of Track Changes in Word) was attached as an Exhibit to the Complaint. The cut and paste job appeared to be the Bellator strategy to ensure it would match the offer made by the UFC and call out the UFC if it claimed that Bellator did not match the offer. The Complaint requested declaratory relief (among other things) which asks a court to make a ruling on an issue: here, to determine that Bellator matched the UFC contract.

After Bellator provided the matching offer, it received an email dated December 16 to Bellator's representatives from Alvarez's attorney claiming that the Bellator offer was illusory. Specifically (1) a Fox (the television network the UFC had a media deal with at the time) event (in which it promised

Alvarez) would be on network television whereas Spike TV (Bellator's television partner at the time, where Alvarez's bouts would be shown) is on basic cable and (2) Bellator's claim that it would have a PPV event by March is contradicted by statements from Bjorn Rebney in the media that it would not have one—thus, no matching of offers. Although the correspondence indicates that these two issues were not Alvarez's only issues with the contract, they appear to be the central ones.

In response, Bellator's counsel argued that the contract matches the UFC contract. Most telling in the correspondence is the fact that Bellator claimed to have a PPV event in the works by March of that year. In addition, Bellator offered three "sweeteners" as described by Bellator's representatives, as well as appearances on Spike TV, which it believed would aid in Alvarez obtaining personal sponsorships. The monetary total amounted to $125,000, but it appeared that Bellator included the exposure on Spike as additional value. Presumably, this is in response to the $250,000 signing bonus and guest commentating spots the UFC offered Alvarez.

Bellator pointed out that Spike would replay Alvarez's bouts at least twice on its network, which would grant him more exposure. Bellator argued that an Alvarez bout on Fox is usually not replayed. A central issue in the dispute was that the UFC could offer PPV percentages while Bellator could not. Bellator indicated that it might have a PPV event by March and would offer similar percentages for Alvarez. Also, a title shot by March would be offered on both contracts.

As for the second cause of action for tortious interference, it named a John Doe as interfering with the Bellator-Alvarez contract. Generally, a tortious interference claim occurs when a party intentionally damages a contractual relationship. In this claim Bellator requested injunctive relief which would preclude the "John Doe" from interfering with the contractual relationship as it would cause Bellator an economic loss. Could Bellator have added the UFC? This would seem unlikely since the promotion granted Alvarez the opportunity to solicit an offer from the UFC. Yet, was there a plan to bring in the UFC?

Alvarez Files for Preliminary Injunction

Alvarez struck back with denials to the lawsuit as well as counterclaims for tortious interference with a prospective economic advantage and breach of contract.[8] According to court papers, he lost out on an opportunity to fight at a UFC event in March 2013. He was then scheduled to fight again in April 2013 if he would be able to be released from his contract. But, in order for Alvarez to fight in April, he had to obtain an injunction to do so. Eddie Alvarez's attorneys sought a preliminary injunction to allow the free agent lightweight to sign a Zuffa contract to fight at UFC 159 on April 27, 2013. An Order to Show Cause hearing was scheduled to determine whether there was sufficient evidence to show it had the prerequisite elements for a court to issue an injunction to allow Alvarez to join the UFC. Also, it was set to show why Bellator should not be restrained from interfering with Alvarez's prospective contract with Zuffa and why Alvarez should not be permitted to contract with Zuffa in order to participate in an upcoming Zuffa event.

According to court papers filed in the U.S. District Court for the District of New Jersey by Alvarez's attorney, Zuffa would not promote or contract with Alvarez until it had court permission. It mandated that it had to within 90 days of the event.

The hearing was to show cause as to "why Bellator should not be restrained from interfering with Alvarez's prospective contract with Zuffa and why Alvarez should not be permitted to contract with Zuffa, so that he may participate in Zuffa's April 27, 2013 event."

As in all preliminary injunctions, the threshold Alvarez's attorneys had to prove for the Court to grant the preliminary injunction was:

1. the likelihood of success on the merits;
2. that Alvarez would suffer irreparable harm if the injunction was denied;
3. that granting the preliminary relief would not result in even greater harm to the nonmoving party (Bellator); and
4. that the public interest favored such relief.

The injunction allowed Alvarez a way to keep active in MMA without having to wait for the resolution of the lawsuit by Bellator and his countersuit against the promotion.

Alvarez argued that he was likely to succeed on the merits of his claim because he believed that the Bellator offer contained numerous and significant substantive changes to the Zuffa offer. Alvarez's attorneys pointed out the discrepancy in networks which have different viewer exposure and demographics. It also noted that the UFC does PPV, unlike Bellator, and as a result can offer bonuses for events that meet sales goals. Next, Alvarez claimed that if the injunction was not issued allowing for him to fight in the UFC, he would be irreparably harmed. In a rather persuasive argument, Alvarez stressed the small window of time that an elite MMA fighter can compete. "Every fight opportunity that passes constitutes irreparable harm," argued Alvarez in the brief. He also pointed to a clause in his contract which identified his services as unique and of a peculiar value which cannot be compensated by damages.

He then argued that Bellator would not be at a greater harm if Alvarez was allowed to go to the UFC. Alvarez stressed that he would be significantly harmed if he was not permitted to earn a living during the lawsuit. Similarly,

Alvarez argued that the public interest favored an injunction since it was in the public interest to allow him to engage in his profession instead of "sidelined" until the resolution of his lawsuit.

In the pleadings, Alvarez's attorneys hypothesize that the court should grant the preliminary injunction notwithstanding the fact that the court may decide in favor of Bellator on the merits. Thus, creating the scenario that Alvarez fights on the April card for the UFC but then Bellator will have the rights (although limited) to re-sign Alvarez. The attorneys for Alvarez also point to a $500 bond indicated in the Bellator contract. Usually, posting bond is much more and this would be a nominal amount. If the court granted the injunction, Alvarez's attorneys would need to post bond pending the outcome of litigation. A $500 bond would be worth the amount he could make at UFC 159 based on the proposed contract Zuffa has already offered Alvarez.

In its opposition, Bellator noted that he's been paid approximately $835,000 by Bellator. Similar to the Alvarez pleadings, they noted the First/Last Refusal (also known as the right to match) provision in the contract. They argued that the type of "right to match" provision in Alvarez's agreement was similar to that of others in combat sports. This is due in part to the amount of investment it puts in to promote athletes. Bellator pointed out that the agreement was negotiated and had representation to handle the contract terms. Therefore, it had an opportunity to address, negotiate and amend if possible, the "right to match" terms. But the terms remained in the contract.

Bellator claimed that not only did it match the contract offered by Zuffa, it added three additional items which made the offer "better." A curious factual argument by Bellator with respect to the argument that the Viacom-based company could not match PPV bonuses offered in the UFC contract. Bellator used the declaration of a television industry expert to predict that the PPV on which Alvarez was scheduled to appear would not amass the requisite number of buys for him to attain the bonus money due to him in the proposed contract offer. The expert noted that the guaranteed income was a better outcome than the prospect of a bigger payout and that the contract terms were matched based on the language in Alvarez's Bellator contract.

Court Denies Preliminary Injunction

The court denied Alvarez's request for Preliminary Injunction.[9] The court heard oral arguments in the morning and rendered its decision the same afternoon. It held that Alvarez could not satisfy the first two elements for issuance of a preliminary injunction. It first believed that Alvarez could not show a reasonable probability of success on the merits. Second, he could not show irreparable harm.

The court held that Bellator had satisfied its matching rights of Zuffa's contract. It would not look into the word for word matching of terms but determined that it would apply a "common-sense interpretation to the word 'match.'"

Notably, the court would not examine the issues regarding weighing Fox versus Spike TV or the issue of Zuffa's PPV offer. Rather, it stated that while Alvarez may prevail at a later date, would not that day.

In a footnote, the court indicated that it would not and could not find Bellator in breach of contract if it didn't provide its own PPV. So, despite the fact that Bellator has not put on a PPV event and there have been no indications of a PPV outside of these legal negotiations, the court would not decide on an event that may or may not occur in the future.

Even if the court ruled in its favor with element 1, it did not determine element 2 to satisfy the burden. The court held that Alvarez was basing the fact that he would be irreparably harmed on speculation. Specifically, the argument that Alvarez would lose out on "notoriety, endorsements and a wider exposure to viewers" would require the court to make speculative assumptions on what might or might not happen as a result of his participation on April 27, 2013.

Furthermore, Alvarez's brief cited two cases in which preliminary injunctions were granted on behalf of professional athletes based on the fact that they would be irreparably injured if they would not be able to pursue their career in the manner in which they saw fit. However, those cases differed as in each there was an illegal restraint that necessitated the players to be granted an injunction. The court held that Bellator was not imposing an illegal restraint on Alvarez and he was not precluded from competing professionally if the injunction were not granted. Thus, Alvarez could not prove the second element.

It is worth noting that the court did not render a decision on one of the more interesting issues in the matching rights debate: the comparison of networks and pay-per-view. Bellator was on Spike TV at the time while the UFC was on Fox networks, which included the main network as well as cable. Secondly, the UFC used PPV as one of its key drivers, whereas Bellator was just introducing it.

In the end, Alvarez and Bellator came to terms on a settlement of their lawsuit with him fighting Michael Chandler for the lightweight world title in November 2013. Alvarez won the fight via split decision to win the Bellator lightweight world title. It was one of the most exciting fights in Bellator history and a rematch was set for PPV on May 17, 2014. But Alvarez sustained an injury a week before the fight and was forced to pull out. In August 2014, Scott Coker, appointed the new Bellator MMA President after Bjorn Rebney parted ways with the company, granted Alvarez's release. Alvarez finally signed with the UFC and made his Octagon debut in September 2014 where he lost his to Donald Cerrone at UFC 178 via unanimous decision.

Conclusion on Jackson and Alvarez Cases

Both Rampage Jackson and Eddie Alvarez were looking for better deals from their promoters which led to litigation. In some ways, both forced the issue via litigation. Jackson determined that his deal was breached due to the lack of action by the promotion which promised him a lot of extra-curricular items outside of fighting. Jackson's management believed his contract to be similar to an entertainment contract rather than a fight contract. Alvarez believed that he was able to extract himself away from Bellator since it could not match the rights of the UFC. But he found out that it was not as easy as it seemed. Bellator did everything to keep Alvarez, which included cutting and pasting the UFC's offer and offering essentially the same to Alvarez to "match" the offer. Notably, both injunctions in each lawsuit did not go the way of the fighter. While the trial court initially sided with Jackson, it was overturned on an emergency appeal. Alvarez's injunction was denied as the court would not look into the matching terms "word for word" despite discrepancies and differences in the contract.

The cases show that the injunction process is not a definitive option when attempting to have a court enforce a term or determine a breach. It shows the seriousness of the action of enjoining an action. In the alternative, it seems that the courts defer to monetary compensation in lieu of specific performance. While Alvarez had pointed out the uniqueness of his vocation, the court did not believe that he could prove that his case would likely prevail or that there would have been irreparable harm.

6

Contractual Ties and Attempts to Break Them

Introduction

The UFC contract is a mysterious document for most. There have been concerted efforts to protect the document from public consumption. The UFC is concerned with potential trade secrets being disclosed and the exposure of business strategy so that competitors may take advantage. In 2007, the standard Zuffa Contract was discussed in detail for one of the first times in the modern era of the UFC as a clause in Randy Couture's contract with the company was in dispute. At that time, only clauses of the contract were discussed, yet a complete copy of a signed contract was not disclosed. For most, it was not until Eddie Alvarez and Bellator became embroiled in a legal dispute that the public saw a UFC contract. In that legal dispute, the Alvarez contract was provided as an unsealed exhibit in the lawsuit. Since then, the exhibit has been used as a template to interpret UFC contractual issues. In subsequent litigation, Zuffa has moved to seal the use of the contract, citing confidentiality. The three cases discussed below address contract breaches involving Zuffa. Each of these lawsuits occurred prior to the Alvarez revelation. They provide a context to the strict construction of the Zuffa enforcement and the beliefs of the athletes signing the contracts.

B.J. Penn Sues UFC

Jay Dee Penn, better known as B.J. Penn, was the first non–Brazilian to win the black belt division of the World Jiu-Jitsu Championship, held in Rio de Janeiro, Brazil, in 2000. He made his move to MMA and a year later made his debut in the UFC. He fought six times in the UFC from 2001 to 2003, earning 5 wins, 1 loss and 1 draw. He then was granted the opportunity to fight for the Rumble on the Rock promotion in his native Hawaii and defeated future Pride lightweight champion Takanori Gomi for that promotion's light-weight title.

Penn signed an Exclusive Promotional and Ancillary Rights Agreement with Zuffa in June 2002. Penn challenged the Promotional Rights clause in his contract as it was to last one year from the date of his promoted bout by the UFC or the date on which Penn has participated in at least three bouts promoted by the company. The clause called for an extension of the agreement of one year or another three bouts if Penn was champion. The latter clause is typically known as the "Champion's Clause" as it automatically extends the contract if the contracted athlete is champion. His first fight under the contract occurred on September 27, 2002.

After the one-year contract anniversary, September 27, 2003, Penn had two fights under his contract prior to the expiration of the one year from his first bout. He was not a UFC champion at the time so the Champion's Clause would not apply and there were no alterations made to the existing contract. After September 27, 2003, Penn signed a "Bout Agreement" that he would fight on January 31, 2004. On that date, he defeated Matt Hughes to win the UFC welterweight championship title.

On that same date, he signed with the K-1 MMA promotion with his first bout with the company occurring on May 22, 2004. He notified Zuffa of his deal with K-1 and allowed the company to match the terms of the agreement, but it decided not to match. The UFC decided to strip him of his welterweight belt. A press release stated that Penn was stripped of the title he won from Hughes due to signing with K-1. It also stated that Penn would no longer be allowed to fight in the UFC.

Penn sued the UFC for breach of the implied covenant of good faith and fair dealing in contract, among other claims, which included negligent and intentional infliction of emotional distress and a request to return the title to Penn.[1] Additionally, he requested the court grant a preliminary injunction which would issue an order preventing Zuffa from having a bout for Penn's welterweight title which the UFC "stripped" from the fighter once he signed with K-1.[2] In its motion, Penn cites an interview in which Dana White would have allowed Penn to fight in another organization if Zuffa would have been involved.[3] This infers that Zuffa would have allowed Penn to fight in another organization so long as he would have done it through the company.

In a Declaration in support of the Preliminary Injunction, B.J. Penn stated that the UFC welterweight title was more than just a belt he was awarded. According to Penn, the title had economic value and garnered attention from fans and promoters. He also stated that the title symbolized his athletic achievements.[4] Penn claimed that the UFC stripping him of his title hurt his legitimacy. Penn had served as a spokesperson for his native Hawaii in the local county's fight against the harms of drug abuse.

Zuffa acknowledged the notice it received from Penn about his contract signing with K-1. This was due to the "matching rights" in Penn's Promotional Agreement. However, it decided not to match the rights for business reasons. Zuffa argued that Penn knew that he could not fight for both organizations. Moreover, Zuffa claimed that Penn could not prove "irreparable harm," a requirement for a preliminary injunction because the evidence he provided was based on speculation.[5] Irreparable harm is harm for which compensatory or monetary damages would be inadequate. Zuffa pointed to Penn's Declaration as well as the Declaration from his manager/brother as faulty evidence Penn relied on in proclaiming that he has been harmed beyond monetary compensation due to being stripped of his UFC title. This evidence did not provide admissible evidence which could be verified. Rather, Zuffa argued that these arguments of harm were based on conjecture.

In response to the claim that Zuffa breached the Implied Covenant of Good Faith and Fair Dealing, the promotion premised its argument based on Penn's retention of the UFC welterweight title. The promotion stated that a contract was not made from Penn winning the title. Thus, no obligations were attached to Penn winning the title and so when he went to K-1 it was in Zuffa's right to strip him of the UFC title. In the alternative, Zuffa claims that even if a contract were found in this instance, there would have been no breach of the implied covenant of good faith and fair dealing. Highlighting this argument was the notification of Zuffa by Penn's lawyer that K-1 had offered Penn a contract and notifying them of their right to match per the terms of his Zuffa deal.[6] The fact that Zuffa denied the right to match shows no evidence of a breach of the good faith and fair dealing in the contract.

Zuffa claimed that they allowed Penn to fight for another promotion while under contract with the company since it was his brother's promotion. Even then, Zuffa argued that it was just a one-time exception, and it was inferred that it would not have allowed Penn to fight anywhere else. It was more of a favor due to the familial interest of Penn.

The Court denied Penn's Preliminary Injunction request based upon the arguments made by Zuffa. From one perspective, Penn argues that Zuffa's stripping him of the title when he decided to sign with K-1 was in bad faith. But one might also see Penn's business move as maybe overplaying his leverage. He was the UFC welterweight champion at the end of his contract and had hoped that his offer from K-1 would have required Zuffa to match and/or give him a better monetary deal. Neither happened and the company moved on from him which Penn realized was a mistake.

Penn's lawsuit is unique in that based on the terms of the contract, according to the fighter, he was under an exclusive contract with Zuffa for one year from the date of his first fight *or* the duration of three fights within a year's time. Penn fought just twice and was not champion at the time of the one-year anniversary of his first fight. The fight in which Penn won the UFC welterweight title occurred outside of his first UFC contract terms. Yet, the UFC stripped Penn of the title due to the fact he signed with another promotion. The action of stripping Penn seemed like a necessity from a public relations standpoint since the promotion did not want Penn to be known as the UFC champion but working outside of the company. This is the reason for the UFC's decision to include a "Champion's Clause." The purpose of an automatic extension of an athlete's contract is to ensure that they stay in the company if they have a title. The term in Penn's contract would have extended his time in the UFC for one year or three fights. One may surmise this additional time would ensure that either the promotion has time to decide on a longer-term contract for the fighter or the fighter loses the title within the three fights they are extended.

On November 22, 2005, the parties settled the case and the lawsuit was dismissed. Penn went on to fight in the K-1 Promotion but returned to the UFC in March 2006 to face Georges St-Pierre.

Reason for a Champion's Clause

Penn's legal dispute gives the promotion a reason to utilize a "Champion's Clause" which is an automatic renewal of an athlete's promotional contract if they are a champion at the time of the end of their contract. Although it is rare to happen, a typical Champion's Clause would renew an athlete's contract for three more fights and/or another year. This would ensure that the athlete remains in the promotion and does not leave as the champion.

In this case, it appears that Penn and Zuffa were arguing two different theories. Penn argued that the UFC stripping him of his UFC welterweight title caused him irreparable harm to his personal brand and reputation. Penn did win the title from Matt Hughes after the expiration of his promotional contract. Technically, it was Zuffa's error for putting Penn in a match where he could have won a UFC title and then leave the organization. If the UFC was prudent, it would have secured Penn to a multiple match contract before the fight for the title. Of course, Penn may have known this as Zuffa inferred in legal pleadings that he was already contemplating an exit having secured the K-1 contract shortly after winning the title. Thus, Penn may have blocked a contract extension to see if he could yield leverage with a win over Hughes. As we see, this did not happen.

Shamrock vs. UFC

Ken Shamrock is one of the pioneers of mixed martial arts. He was on the card for UFC 1 when the company began. He headlined numerous UFC events and PPVs. His career in MMA landed him as one of the first individuals inducted into the UFC Hall of Fame. Shamrock was coming off a loss to Tito Ortiz in 2006 and the UFC wanted to re-sign him to a contract with Zuffa to fight Ortiz once again. Zuffa proposed a two-fight contract for Shamrock to appear in the Ortiz rematch and then the next fight after.

Shamrock entered into the contract with the UFC and fought Ortiz in October 2006. Yet again, Shamrock lost to Ortiz via stoppage. After this fight, Shamrock decided that he would retire from the sport. Exercising its right in Shamrock's promotional contract, Zuffa would have the right for Shamrock to fight in at least one more fight in the UFC if he were to ever decide to return. Or, in the alternative, it could terminate his contract. The contractual term read:

> 10.3 If at any time during the Term, Fighter decides to retire from mixed martial arts or other professional fighting competition, ZUFFA may, at its election, (i) suspend the Term for the period of such retirement; (ii) declare that ZUFFA has satisfied its obligation to promote all future Bouts to be promoted by ZUFFA hereunder, without any compensation due to Fighter therefor, or (iii) elect to provide Fighter with notice of an Acceleration.[7]

In fact, as happens more often than not in MMA, a fighter wants to return. In June 2007, Shamrock had a change of heart and wanted to "unretire." But, after much negotiation on his return, the UFC decided not to exercise the second fight on Shamrock's contract. Shamrock indicated that he had been under the impression that Zuffa had suspended his contract and thus did not contemplate signing with another organization despite the fact he could have solicited other offers if he knew that the contract was terminated. He did not know that Zuffa could change its election to the terms of the contract.

In April 2008, Shamrock filed a lawsuit against the UFC for Breach of Contract.[8] As one might expect, Zuffa filed a Motion for Summary Judgment which was opposed by Shamrock and denied by the court. A two-day bench trial took place in February 2010 with the court ruling in favor of Zuffa. The District Court interpreted the contract in favor of Zuffa in that it did not have to comply with providing Shamrock a second fight after coming out of retirement. As the prevailing party, Zuffa filed a motion to recoup its attorney fees. The Court ordered that Shamrock had to pay Zuffa attorneys approximately $175,000.

However, the legal saga was not over as Shamrock's attorneys filed a Notice of Appeal to the state Supreme Court seeking to overturn the District Court's decision. Shamrock's lawyers hoped that they could persuade the Nevada State Supreme Court, the highest court in the state, that the contract Shamrock entered into required two fights and Zuffa was in breach for terminating it prior to offering Shamrock his last fight.

In its appeal brief, Shamrock pointed to key parts of the contract. The provision in the contract at issue on the appeal was Recital G:

> G. Fighter has determined the first Bout will be his final, after which he will retire, but has agreed to one additional Bout with ZUFFA in the event fighter should either elect not to retire, or to come out of retirement to fight again.[9]

The purpose of this clause was to ensure that if Shamrock decided to retire after his first fight of the contract, he would not be sued for breach of contract if he decided not to go through with the second fight. Ironically, it was Shamrock that wanted another fight and Zuffa that wanted to terminate the contract. Recital G allegedly gave Zuffa the unilateral option for the second bout. Shamrock argued that Zuffa was required to promote a second bout if Shamrock came out of retirement.

Secondly, Shamrock argued that the District Court erred in ruling that Zuffa could terminate the contract under section 10.3 (cited above). He claimed that the company could not have unilaterally made a decision to change its election on how it categorized Shamrock's contract. Also, Shamrock challenged the trial court ruling that he waived his right to sue Zuffa for breach of contract for failing to give timely notice of the breach and opportunity to cure. The contract included a clause that required Shamrock to give notice of a lawsuit as it would trigger a right for Zuffa to attempt to cure the issue short of filing a complaint. Since Shamrock did not provide notice, Zuffa claimed that he waived his right to file a lawsuit against the company.

Zuffa countered Shamrock's appeal by maintaining that Recital G was an option, and the UFC simply did not pick it up. It sided with the District Court's interpretation of the contract in that Shamrock was signed on to fight against Tito Ortiz and then there was an option for another fight. According to the UFC, the second fight was included in the case that the first fight under the contract ended in some sort of controversy. The UFC pointed to the Ortiz fight which ended in a first round stoppage, which many believed was stopped too soon, as the reason for an option fight for Shamrock's contract.

In November 2011, the state Supreme Court affirmed the trial court's decision. It noted that, "there is nothing within the language of Recital G that indicates the promise [of two fights] was mutual or, in other words, that Zuffa was obligated to promote a second fight for Shamrock if he chose not to retire or decided at a later date to come out of retirement."[10]

Notably, Shamrock went on to fight in other organizations, including rival Bellator. Despite the hard feelings, Dana White and Shamrock were able to work out their differences in 2014; the two talked things over and were able to come to terms over the dispute. Still, the harsh lesson for Shamrock was having to go through the process of losing the trial and then the appeal. In retrospect, Shamrock was paid $1 million for his first bout with Ortiz and would have been paid $230,000 for his second bout. Thus, the amount of money he was disputing with Zuffa was for his unpaid second bout of $230,000.

Was the Contract Interpreted Correctly?

The Shamrock-Zuffa legal dispute enforces the contractual weight Zuffa had over its athletes. One might paint the problem on Recital G. Admittedly, it appears the court sided with Zuffa in its interpretation that Shamrock's second fight was an option. One would have to place some level of culpability on Shamrock's agent that purportedly pushed for the recital. Of course, Zuffa likely had some say in the negotiation in the drafting of this clause. But how it reads does make it ambiguous in certain ways. The clause could have indicated that Shamrock would be fighting two fights under the contract with the first being Ortiz and the second to be mutually determined at a later date. If the parties did not mutually agree to a second fight, there would be no second fight. However, if Shamrock decided to retire again after the Ortiz fight then the contract would terminate. Instead, Recital G was drafted in a way where it could be interpreted as an option for a second fight instead of for two.

Couture vs. UFC

One of the more interesting cases involving UFC contracts is the Randy Couture lawsuit which was based on both his employment with the company and his fight contract with Zuffa.[11] The legal dispute between Couture and Zuffa highlighted several issues with fighters and promoters. The exclusive nature of the deal that athletes signed had potential for harm if the fighters experienced success. In Couture's dispute there were two contracts with Zuffa. First, there was a non-compete agreement in Couture's employment contract which Zuffa said was violated when the former UFC champion appeared in marketing for rival International Fight League. Second, Couture's attempt at resigning from his fight contract with the UFC was met with opposition. With fights remaining on his contract, Couture opted to leave the organization with hopes of signing somewhere else. However, the UFC was unwilling to allow this. This caused a third party that wanted to sign Zuffa to step in and press the case via judicial intervention. The dispute highlights Couture's contractual problem in attempting to void his own contract.

Randy Couture was a standout collegiate wrestler, a Greco-Roman wrestling champion and an army veteran. His accolades made transition into mixed martial arts seamless when he started his professional career in the UFC in 1997. He won the UFC title in two divisions and was a favorite among MMA fans. Couture decided to retire in 2006 despite having two fights left on his contract. This is when he had entered into an Employment Agreement with Zuffa to act as an ambassador of the sport. He switched from independent contractor as a fighter to an employee of the company. But, like most MMA athletes, Couture made a comeback.

In January 2007, Couture signed a contract with Zuffa to fight in the UFC for 18 months or 4 fights. Zuffa wiped out the last two fights of his prior contract despite the potential of having Couture honor the contract. Prior to the end of the January 2007 contract, Couture decided to resign. In March 2008, prior to the end of the contract, the UFC filed a Complaint against Couture for breach of contract.

Zuffa claimed that it acknowledged Couture's resignation letter, which it points out was dated September 18, 2007, yet delivered on October 11, 2007, but determined that it still retained the exclusive rights for Couture to fight. In a letter sent by Dana White on the same day as Couture's resignation, White reiterated that Section 6 of his Employment Contract prevented working with other promotions and disclosure of confidential information.[12] In a separate letter dated the same day, White addressed Couture's resignation and "presumed" that Couture was retiring from MMA. He cited section 10.3 of his Promotional Agreement (the same section cited in Ken Shamrock's contract) notifying Couture it was suspending Couture's contract.

One might assume that based on the resignation, he was not going to retire. Moreover, he was attempting to get out of his contract, wait out the timeframe outlined in his contract, and then move to another company. Seeing the value of Couture with a competitor, the UFC elected to categorize his departure as a retirement which would mean that Zuffa would claim ownership of Couture's exclusive right to fight in MMA with the UFC. This was problematic for Couture who sought to continue his career elsewhere. Specifically, Couture wanted to fight Fedor Emelianenko. The Russian heavyweight MMA champion was considered the No. 1 MMA fighter in the world, but due to contractual issues, Emelianenko would not sign with the UFC. With Couture considered the No. 2 fighter in the world, a "superfight" of this magnitude would not take place.

However, there was the idea that if Couture would be able to sign with another promotion, a fight with Emelianenko could happen. Thus, Couture signed with HDNet Fights, an upstart promotion founded by Dallas Mavericks owner Mark Cuban. The intent would be to have Couture wait out the duration of his contract with Zuffa and then come aboard with HDNet to have the highly anticipated showdown with Emelianenko. In fact, HDNet filed a lawsuit in Texas seeking a declaratory judgment to determine the status of Couture's contract.

From Zuffa's perspective, one might have to be concerned with the prospect of Couture leaving and then brokering a fight with Emelianenko. This would be a huge win for the promotion that could pull this off and be the spark that would create a formidable competitor to the UFC. Thus, you could understand why the UFC would want to attempt to hold onto the rights of Couture to at least have him fight out the contract he signed. Feasibly, even if this was not the plan, it might give time for Zuffa to attempt to sign Emelianenko to hold this fight in the UFC.

In the end, Couture settled with the UFC in order to save legal fees. He admitted to spending $500,000 in legal fees, with Zuffa intent on dragging him into a courtroom battle.[13] Despite the settlement and actual return to fighting in the UFC, Couture remains angered by what Zuffa does with its contracts to stifle the livelihoods of its independent contracts. Couture has been outspoken about the coercive contracts which bound its athletes to exclusivity.

Conclusion

For Zuffa, the contracts have proven to be legal and effective. Despite the perceptions of Penn, Shamrock and Couture, the contracts reflect the leverage Zuffa has had over its fighters. The terms are almost non-negotiable and hard to void. Even with terms that are drafted in favor of the ones who created the contract, the athlete is ultimately responsible for what they sign. Certainly, the above cases reflect issues with these agreements.

Whether it was the perceived "Champion's Clause" which B.J. Penn seemingly avoided, the late-changing election of terms which negated an additional fight for Ken Shamrock or Randy Couture's attempted resignation, the power of the Zuffa contract and its zealous defense of it have proven effective both in leverage and attaining (and retaining) the best talent.

7

The Athlete-Agent Relationship

Introduction

Like most sports, athletes are in need of representation to help them with the details off the court, field or ring. MMA is the same. As the sport has grown, there is a need for fighters to seek help from agents to review contracts, help secure sponsorships and find fights. But, the agent-athlete relationship can be strained. The best example of this in MMA is the case of *Fight Tribe Management vs. Ronda Rousey*.

Darin Harvey, the long-time manager of Ronda Rousey, sued the former UFC women's bantamweight champion claiming that Harvey's MMA Management firm was owed money for managing Rousey. Harvey argued that he had helped "find" Rousey and now that she emerged as a star for the UFC, she was trying to exit out of her contractual obligations with Fight Tribe Management ("Fight Tribe"). He claimed that Rousey owed $86,000 stemming from his representation of the fighter. Rousey sought to be released from her contract from Fight Tribe citing the contract was void as to the Agreement's provisions related to professional fighting services.

This chapter will take a look at the California State Athletic Commission's Arbitration Decision and inquire as to the specifics of representing fighters using California as an example. It will also examine the argument of "quantum meruit" posed by Harvey. Looking at this case, it's clear that Harvey's situation is similar to the cutthroat industry of agents in other sports.

A Star Is Born

Ronda Rousey became the UFC's first major mainstream superstar. In 2011, UFC president Dana White proclaimed that no woman would fight in the UFC. He was woefully wrong, as Rousey came on the scene, making her UFC debut in February 2013.

Rousey was not just another pretty face. She was the first American woman to earn an Olympic medal in Judo at the Summer Olympics in Beijing since its inception as an Olympic sport in 1992. She qualified for the 2004 Olympic Games in Athens and was the youngest judoka in the Games. She won a gold medal at the 2004 World Junior Judo Championships in Budapest, Hungary.

Rousey became a star due to her dominance and her girl next door looks. She was undefeated in Strikeforce, another MMA promotion that eventually was purchased by the UFC, and her debut with the UFC was met with great anticipation. After her win against Liz Carmouche at UFC 157 in February 2013, she ran off 5 dominant wins in the UFC and drew a huge following of fans, especially younger women that now had an MMA hero.

Rousey Finds Fight Tribe

Manager Darin Harvey was there from the beginning. He met Rousey in the spring of 2010 while still an amateur mixed martial artist. She contacted Harvey, who is also a martial artist practitioner, to help her set up fights and manage her career. According to the arbitration records, Rousey testified that Harvey arranged and paid for her MMA training, including training with her strength and conditioning coach.[1] He also paid for Rousey's medical exams and expenses related to her MMA activities and helped promote her first three amateur fights which she won. Harvey testified that his company, Fight Tribe Management, LLC, provided everything for his fighters so they didn't have to worry about anything but fighting. This included public relations, legal services, photo shoots, fighting and living expenses.

Despite the uncertainty of Rousey ever making it in the UFC, Harvey shepherded her career when she turned pro in March 2011. Harvey paid for an attorney to represent Rousey in their negotiations with the UFC to finalize their contract.

It was not until May 15, 2012, that Rousey and Harvey entered into a written contract identified as a "Service Agreement."[2] However, it took several months to draft and finalize, and it was finally executed by Rousey and Harvey on January 29, 2013. The commission noted that the service agreement was not drafted on the commission's preapproved two-page form, and neither did either party seek approval of the agreement by the commission. Moreover, the agreement was not filed with the commission—all requisites that would have verified or denied the agreement.

Harvey claimed that the service agreement was not a fighter-manager contract but a talent agreement which provided Harvey 10 percent of all of

Rousey's professional compensation including payments from her professional fights.[3] The service agreement included acting and modeling jobs according to Harvey.

However, Harvey stated that Rousey owed him money apparently loaned to her. This coincided with her wish to be released from Harvey's fight contract. The $85,818 claimed by Harvey's management company was related to his representation of the fighter. Rousey argued that the agreement was void as to the provisions related to fighting services.

Rousey and Fight Tribe Go to Arbitration

Harvey filed a lawsuit and a Petition to Compel Arbitration against Rousey but per the terms of the contract, it was to be decided by the California State Athletic Commission (CSAC).[4]

After a CSAC arbitration hearing, the Commission held that the portion of the contract that was related to professional fighting services was void. It determined that the portion of the contract that was entertainment in nature should be determined by the lawsuit filed by Harvey in Los Angeles Superior Court.

It appeared that Harvey used a contract that was part fighter representative services and part entertainment contract. While an agent may be able to perform both services, California required certain conditions of an athlete fighter representation agreement. The commission discovered that the agreement was not on the requisite form used by the state of California.

At the arbitration, he claimed the following income and expenses:

Income received from fights:	$25,608
Income from pay per view fights:	$23,180
Income from sponsorships:	$20,830
Expenses:	$170,376

While the expenses were not itemized, one can imagine that Harvey advanced money to Rousey for training, nutrition, travel and other expenses.

The simple profit/loss outlined by Harvey reflects that he lost $85,818. Or, he sought to recoup this amount from Rousey.

The findings by the California State Athletic Commission may be tailored to the specific state but are certainly instructive.

Despite Harvey's assertion that Rousey's MMA career was incidental to the overall representation agreement, the CSAC arbitrator held that Harvey was in fact her manager. Even when Harvey's duties as a matchmaker were eliminated once Rousey reached the UFC (as the company makes its own fights), he still represented her.

The CSAC determined that fight contracts entered into in the state of California are to be issued on specific forms approved by the commission. The CSAC exercised jurisdiction of that portion related to fighting and deferred issues outside the scope of "professional fighting, kick boxing and martial arts" to the Superior Court Case. Thus, issues related to modeling, acting or commercial endorsement were not determined at the hearing.

Harvey argued the contractual legal issue of *quantum meruit*, which stands for the recoupment of the fair market value of his professional management services. In this case, Harvey was seeking money he spent for Rousey from May 1, 2012, until April 3, 2014. The Commission determined that a finding of quantum meruit "would be inconsistent with the provisions of California law requiring prior written fighter-manager contracts." A contract made in violation of a regulatory statue is void. The policy behind this is grounded in the belief that it would act as a deterrent to managers drafting contracts as "managers are less likely to enter into illegal arrangements." The Commission sternly denounced any help via quantum meruit. "Harvey violated the statutory schemed designed for the protection of athletes, like Rousey, and therefore, Harvey will receive no help from this commission in enforcing this illegal fighter-manager contract."

A Fair Result?

While one might feel bad for Harvey as the Commission ruling left him out of luck in recoupment of fees he expended for Rousey, the rules are stringent as they relate to drafting fighter contracts. The harsh reality is that the policy of protecting fighters from unsavory contract deals takes precedence over returning value for professional management services. It also highlights the responsibility of managers to ensure compliance with the relevant rules within the jurisdiction in which they operate.

Investing in a young prospect with an unknown future is risky. For a manager to undertake this investment, it takes time, energy and money. For a young prospect, the advance of money is a short-term payoff but might impact them long-term. If the service agreement entered into by Rousey-Harvey was viable, it would have tied up Rousey's overall career, not just her fight career. Moreover, there's no indication that Rousey knew the terms of the contract. This is likely why California has standard form contracts approved by the athletic commission to curb unsavory terms.

In addition, the most important thing to remember is that managers have a duty to follow the rules. The Commission was unforgiving of the contract drafted by Harvey. The record reflects Harvey's management team managed fighters and for him not to know the rules, or show disregard for them probably upset the Commission. It was likely that a request for quantum meruit would be denied, since Harvey did not comply with the forms or request confirmation of his representation agreement.

While Harvey claimed it to be a talent agreement and the fight agreement was ancillary to the overall managing agreement, it would have been prudent for Harvey to have made two agreements to ensure each was valid.

The parties decided to settle the court case over the talent agreement after the arbitration hearing in what was described as an "amicable" settlement. But, issues remained and the two sides had to settle a potential defamation claim threatened by Harvey regarding how he was portrayed in Rousey's 2016 autobiography, *My Fight/Your Fight*. There was an agreement that there would be no lawsuit if the subsequent reprints of the book altered a passage related to Harvey.

Something to Consider

Notably, the hearing uncovered the fact that Rousey had not signed her contract with Harvey until several months after he had begun representing her. While this might be considered a formality, it is one that should be done at the outset of a representation matter. Certainly, the athlete agency business is by far one of the most competitive industries out there. Some recall the scene in the Tom Cruise film *Jerry Maguire* where the agent (Maguire) played by Tom Cruise stops his prospect client and wants him to sign an agreement that Cruise represents him. However, the prospect is unwilling to put his signature to paper because he confesses that he has signed with another agent and was using Maguire. While the cinematic drama played out, it is clear that this is a valid scenario in real life. The time and energy needed to secure a client can be precarious. Reducing an agreement down to paper might seem like an afterthought, but it's clear from the Rousey situation that it is a necessity.

Heavyweight Signs with UFC, Sues Agents

In January 2012, MMA fighter Alistair Overeem was sued by his representatives at Knockout Investments (KOI) which owned the gym where he trained. The lawsuit stemmed from a dispute over payment by Overeem's gym and payments made to the fighter when he signed with the UFC. The dispute revealed a unique payment arrangement which tied the management group to the fighter and granted it an unwarranted renewal of the contract.

Alistair Overeem split with his longtime training gym and management group in September 2011, citing "a breach of trust" and that there was "no turning back and no way to continue a positive, working relationship."[5]

KOI represented fighters in MMA, including the UFC Heavyweight

Overeem. According to its management contract with fighters it was to receive 30 percent of all revenues generated by Overeem's participation or promotion. According to the terms set forth the contract was set to expire after five years or July 2012, but it was subject to an automatic renewal unless one of the parties gave a written notice at least six months prior to the expiration of the initial term.

According to KOI, it had spent time and effort in securing fights for Overeem in several promotions. It also spent money promoting the fighter as it is related to his contract.

In November 2011, KOI claimed Overeem officially breached the Management Contract through his attorney demanding money from KOI, alleging the gym breached the lawsuit. According to KOI, the UFC's Lorenzo Fertitta told Overeem that he would have a $1 million signing bonus for contracting with the UFC and that it was his money. He also told Overeem that KOI and his gym, Golden Glory, were "ripping him off." This may have been the impetus for Overeem to think about filing a lawsuit against his management.

The lawsuit claimed that Overeem neglected to pay commissions from certain bouts made in the Strikeforce promotion. Overeem was cut from Strikeforce in July 2011.[6] It was believed to be due to a disagreement regarding payment methods. KOI also claimed that it did not receive its payment during the negotiations with his UFC contract.

According to the lawsuit, his guaranteed "bout fee" was $264,285 and he would receive a "win bonus" of $121,428 if he defeated Brock Lesnar in his fight on December 30, 2011. He would also receive a "Pay Per View" bonus of $2.00 per view for each viewer, for all revenues received by UFC–Zuffa for telecast of the Lesnar fight in the United States, Canada or over the internet in excess of $500,000.[7]

According to PPV reports, the UFC 141 event drew an estimated 535,000 PPV views. This would equate to approximately $70,000 for Overeem.

Overeem sued KOI and GG, citing that some of the terms in his contract were ambiguous and unenforceable in a personal services contract.[8] He notes that the contract included a provision that fines the fighter $10,000 for any breach of the agreement and a $5,000 per-day penalty for each day the violation continues.[9] The heavy-handed penalty seemed punitive and likely unenforceable. Yet, it shows the oppressive nature of the contract, which seems to be drafted in favor of KOI.

In the Complaint, Overeem lists "failures" on the part of KOI which could be deemed as a "breach" of his contract and thus excuse him from the agreement. Some of the allegations paint KOI in a bad light, as they allegedly managed him in jurisdictions where they were not licensed as well as allegedly pushed him to fight when injured. One might infer that the influence would be so that the company could obtain their percentage for its management fee. KOI saw the lawsuit as retaliation for its claim that Overeem had yet to pay on its commissions.

Overeem claimed that KOI was sent his fight purses. Then, KOI would take its percentage and send Overeem the remainder. After Zuffa purchased Strikeforce, it refused to continue this practice. As a result, the company fired Overeem and other fighters managed by KOI over this. However, they were later reinstated by the UFC after KOI relented and allowed the promotion to pay the fighters directly.

The practice of withholding pay to fighters and directing them to the management team has advantages and disadvantages. While it ensures payment by the athlete, which was of chief concern to KOI, it also withholds the amount of money due. If the athlete is given a percentage of the total purse without a detailed accounting of what was being withheld, it would seem unfair to the athlete. One might assume that in addition to the fee, costs are also withdrawn from the total purse. In some instances, the athletic commissions that regulate the events deduct the costs associated, including licenses to fight within the state. Moreover, it would appear that once the money is deducted from the purse, there would be no direct way to protest a payment if the fighter did not agree with what was deducted. The only recourse would be to dispute the fee and/or file a lawsuit against the management.

Notably, KOI filed a writ of attachment and request to garnish Overeem's wages from his main event at UFC 141.[10] The strategy to garnish wages was an attempt to "make good" on the commissions Overeem allegedly owed to KOI. However, the attempt to garnish Overeem's wages did not transpire as KOI did not post a bond, a requisite in filing for a writ of garnishment. The reason being is that in an attachment hearing (to garnish someone's wages) there only need be a showing that the claims have "probable validity" and have "probable cause." Thus, the threshold to prove something could still be in doubt. In Nevada, KOI and GG had to put up a surety bond of $200,000 to garnish a portion of Overeem's $385,000 fight purse. For whatever reason, it did not do so.

Observations and Conclusions

This legal dispute shows the extent that training gyms had with its fighters. It is still an ongoing practice that gyms have their own in-house management team, which seems like a smart business move but might prove to be a detriment to the athlete, as they are extrinsically tied to the gym. The business side of MMA has overridden the once familial and fraternal culture of training partners and coaches. In this case, the contract was made in Holland and seemed to have a lengthy duration in addition to an automatic renewal if a party did not notify the other in time. This type of contract favors the management group, as it grants them a substantial percentage (30 percent). Moreover, the practice of having the full purse amount of a fight to be directed to the management team seems unfair to the athlete. It reflects a certain undue control that the management would have over the athlete.

In an interesting twist, the UFC let go of KOI-represented fighters in what looked like a strong-arm tactic.[11] While the strategy may be questionable, it brought to light the problem with the practice. Overeem was reinstated by the UFC and no other problems between himself, the UFC and management surfaced after his return.

St-Pierre Split with Long-Time Manager Causes Lawsuit

Georges St-Pierre ("GSP," as he's known) split with long-time manager Shari Spencer in 2011. Spencer had represented GSP's business interests since 2007. He had signed on with Hollywood talent agency Creative Arts Agency but retained Spencer as his personal manager.

As the UFC was beginning to be a part of the mainstream, GSP was given opportunities through Spencer including a feature in the *New York Times* Style Section in September 2010.[12] The article chronicled GSP's foray into New York fashion week. An underlying theme in the piece was that GSP seemed uncomfortable with the mainstream New York scene and perhaps his role as the spokesperson for the UFC. Spencer's work had helped GSP obtain mainstream sponsors (Gatorade and Under Armour) as well as appearances on ESPN and non–MMA magazines.

But the split between GSP and his former manager was acrimonious. An arbitration took place over alleged unpaid payouts from their athlete-manager contract.

Although GSP is known as one of the nicer guys in MMA, his fallout with his manager highlights an issue between talent and the business managers and agents that work with and for them. While there may be friendships, the business side takes over.

8

Should the Ali Act Include MMA?

Introduction

The Muhammad Ali Act ("Ali Act") was enacted to help boxers combat unsavory aspects of the sport outside of the ring. The legislation amended the Professional Boxing Safety Act of 1996. Among the rules included in the bill, which was introduced in 1999 and passed in 2000, the legislation specifies that a sanctioning organization may not receive any compensation from a boxing match unless it files its bylaws and a complete description of its ratings criteria, policies, and general sanctioning fee schedule with the FTC.[1] It also created safeguards to protect the rights and welfare of professional boxers from managers and promoters. The law was named after famous heavyweight boxer Muhammad Ali. He was one of the most recognized figures in sports and pop culture. In 2005, he was awarded the Presidential Medal of Freedom, the highest civilian award in the United States. The award recognizes people that have made contributions to world peace, culture and other significant public and private endeavors. The Ali Act would serve as a measure to protect boxers. In May 2016, an Oklahoma congressman introduced a bill to amend the Ali Act to expand it to mixed martial artists.

Congressman Markwayne Mullin, a Republican out of Oklahoma, introduced a bill to amend the Muhammad Ali Boxing Reform Act of 2000.[2] The bill targets mixed martial artists in expanding the federal law's coverage to all combat sports athletes. Mullin, a former MMA fighter, believed that it was time that athletes are protected and given the same protections that boxers are provided under the Ali Act. Mullin believed that the business of MMA was slanted toward organizations and fighters suffered from the lack of insurance benefits, low pay and unfair contractual provisions. Although the Ali Act has been criticized, it provides certain rights that MMA fighters currently lack. This included health care benefits and a ranking system to determine fights for titles, which presumably equates to better compensation and contractual rights favoring the promotion.

As of December 2018, there have been two congressional hearings held regarding the sport of MMA. The hearings were informational in nature although several issues arose about the structure of MMA business and the plight of fighters.

Background on the Muhammad Ali Act

The Muhammad Ali Boxing Reform Act ("Ali Act") was signed into law on May 26, 2000.[3] Lawmakers were concerned with the exploitation and anti-competitive practices of boxing managers and promoters. The boxing business lacked a set of checks and balances and the Ali Act was a method to address the problems.

According to the Ali Act, it had three purposes. The first was to protect the rights and welfare of boxers. Second, it was to aid state boxing commissions with the oversight of the sport. Finally, it was to promote honorable competition in professional boxing and enhance the overall integrity of the industry.

The Ali Act enacted major reforms in the sport including a "firewall" between managers and promoters that prevents an individual serving in both roles for a fighter. It also protected boxers from coercive contracts and required disclosures regarding pay before bouts.

The Ali Act carries penalties, including monetary damages, court costs and reasonable attorney's fees and expenses. There is also the possibility of serving "not more than 1 year" in prison. The Attorney General may bring charges based on the Ali Act against an individual that is found in violation of the Ali Act.

Ali Act Congressional Hearings

First Congressional Hearing

The first Congressional meeting on MMA as it related to the possible expansion of the Ali Act took place on December 8, 2016. Described as a new concept for its jurisdiction, the Chairman of the Committee admitted he had no previous knowledge of the sport and regulation. The hearing was a way to bring Congress "up to speed."[4]

There was some controversy at the outset as the UFC indicated that it would not participate in the hearings if Randy Couture would participate. Couture, a former UFC champion, was embroiled in a legal battle during a contract dispute with the company in 2007. The parties settled and Couture returned to the UFC. He had his last fight with the company in 2011. But, after leaving the company, he was critical of Zuffa's business practices. "This company [Zuffa] has been signing fighters to coercive and literally awful contracts for years. It's been one of the things that I've fought with them over since day one, since they bought the company, over ancillary rights, over (right to match) and retirement clauses, and having a little bit of leverage as their heavyweight champion when they bought the company, we fought over all these things. It's one of the reasons I'm persona non grata with the company now," Couture said in a 2016 interview.[5]

Couture was asked by the bill's sponsor to explain to the lawmakers about the flawed rankings system. Couture talked about how the UFC filed a lawsuit and sought an injunction to prevent a fight with Fedor Emelianenko which would have been a matchup between the presumed number 1 and 2 ranked fighters in the world. The UFC did not want Couture to fight Emelianenko, since he was not contracted with the UFC.

Jeff Denham, a congressman from California and co-author of the bill, testified that there was a need for "minimum standards" for fighters. This would include a baseline for fighters to determine when one might be able to return to fighting. A former boxer, he expressed concern that fighters were coming back too soon from injury without properly recuperating from a fight. Denham noted that he wanted minimum federal oversight. Aside from safety standards, he wanted transparency between manager and fighter.

On behalf of the UFC, Jeff Novitzky, the Vice President of Health and Performance, represented Zuffa at the Congressional Hearing. Novitzky focused his time on the health of the athlete. He spoke to programs that focused on working on the effects of head trauma for safety reasons. This included stressing the UFC Performance Institute in Las Vegas which aimed to help its contracted fighters with injury recovery, nutrition and health. He also spoke about the UFC Anti-Doping Program and described it as "the most comprehensive, robust anti-doping program in the world."

Lydia Roberts, Treasurer of the Association of Boxing Commissions and Combative Sports ("ABC"), testified about the organization and how it oversees MMA promotions and their health. She noted that the ABC is a 501(c)(3) and does not receive any federal funds. She indicated that the ABC mission is how to protect its fighters. She praised both fighters and promoters which make the sports and highlighted the delicate balance between the both. She testified that the Muhammad Ali Act has greatly impacted the industry in a positive manner. ABC would probably support a bill that would support fighter safety. "There is a balance between a business model and a sports model," said Roberts in highlighting its position as both advocate for fighters and promoters but said the ABC would also be wary of overreach in regulation that might inhibit the sport.

Dr. Ann McKee, a Boston University professor, spoke about head injuries and CTE. Dr. McKee indicated that there was not enough research at the time to determine whether there is a correlation between MMA fighting and head trauma. She did note that in the one brain studied, a 25-year-old MMA fighter who passed away, evidence of CTE was found. It was the first person that they were able to examine with head injuries. While there has not been a major stir about head trauma litigation in MMA, sports like the NFL and NHL, and the sports entertainment product of pro wrestling, have seen head trauma lawsuits arise stemming from their activities.

Although an aside for this chapter, the hearings addressed the health of the fighters and could be revisited at a future date if and when CTE becomes a legal issue in MMA. Dr. McKee also advised that children and young adults not participate in full contact MMA with head strikes, that fighters be educated to limit their exposure to head strikes in training and that limitations be placed on the number of head strikes per match. Her advice does not conform with the rules of combat sports, where blows to the head are fair strikes; in fact many of the strategies in combat sports deal with punches, kicks, knees or elbows to the head.

The first hearing did not culminate in any further development. It did bring publicity to the bill and the bill's sponsors as they sought more lawmakers to sign onto the bill. The hearing did shed light on the industry as many had no idea about its inner workings. For supporters of the law, it was a chance to exhibit the value of a law that preserves the health and well-being of athletes. Although there was the Muhammad Ali Act, some were skeptical about expanding the law to mixed martial arts. Those in favor of the political philosophy of smaller government and opposed to governmental overreach and regulation opposed the law.

Second Congressional Hearing

A year later a Congressional Hearing was held, in December 2017, to discuss the issues with the sport of mixed martial arts.[6] The issues remained similar to the first, with Couture returning to testify along with UFC representative Marc Ratner, Pennsylvania Athletic Commissioner Greg Sirb, and Associate Professor of Neurology and Co-Director of the Brain Injury Research Center of Mount Sinai, Kristen Dams-O'Connor. Similar to the first hearing, the invited individuals testified before lawmakers skeptical of the sport and those wanting clarity on the issues.

Couture testified that signing a promotional contract with Zuffa means that the company "retains sweeping ancillary rights to utilize the athlete's likeness in perpetuity for all commercial purposes."

In his public comments,[7] he cited four key areas where the UFC's practice has stunted the growth of MMA:

1. The use of exclusive and non-public contracts;
2. The assignment of ancillary fights from the athlete to the promoter far beyond the term of the promotional agreement;
3. Champion's clauses that prevent champions from ever becoming really marketable; and
4. Secret discretionary payments that are utilized to keep the athletes subservient and silent.

Another issue he brought up was the ineffective rankings system employed by the UFC. He stated that MMA promoters are not required by the athletic commissions to utilize independent or objective rankings. Promoters issue their own titles and athletes are only allowed to compete for those titles if they sign exclusive contracts with the company. Couture indicated that the contracts are long-term and inferred that the fighter has little, if any, leverage when negotiating terms of the agreement.

He claimed that, due to a lack of independent and objective rankings, it is hard to quantify the seemingly arbitrary nature of what fighter will receive a title shot. The inference is that having a title and title shot equates to higher pay and more chances to capitalize on potential monetary opportunities. Challengers for titles are also paid more for the opportunity and winning the title. Couture points out that despite UFC rankings that seem to outline a top challenger for the champion, they are sometimes skipped over for a fight that the promotion feels would be more appealing, a better matchup, at the champion's request or deemed a "superfight."

One of the constant marketing talking points by the UFC is that they will give the fans the fights that they crave. For the UFC, if that means that a fighter who is set to receive a title shot is skipped over due to the fact that another is more popular, it will both appease the fans and increase the revenues for the UFC.

A month prior to the hearing, former UFC welterweight champion Georges St-Pierre made his return to the Octagon and was given an immediate title shot against middleweight champion at the time, Michael Bisping. Prior to the November 2017 fight, St-Pierre's last appearance in the UFC happened almost four years prior, in 2013. He had not fought in any other organization and was not active in the UFC. Thus, St-Pierre "skipped the line" of title contenders waiting for the chance to fight Bisping. The event took place at New York's Madison Square Garden. It was the company's second time at the venue and it wanted a big fight for its return. Prior to St-Pierre's prolonged sabbatical from mixed martial arts, he was considered one of the UFC's top stars and a big draw on pay-per-view. St-Pierre defeated Bisping to win the middleweight title.

However, St-Pierre relinquished the title soon after his victory, leaving the title vacant to the consternation of many of the athletes who were ranked ahead of the former champion. Since his fight in 2017 against Bisping, St-Pierre had not returned the Octagon, making the fight seem like a "one-off" for the purposes of making a fight for fans—but, also for the purpose of selling the most tickets, merchandise and pay-per-view buys.

Couture characterized the championship belts of promotions as "ceremonial" and fighters have no property or "contractual" right to enforce their status as champions and the promoter can strip a fighter of the title at any time. This seemed to be the case as GSP won the middleweight title and eventually forfeited the title, as he declined to face the top contenders ready to fight him. He identified what is known as the "Champion's Clause," which refers to contractual language which requires a champion's contract to be extended once they become champion. Even if a fighter wins a promoter's title and is at the end of his or her contract, their existing contract is automatically extended for a requisite period of time. Additionally, a fighter cannot retire or voluntarily sit out the remaining term of the promotion agreement as the UFC "tolls" it for the entire period of the "retirement" or refusal to compete.

In his testimony, Couture analogized this perceived unfairness to that of a professional tennis player or golfer signing an exclusive, long-term contract with a promoter of a tournament and not being allowed to play in another tournament unless they received permission, and only being able to play against those opponents approved by the promoter.

In a footnote to his written statement, he made another analogy to the Wimbledon tennis tournament. If top tier tennis players had to sign exclusive contracts to the tournament, it would make all other tournaments obsolete or considered minor-league. Couture stated that this has happened in MMA, "with the tacit approval of the athletic commissions." This was the argument Couture gave for prohibiting the UFC from issuing titles and requiring exclusivity.

The clause protects promotions from having their champion utilize their status as the "champion" of one company and then appear in another without notice of leaving the title with their previous employer. For the promotion with a departing champion, it is a public relations problem and is a sign of disrespect for the company. But, it also is a sign that the champion either felt disrespected or was not paid enough to remain as champion. The contractual clause invoked in the MMA contracts referred to by Couture would ensure that the champion remains with the organization. This would enable the company and fighter to come to terms on a new contract and/or the fighter would lose the title to a contender. From a promotional point of view, the contract clause provides continuity with its business. It prevents a disruption with its promotion, as the champion is viewed as the most important fighter in the division, and without the fighter, there is a void that must be filled.

The Interim Title

In the event that the champion is injured, or cannot make a defense in a reasonable amount of time from their last fight, the UFC has come up with "interim" championship titles. The moniker creates the same scenario as if the champion were able to fight. The likely scenario is that the winner of the interim championship is to face a returning champion to unify the titles. The "interim" title buttresses Couture's argument that the championship belt is "ceremonial" since the purpose is to incentivize a matchup between two contenders and sell to fans while the titleholder is able to return.

This practice can cause some obvious concerns. What happens if the fighter that wins the interim championship gets injured and the original champion is unable to return in time for another defense? Would there be another interim championship? Is the divisional title put on hold? Many title contenders, looking for a shot at the championship, embraced the motto "Defend or Vacate," meaning that the fighter should either defend the title or vacate it to allow another the shot.

For instance, Conor McGregor left the UFC as titleholder of the Featherweight title and the Lightweight title to pursue a fight with Floyd Mayweather, which happened in August 2017. Both divisions had "interim" title bouts to determine who would be the eventual challenger to McGregor. But, McGregor's sabbatical away from the UFC left a chasm of uncertainty. Despite being "stripped" of the title, McGregor claimed to be champion in both divisions because he was never defeated for the title.

While an "interim" title may have the promotional intent of generating interest, it also reflects the "ceremonial" nature of the prize.

Promoter Disclosure

The Mixed Martial Arts Fighters Association cites the Ali Act's provision which requires a promoter to disclose "the amounts of any compensation" a promoter will receive from a fight as beneficial and necessary. But even boxers have had issues obtaining this information from promoters. In April 2016, boxer Chris Algieri had issues obtaining disclosure information from his promoter.[8] One of the issues with the current Ali Act is that it does not provide a time prior to the bout by which the promoter must disclose the information to the fighter. A promoter waits until the last minute to produce this information, as they do not know how much the event will produce and therefore cannot provide the fighter with the information. For instance, there is not a solid figure on pay-per-view numbers and/or closed-circuit receipts. Of course, the promoter can probably estimate this figure, along with the numbers it should have for the advanced ticket sales. But, this information may be incomplete and not account for walk-up tickets from fans that wait until the day of the event to purchase a ticket. It also cannot account for pay-per-view. There is the issue that if a promoter were to provide a fighter with the information some time before the fight, the fighter may decide not to show. Or, it would cause the fighter to attempt to renegotiate with the threat of not showing unless his or her monetary demands were met. Still, the fact that there is not a set time per the law to provide a fighter with this information hinders a fighter.

Not knowing about how much a fighter will make handicaps a fighter's ability to negotiate future fights. It also negates the opportunity to evaluate his value and market. It is worthy to note that there has been only one instance in which a UFC contract has been produced in recent years, and that is the Eddie Alvarez lawsuit. The contract has been utilized by reporters, bloggers, fighters and agents to compare and contrast the terms in a standard UFC agreement.

Dr. Kristen Dams-O'Connor and Pennsylvania Athletic Director Greg Sirb also testified at the hearing. Dr. Dams-O'Connor spoke about the health concerns associated with combat sports, specifically, head trauma. Sirb addressed issues regarding coercive contracts in combat sports.

Similar to his first time testifying before a congressional subcommittee, Couture spoke about his time in MMA and the perceived unfairness in pay for fighters. He testified that "[o]ver 90% of all revenue in MMA is generated by the UFC" which infers the monopoly that the promotion has over fighters. Couture spoke about the "sweeping ancillary rights" the UFC has over its fighters and the exclusive long-term contracts they are coerced to sign. He also highlighted the lack of independent rankings and the arbitrary nature in which title fights are given without merit.

On the other end, the UFC's Marc Ratner testified on behalf of the promotion. In favor of the original Ali Act, Ratner testified on behalf of the legislation to fix a broken system in boxing. Yet, he took the other side in this case. He advocated for state legislation which he described as "real and effective." Ratner stressed the "rags to riches" success story of many of the company's athletes which has made several millionaires out of fighters. He also commented on the women's movement within the UFC and how the UFC put athletes first, regardless of gender.

In finding differences between boxing and MMA, Ratner cited the fact that there were no incidents of conflicts of interest or corruption in MMA. This is in reference to the alleged dealings in boxing where individuals act both as managers and promoters for boxers. This would be a direct conflict considering the manager acts on behalf of the athlete which infers maximizing their earning power while a promoter is acting in the interests of his or her event and would likely budget their monetary resources which would include curbing athlete costs. This conflict of interest was one of the reasons that the Muhammad Ali Act came into existence.

The hearing included a heated exchange between Markwayne Mullin—the bill's sponsor—and Ratner. Mullin took the tact of a prosecuting attorney with Ratner as he cross-examined the former Nevada Athletic Commissioner about the promotion's business practices, including the matchmaking process which did not involve a rankings system.

Mullin attacked Ratner's testimony that boxers and MMA fighters were treated the same by commissions. The congressman inquired whether the rankings systems were the same. Ratner defended his testimony, stating that the rankings systems were actually different and noted that he was on the regulator side of the operations for the promotion and could not address the rankings. Mullin indicated that the rankings system utilized by the UFC was made by those covering the sport but could be removed by the UFC at any time.

While most viewing the interaction may have thought it to be curt on the part of Mullin, it was done on purpose to expose the problems with the UFC's ranking system. For his part, Ratner responded appropriately, stating to his knowledge, given his role within the company, that he could not address some of Mullin's accusations, which were disguised as questions. He attempted to switch subjects but was interrupted and redirected to the questions. Mullin brought up a conversation he had with UFC Executive Lawrence Epstein in which he conveyed that Epstein told him regarding titles that it is "an award they [the UFC] bestow on the best fighter on that night." Mullin claimed that this was "insulting" to the fighter. But, Mullin's questioning tone was in part drama. He proclaimed that the Ali Act was the "backstop" for boxers in terms of a law that would prevent abuses by promoters, managers and others. Mullin stated that there was no "backstop" in MMA and ended his time during the hearing by making the analogy that the UFC was the "Don King" of MMA. The pejorative analogy accused the UFC of mistreating its contracted athletes as King had been alleged to do with many of the boxers he promoted. Mullin's aggressive behavior during the questioning was done on purpose to show his disgust for the UFC's business practices and perhaps to persuade the lawmakers in attendance. For those legislators who were uncertain of the reasons for the hearing and the need for governmental interaction in the industry, Mullin's rhetoric displayed the reasons for the need for the expansion of the Ali Act to MMA.

In addition to the public testimony, there were statements filed with the Subcommittee Hearing. Among these, one was from Bellator MMA.[9] Unlike the UFC, it supported the Ali Act's expansion into combat sports.

Bellator's statement gave a historical look at the sport and indicated that MMA's sanctioning "organically developed" under a "league" system. Unlike the UFC, Bellator states that it "co-promotes events with smaller domestic local promoters and international fight promoters to enhance [its] events and allow them [local promoters] opportunities to showcase their league talent."[10]

Bellator noted that it utilizes "multi-year, multi-fight, exclusive promotion contracts," but makes the distinction between these contracts and coercive contracts which are prohibited under the Ali Act. According to its statement, "Bellator invests a great deal of time, resources, and capital into promoting and marketing each long-term athlete and therefore the exclusivity and duration of each contract reflects a desire to seek a return on investment." The multiple fight contracts allow for Bellator to plan and budget for events in advance and they noted that there is a monetary investment made that is not immediately recouped by the company.

Without getting into specifics, Bellator made the statement that the UFC "utilized tactics that made competition in the MMA industry very challenging." It noted the "unimpaired movement of skilled athletes to organizations" as one of the primary things that can overturn UFC market share.

In comparison to Marc Ratner's view of state commission and regulation, Bellator relies upon state and tribal athletic commissions to oversee its events. But, it believes lack of funding, staff and resources have made regulation a challenge. Its statement endorsed the use of federal funds to support the work of the state and tribal commissions.

Former UFC fighter Jon Fitch filed a statement for the Congressional Record.[11] Fitch was an advocate of the Mixed Martial Arts Fighters Association, a group seeking fights for MMA fighters and supporters of the Ali Act expansion. Fitch was briefly fired by the UFC for refusing to give up his identity rights for a UFC video game and other commercial purposes, in perpetuity, with no compensation.

Fitch claimed that while he was in the UFC, he was passed over for fights despite being the ranked number 1 contender in his division. Fitch, an amateur wrestler from Purdue University, did not have a fighting style that entertained a large segment of fans. He focuses on his wrestling to control position in fights and win via control. Most fans like to see fighters either go for knockouts or attempt submissions. Fitch was not known for either. As a result, he was not considered an exciting fighter and would be overlooked for a title shot. According to his statement,

> No other sport allows the owner of an event or promotion to act as its own sanctioning body determining rank and championship status, while requiring the athlete to compete exclusively for that owner. If title shots and rankings are not earned by athletes through competition, what is being conducted is not a sport at all but the equivalent of a reality show promised around athletic endeavors.[12]

Fitch proclaimed that the Ali Act would address the UFC's coercive practices by requiring objective and consistent rankings criteria. He believed that once artificial restraints are removed, there will be organic growth and that there will be investment in MMA. He also proclaimed the same thing in an op-ed piece which ran in a Washington, D.C.–area paper.

Similar to the arguments against made one year earlier, the opposing view argued that the expansion of the Ali Act would amount to government overreach and an unneeded spending of funds. Zuffa devoted resources to lobbying efforts to defeat the expansion of the Ali Act. Some groups with the same mindset as Zuffa joined the cause by authoring opinion pieces against the act with the theory that government regulation should not reach the world of MMA. As a subtle slight on the sport, several opinion pieces inferred that the sport did not deserve the attention it was attracting through this bill. Letters sent to the Committee on Education and the Workforce and the Committee on Energy and Commerce noted that the proposed federal regulation "should not be given any serious attention by lawmakers." It went on to suggest that the government would be placed in charge of ranking fighters and making matches, which would take the control out of the hands of promoters. The opinion muddled the issue raised by Couture with respect to independent rankings of fighters, and seemed to misrepresent the intent of the possibility of the legislation.

Thus far, the expansion of the Ali Act is still in the House's Subcommittee on Digital Commerce and Consumer Protection in the Energy and Commerce committee. There are over 55 Democratic and Republican co-sponsors of the Ali Act expansion. But, the bill has yet to go to a vote in the House; then it would go on to the Senate before achieving the opportunity for the President's signature.

The overall language of the expansion to the Ali Act does not change or alter the current Ali Act for boxing. The application is expected to be the same if the bill is voted into law. Critics of the law cite the ineffectiveness of the Ali Act as applied to boxing. To date, there has not been a result where a boxer has filed a lawsuit under the Ali Act and successfully prosecuted the case to finality. The overwhelming legal fees and lengthy legal process is a built-in deterrent to this route with a promoter. This makes the prospect of an MMA version of the Ali Act sound helpful but probably not useful.

Conclusion

The question of the Ali Act expanding to cover MMA was still open as the sport entered 2019. At this point, the proposed legislation has not been up for a vote as bill sponsors continue to look for support in Congress. In order to look at whether the expansion of the act would work, we should examine the effect of the Ali Act in terms of boxing.

One might argue that the Ali Act has acted as a deterrent for those managers and promoters seeking to take advantage of boxers. However, one might also point out that as of this writing there has yet to be a successful case filed by a fighter where it has prevailed over the manager or promoter.[13] For those that argue that boxing has been "cleaned up" due to the Ali Act, there are limited examples which point to areas where boxers have used the legislation to protect themselves from promoters or managers. Moreover, the legal fees spent to defend themselves from unsavory business practices is oftentimes overwhelming versus the ability of promoters and managers to spend on litigation. In most instances, a promotion or manager usually files a motion to dismiss the case citing issues with the factual and legal claims made by the boxer. Even if the boxer is able to survive a motion to dismiss, there are still hurdles in paying for discovery and the potential of a trial. In most cases, there is a settlement prior to the commencement of a trial. This is usually in the best interests of the boxer as they do not want to burn bridges within the industry and will eventually need to find fights to get paid.

Notwithstanding the business element of the Ali Act, an observer could understand the physical health issues that might persuade a legislator to come up with a law to protect the safety of fighters. With recent head trauma cases occurring in sports, leagues have become more vigilant in ensuring that the safety of players is addressed. Could the Ali Act succeed if it were to focus on the health and safety issues instead of the business issues? Perhaps, although state commissions and regulators would have a say on this subject. But as an end around to address the business "health" of fighter, this might be a way to get lawmakers to take notice.

9

RICO, Defamation and Slavery—More Legal Disputes Featuring UFC and Disgruntled Fighters

Introduction

In this chapter we take a look at more lawsuits involving the UFC. This time we take a look at some of the unusual legal disputes between fighters. Some relate to issues over breach of contract, drug testing and even accusations of RICO violations and defamation. The cases discussed in this chapter are unique for the reasoning behind them and show the acrimony between parties as the fighter-promoter relationship dissolved.

Mark Hunt Sues Zuffa, Dana White and Brock Lesnar

Nicknamed, "The Super Samoan," New Zealander Mark Hunt sued the UFC, Dana White and his opponent at UFC 200 Brock Lesnar for a number of violations. The lawsuit stems from his fight with Lesnar in July 2016. Lesnar was returning from a five-year absence from the octagon and was placed as an attraction for UFC 200. Lesnar, under contract with World Wrestling Entertainment at the time, was not placed into the drug testing pool of active fighters who may be randomly tested pursuant to the UFC Anti-Doping Policy. Under the policy at the time, a fighter that was retired and returned to the organization must be placed onto the active roster of fighters that could be randomly tested. His name would have been made available to the public as one of the athletes that may be tested. This would have sparked major headlines within the world of MMA and professional wrestling with one of the biggest PPV draws in UFC history returning.

Lesnar was tested eight times in just the month lead-up to his fight against Mark Hunt.[1] He took five tests in the first two weeks after it was announced he was returning on June 5, 2016. Multiple tests came up free of any banned substances.

Despite the tests, the UFC policy, handled by USADA, dictated that a returning athlete to the UFC must give the company four months written notice so that USADA can put the athlete in the pool of those it may selectively test. But, the UFC anti-doping policy allows an exemption for a returning athlete that may be subject to drug testing. Per 5.7.1 of the UFC anti-doping policy:

> An Athlete who gives notice of retirement to UFC, or has otherwise ceased to have a contractual relationship with UFC, may not resume competing in UFC Bouts until he/she has given UFC written notice of his/her intent to resume competing and has made him/herself available for Testing for a period of four months before returning to competition. UFC may grant an exemption to the four-month written notice rule in exceptional circumstances or where the strict application of that rule would be manifestly unfair to an Athlete.[2]

The key sentence here is the last sentence: "UFC may grant an exemption to the four-month written notice rule in exceptional circumstances or where the strict application of that rule would be manifestly unfair to an Athlete."

There was some ambiguity in the application of the policy as it related to fighters seeking to return to active status. Since the UFC Anti-Doping Policy did not begin until July 1, 2015, and Lesnar's last fight in the UFC prior to UFC 200 was December 2011, he was considered a new athlete. The UFC claimed that they could not officially place Lesnar into the pool of fighters until they had clearance from his contracted employer, WWE. But, one might surmise that Lesnar and the UFC had contemplated his return as he had been training prior to the June announcement of his July bout. Lesnar could have notified the UFC of his return in the requisite four months to allow for the proper testing to occur. Yet, under cover of the excuse that there were still issues that Zuffa had to clear with Vince McMahon's company, it could not officially put Lesnar into the testing pool.

It would seem that the parties wanted the Lesnar announcement to be a surprise. MMA journalist Ariel Helwani and others from the MMA news reporting web site MMA Fighting were thrown out of UFC 199, an event in June 2016 and Helwani was banned for life due to his report of Lesnar's return prior to the UFC's opportunity to make it themselves.[3] Helwani, along with his colleagues, were reinstated a couple days later.

Hunt demanded that he receive half of Lesnar's $2.5 million purse or else he wanted his release from his UFC contract. Hunt, who made $700,000 for taking on Lesnar, was disappointed to learn that under the UFC-USADA guidelines, any money forfeited by an athlete would be under the UFC's discretion "to be applied to offset the costs of the Program or given to anti-doping research."[4]

A little over two weeks after UFC 200, USADA flagged two tests from Lesnar. One occurred prior to UFC 200 and the other was the post-fight drug test. Per the UFC anti-doping policy, Lesnar was put on a provisional suspension until the drug test results could be adjudicated. Lesnar denied wrongdoing. The banned substance for which Lesnar tested positive, clomiphene, is a medication used to treat infertility in women. However, as an estrogen blocker, it is also used to alter testosterone levels. Multiple UFC fighters have been suspended due to alleged clomiphene use.

Lesnar entered into a settlement with the Nevada Athletic Commission regarding the drug test failure. He received a one-year sentence and a $250,000 fine. Lesnar was issued a one-year suspension by USADA. Lesnar could have received up to a two-year suspension per the UFC Anti-Doping Policy.

A portion of the USADA press release[5] read:

> Lesnar, 39, tested positive for clomiphene and its metabolite, 4-hydroxyclomiphene, following an out-of-competition urine test conducted on June 28, 2016, and an in-competition urine test conducted on July 9, 2016, at UFC 200 in Las Vegas, Nev. Clomiphene is a prohibited substance in the category of Hormone and Metabolic Modulators and is prohibited at all times under the UFC Anti-Doping Policy, which has adopted the WADA Prohibited List.

The exemption granted to Lesnar by USADA and the UFC led to an amendment of rules as well as a lawsuit filed by Mark Hunt against Lesnar, the UFC and Dana White.

Despite receiving the news that he would only serve a one-year suspension, Lesnar notified the UFC that he was retiring again in February 2017, with just five months left to serve on the suspension.[6] After returning to WWE, in July 2018, he appeared in the UFC octagon once again for a potential matchup with Daniel Cormier. As a result, he returned to the USADA testing pool. Unlike last time, the announcement was made public immediately.

The Lesnar situation brought up the question of the merits of the UFC Anti-Doping Policy. Even with the multiple tests and abundance of care in explaining the policy to Lesnar, the WWE superstar still tested positive on two occasions. It should be noted that while the WWE randomly drug tests its performers for performance enhancing drugs, Lesnar is exempt as a performer according to multiple reports.[7] While this does not mean that Lesnar utilized banned substances while in the WWE, it paints a murkier picture as to whether the UFC should have granted Lesnar an exemption prior to signing him back on to the active athlete roster and placing him in a bout without the requisite time to test him.

Details of Hunt Lawsuit

In January 2017, Mark Hunt filed his lawsuit in federal court in Nevada.[8] Hunt claimed that the UFC, Dana White and Lesnar conspired to allow Lesnar to fight while using performance enhancing drugs which were banned under the UFC's Anti-Doping Policy. The lawsuit claims that the UFC had a pattern of allowing fighters to participate in events with the knowledge that they were using performance enhancing drugs such as anabolic steroids which gave them an advantage over Hunt who said that he did not use steroids. This was the basis for a Civil RICO violation. In addition, Hunt sued under a theory of breach of contract, duty of good faith and fair dealing, and negligence against the UFC and Lesnar. He subsequently amended his complaint to replace the negligence cause of action with a battery claim. It suggests that Hunt was not under contract to face an opponent that was using PEDs and as a result, the fight was an unauthorized use of force by Lesnar against Hunt.

The RICO claim was unique as never had a lawsuit involving MMA athletes involved such a claim against the UFC. Moreover, the personal claims against the promoter and the fighter he faced were unusual.

As of January 2019, the lawsuit had yet to go to trial as the parties litigated the defendants' motion to dismiss the lawsuit. In September 2017, Hunt wrote an article for a news outlet stating health issues which he related to years of fighting in MMA.[9] He stated that he could not sleep and was affected by slurred speech which he attributes to his time fighting. After learning of the article, the UFC pulled Hunt from a scheduled fight in Australia. The UFC claims that the decision to remove him from an event stemmed from their concern about his safety. Dana White stated that he wanted Hunt to be tested by one of their physicians prior to allowing him back in the octagon. Eventually, Hunt was allowed back into the UFC after he was medically cleared to fight again.

The case is one of the truly unique situations in MMA as Hunt maintained his contractual relationship with the UFC (and notably is one of the top paid fighters in the promotion) during an ongoing legal dispute. At this juncture of the case, all three defendants have filed for a motion to dismiss the case based on the inclusion of the additional information of Hunt's article and subsequent removal from a UFC event.

The prospects of the lawsuit going to trial seemed slim given Hunt's ongoing contractual relationship with the company and the legal costs incurred by the UFC and Lesnar. One may assume that the UFC will indemnify White from personal liability since it would appear that he was acting on behalf of the promotion.

Hunt v. Lesnar

The claims against Hunt's opponent, Brock Lesnar, are unique since the pragmatic view was that Hunt signed a bout agreement to fight Lesnar and knew that this would mean the distinct possibility of physical injury. But, his claim was that he did not know that Lesnar had taken performance enhancing drugs. In his lawsuit, Hunt filed a negligence claim against Lesnar for physical injuries he sustained in their bout at UFC 200. He then amended this claim to an intentional tort of battery. Hunt alleges that Lesnar intended to cause harmful and offensive contact to Hunt without Hunt's consent to a bout with "a doping competitor."[10] Lesnar caused 137 total strikes to Hunt and 51 significant strikes in the UFC 200 bout.[11]

Lesnar's legal counsel asserted that Hunt consented to the bout and pointed out that Hunt assumed the risk when he entered into the contest. As Lesnar points out, Hunt signed a promotional agreement which contains an express, broadly-worded assumption of the risk provision and waiver of all claims arising out of the inherently dangerous sport of MMA. As part of his Bout Agreement to face Lesnar at UFC 200, he expressly agreed to a similar assumption of the risk and waiver provisions.

There are few cases in sport where athletes sue each other. Two such instances occurred in the NHL and NFL. Both cases question the theory of assuming the risk on the basis of the extraordinary actions by the defendants.

Todd Bertuzzi Lawsuit

In recent memory, the most notable lawsuit involving fighting outside the scope of the sport involved the NHL in February 2004. Although fights in hockey are common as compared to other team sports, Vancouver Canucks' Todd Bertuzzi sought after Colorado Avalanche player Steve Moore to fight. In a previous game, Moore had injured Bertuzzi's teammate, Markus Naslund. Bertuzzi attempted to instigate a fight with Moore as revenge for injuring his teammate. As a result, Bertuzzi grabbed Moore's jersey from behind and punched him in the jaw and then fell on top of him as he went down.[12] Moore was seriously injured and his career was effectively over due to the incident. Bertuzzi was suspended by the NHL for 17 months.[13]

Criminal charges were filed by the Attorney General of British Columbia in June 2004 as Bertuzzi was charged by the Canadian court with assault causing bodily harm.[14] Avoiding criminal penalties which may have carried one-and-a-half years in prison, he entered into a plea bargain with prosecutors and avoided any jail time.[15]

Moore filed a civil lawsuit in February 2005 in Colorado against Bertuzzi, several of his teammates, the team and the organization that owned the

Canucks. The case was thrown out by the Colorado court citing that the litigation should occur in Canada. He refiled in Ontario Superior Court.[16] The lawsuit lingered on for several years and involved Bertuzzi filing a Third-Party Complaint against his former coach in 2008 stating that he received instructions to go after Moore. The lawsuit between Bertuzzi and the coach were settled as was the original lawsuit in July 2011. Details of the settlement were confidential. In 2014, over 10 years after the incident took place, Moore settled his lawsuit with Bertuzzi and the Canucks a week before the case was to go to trial.[17]

Bill Romanowski Lawsuit

Bill Romanowski was a fierce linebacker during his time with the Oakland Raiders and Denver Broncos. He was fined by the NFL for his play which included headbutting, headkicking and spearing opponents. In August 2003, his ferocity may have exceeded the bounds of football during a training camp fight with teammate Marcus Williams. During a scrimmage Williams blocked Romanowski. After the play, Romanowski came up on Williams from behind, took his helmet off and punched him. The punch caused brain damage when his eye socket was crushed. The hit caused the end to Williams' short-lived career. Williams sued Romanowski for millions of dollars in damages claiming that the punch was outside the bounds of playing football. Williams claimed damages for battery, negligence and intentional infliction of emotional distress. The Raiders denied liability for Romanowski's behavior. The team did fine Romanowski $60,000 for the altercation. Romanowski claimed he did not recall the punches he threw at Williams. Williams' attorney inferred that Romanowski's alleged steroid use may have fueled his reaction and aggression toward Williams.

In the end, the case went to trial and Williams was awarded $340,000 which covered medical expenses and lost wages.[18] Although Williams threatened to appeal the verdict, the parties settled for a higher dollar amount prior to the case going any further.

Avila v. Citrus Community College District

A college baseball pitcher threw a fastball at an opponent batter's head in retaliation for one of his teammates being hit by a pitch. The pitch shattered the batter's helmet and caused permanent injury to his brain. The batter sued the county and the defendant took the position that the batter assumed the risk of playing even with the possibility of being hit with a "beanball."[19] The batter, Jose Avila, claimed that Citrus College was negligent in failing to properly supervise its pitcher, failing to provide umpires or other supervisory personnel who would keep control of the game, and failing to summon or provide medical care when he was obviously in need of it.[20] The Supreme Court of California determined that "even beanings that were intentional were an inherent risk of playing baseball."[21] In Avila, the Court looked to the issue of public entity tort immunity statute.[22] In determining that the district did not owe Avila a duty of care, it stated that Avila availed himself to an assumption of risk inherent in playing baseball. The opinion notes that assumption of the risk bars a claim for a failure to supervise. In that case, there was no liability for failing to supervise a pitcher from hitting a batter. Being hit by a baseball is a known and apparent part of baseball. It is known that it can result in serious injury and even death.[23] The court states that "[i]t is not the function of tort law to police such conduct."[24]

The dissent states that the majority's opinion of finding no issue with the intentional throwing at an opposing batter "a startling conclusion."[25] It argues that "whether being hit by a pitched ball intentionally aimed at one's head is an inherent risk of baseball, whether professional or intercollegiate, is a question of fact to be determined in the trial court."[26] The criticism of the majority decision as to how it came to the conclusion that a "beanball" is a part of the game and any claim is barred by the assumption of the risk doctrine is based upon its anecdotal theory based on empirical data. It is argued that this is a question of fact, not premised upon law. The dissent contends that assumption of the risk should be based on "what risk the plaintiff consciously and voluntarily assumed" and not what risks are inherent in a particular sport.[27] Broadly, the dissent is concerned with the opinion as it "is tearing at the fabric of tort law."[28] The reasoning is that it distorts the negligence concept of due care to encompass reckless and intentional conduct.

The dissent contends that the case should have been analyzed under the traditional doctrine of assumption of risk and ask what risk did the plaintiff "consciously and voluntarily assumed."[29] Thus, any action that may be unreasonably risky conduct that might cause harm would be within the ambit of a colorable cause of action.

Knight v. Jewett

In *Knight v. Jewett*, the California Supreme Court determined that those involved in a sporting activity do not have a duty to reduce the risk of harm that is inherent in the sport itself. They do, however, have a duty not to increase that inherent risk.[30] The duty of care is to refrain from intentionally injuring one another or engaging in conduct that is "so reckless as to be totally outside the range of the ordinary activity involved in the sport."[31] In that case, an impromptu football game during halftime of a Super Bowl party caused injury to an individual when her hand was stepped on. Her injury led to the eventual amputation of one of her fingers. A lawsuit was filed based on the claims of assault and battery and negligence. There were multiple factual questions as to the level of play during the game by the participants. In the end, the Court held that the plaintiff could not recover for her personal injuries since the injury occurred in the ordinary course of the football game.

The Hunt situation is different from the cases discussed above. While Hunt may be willing to concede that he is assuming the risk in fighting against an opponent that may cause him bodily harm, he did not sign on to fight an individual that utilized performance enhancing drugs. The UFC Anti-Doping Policy would bolster Hunt's claim in that he could argue that he reasonably relied on USADA and the UFC to enforce its policy. Under the string of cases discussed here concerning assumption of the risk, the question would be whether Lesnar intentionally injured Hunt (as the Bertuzzi case exemplifies) or engaged in conduct that is "so reckless as to be totally outside the range of the ordinary activity involved in the sport." One may concede that Lesnar did not specifically take performance enhancing drugs to *injure* Hunt but he did take the banned substance to be able to *compete* with Hunt. Whether taking a banned substance is "reckless" seems to be a factual claim. On the other hand, the UFC Anti-Doping Policy anticipates the possibility of athletes using banned substances and Lesnar's flagged tests reflect the fact that his behavior was not reckless but negligent. Lesnar disputed he knowingly took the banned substance despite failing two USADA tests. Rather, he believed that clomiphene and clomiphene metabolites may have been found in eye medication or foot cream he used before the fight.[32]

Under an assumption of risk theory discussed above, one would inquire whether Lesnar had a duty not to increase the inherent risk of the sport. While the banned substances used by Lesnar are not anabolic steroids, they are used as an "estrogen blocker" to disguise the use of synthetic testosterone.[33] Lesnar tested positive for clomiphene and its metabolites. It cannot be proven from his tests that he purposefully used this to disguise the use of testosterone, steroids or other performance enhancing drugs. But, if it is determined through discovery, expert testimony or through some other means that Lesnar attempted to use the banned substance to mask another, one might argue that Lesnar purposefully increased the inherent risk of the sport. Thus, Hunt's claim for battery might be viable.

Avila and Knight exemplify the issues with athletes suing each other citing torts outside the scope of the sport. The doctrine of assumption of the risk is key to the legal analysis in these cases. In Avila, a baseball player getting "beaned" by a pitch during a game, the court held that "[i]t is not the function of tort law to police such conduct." The court concluded that being hit by a pitch is known and apparent and a part of baseball. However, the dissent in the court opinion noted that "whether being hit by a pitched ball intentionally aimed at one's head is an inherent risk of baseball, whether professional or intercollegiate, is a question of fact to be determined in the trial court." Here, the dissent takes issue with the majority opinion's interpretation of assumption of the risk. According to the dissenting opinion, assumption of the risk should be based on "what risk the plaintiff consciously and voluntarily assumed" and not what risks are inherent in a particular sport. Broadly, this viewpoint is concerned with the opinion as it "is tearing at the fabric of tort law." The reasoning is that it distorts the negligence concept of due care to encompass reckless and intentional conduct. In the baseball scenario, the court should have analyzed the traditional doctrine of assumption of risk and ask what risk the plaintiff "consciously and voluntarily assumed." Thus, any action that may be unreasonably risky conduct that might cause harm would be within the ambit of a colorable cause of action.

In light of the dissent in Avila, the Hunt case would have a different outcome. Rather than the eventual dismissal of his claims, it would be reasonable to believe that Hunt's claims would survive a motion to dismiss.

Following the line of sports cases involving personal injuries occurring during the sport the threshold question to analyze is whether the claimed injuries were caused arising out of risks deemed inherent in a sport. As previously identified, USADA served as a monitor to ensure that fighters would not utilize drugs deemed to provide an unfair advantage to athletes. Enacting an anti-doping policy by the UFC can be seen as evidence that it was aware of the potential issues with those seeking to take performance enhancing drugs that may help one become stronger, faster, lose weight without physical depletion of their muscles, or something else. One might infer that these measures would be a part of mixed martial arts due to the inherent risks of the sport and what might occur if someone were to use performance-enhancing drugs against an unknowing opponent. This may bring one to the conclusion that performance-enhancing drugs deemed illegal or unwarranted by a promotion like the UFC is part of the sport. If so, this could be seen as inherent in the sport.

The conclusion that the use of banned performance enhancing drugs is a part of the sport of MMA as a "beanball" is a part of baseball may seem like a strained analogy. Certainly, other MMA promotions haven't tailored a policy to prevent the use of banned substances. Avila advises "A court must evaluate the fundamental nature of the sport and the defendant's role in that sport in order to determine whether the defendant owes a duty to protect a plaintiff from the particular risk of harm."[34]

It's easy to suggest that the sport of MMA relates to what happens between the combatants inside the Octagon, cage or ring. Suggestions that a drug test or taking anything to "cheat" the system would be beyond the realm of the "fundamental nature" of the sport. But, with respect to the uniqueness of Hunt's claim, one might argue that the necessity of drug testing a combatant prior to and/or after a fight is required to ensure fairness and safety for the athletes. The "beanball" described in Avila is an unsportsmanlike act, yet intertwined with the sport.[35] The Bertuzzi and Romanowski cases were cases where athletes' unsportsmanlike acts were deemed outside the normal course of the sport. You might analogize that taking a banned substance would be so as well.

The natural opposition to this theory is that Avila, Bertuzzi, Romanowski and even Knight occurred "on the field of play," or ice in the Bertuzzi matter whereas an argument for Hunt would encompass something occurring outside the realm of the actual action of the sport.

Court Dismisses 9 Out of 10 of Hunt's Claims

On February 14, 2019, the United States District Court of Nevada dismissed all but one of Hunt's claims. U.S. District Court Judge Jennifer A. Dorsey issued a 28-page opinion which primarily determined that Hunt had not proved a causal connection between his claims and financial losses or that they were "non-cognizable damages."[36] Thus, Hunt did not overcome the initial hurdle of providing factual information to defeat the defendants' Motion to Dismiss.

The lone remaining cause of action, a claim for the breach of good faith and fair dealing in contract left Zuffa as the last defendant. The court mentioned in a footnote that the claim that the UFC enforced the UFC Anti-Doping Policy inconsistently could possibly be a breach. Lesnar and White were discharged as defendants when the other allegations were dismissed.[37] The court ordered the parties to a settlement conference which would infer that an agreement will be entered to end the case short of having to expend any more resources to litigate.

Hunt's claim rested on the theory that White and the UFC intentionally concealed Lesnar's return to help circumvent the UFC's Anti-Doping Policy and to conceal the fact that Lesnar was training with banned substances.[38] It seemed plausible from Hunt's perspective that providing the court with a roster of fighters he had to face that were found to have failed drug tests provided a theory for his claims. But, the facts for Hunt were not sufficient to survive a motion to dismiss. Simply put, the court could not side with Hunt's alleged damages due to his loss to Lesnar because he could not support his claims that, since the former WWE champion failed a USADA drug test, it caused him ancillary injuries. Moreover, the court opined that Hunt's loss may have been rooted in the fact that Lesnar was the better fighter on that night. The court did not agree with Hunt's damages allegation that his loss to Lesnar was directly connected to his use of a banned substance. Hunt's "promotional and ancillary rights agreement" with the UFC entitled him to a fixed lump sum payout without an additional sum for winning so any damages theory that rested on Hunt winning was moot.

The RICO claims Hunt alleged were dismissed by the court under both state and federal statutes because he did not establish that the alleged harm qualified as injury to his "business or property." Hunt cited the *Mendoza v.*

Zirkle Fruit, Co., case in which the defendants sought to manipulate the work force by hiring undocumented laborers to depress wages of documented workers. Hunt claimed that the UFC and White wrongfully manipulated the market to depress wages of clean fighters by hiring doping fighters.[39] The civil RICO claim in the *Mendoza* case was not dismissed because there were alternative theories to the damages from the plaintiffs. Also, Hunt cited an antitrust lawsuit in *Knevelbaard Dairies v. Kraft Foods, Inc.,*[40] in which the plaintiffs' civil RICO claims were reinstated for similar reasons. In that case a group of milk producers alleged that the defendant cheesemakers conspired to fix prices to artificially depress prices in California. In response, the court noted a Ninth Circuit case, *Canyon County v. Syngenta Seeds, Inc.,* which found proximate cause lacking because "the cause of the plaintiff's asserted harms [was] a set of actions...*entirely distinct* from the alleged RICO violation."[41] As the court concluded in this case, the proximate cause in the *Canyon County* lawsuit was attenuated and dismissal of the lawsuit was proper. It also distinguished *Mendoza* and *Knevelbaard* as both were decided prior to the heightened pleading standard in the *Twombly* decision requiring enough facts in the complaint to make the claims plausible. As a result, the court does not address the second prong of establishing RICO standing: whether "by reason of" the RICO violation, the plaintiff could establish proximate causation.

Hunt pointed to the triumvirate of fights in which he faced opponents who tested positive for performance-enhancing drugs. In each, he claimed injury due to the fact that the fighters had taken banned substances. But the court noted the lack of standing due to its finding that Hunt could not identify a qualifying harm that resulted "from either of the first two fights."[42] In the first fight against Antonio Silva, Hunt claimed he injured his hand as a result of the fight which left him unable to continue training, resulting in a loss of economic income. Yet, case law is instructive in that personal injuries are not recoverable under RICO and damage flowing from are not compensable. The court found that Hunt's claim in the Frank Mir fight was "vague and abstract" and was not considered a concrete loss. Hunt asserted that Mir was granted a "Therapeutic Use Exemption" to use a banned substance based on medical needs. Hunt concluded that Mir should not have been in the pool of available heavyweights that he could have fought.

As for the allegation that Lesnar committed battery on Hunt as a fighter that exceeded the scope of consent, the court cited the *Avila* decision. Similar to that case, where a pitcher threw a "beanball" to intentionally hit a batter in the head, it was still an "inherent risk of baseball." The Court analogized the "beanball" with this case as it stated that while the alleged doping violated the bout rules, it did not establish that Lesnar exceeded the ordinary range of activity in an MMA fight. Despite any hypotheses that Lesnar may have had an advantage to hit harder or move faster, Hunt does not indicate that Lesnar's conduct was atypical. He also does not argue that his injuries exceeded those typical of an MMA bout. Therefore, the court dismissed the purported tort claim and the aiding and abetting claims that were associated with it.

Conclusion

The thrust of Hunt's claims rested on the proximate cause that he could tie-in with his claimed injuries. Having three opponents failing drug tests must have infuriated Hunt as he suffered physical injuries as well as lost the potential economic benefits of winning fights. Of course, this is based on the assumption that the banned substances provided the necessary assistance for his opponents to win. This was the issue with Hunt's lawsuit. He could not find the causal connection with his civil RICO claim and his other claims began to unravel.

Only the allegation that the UFC does not consistently enforce its UFC Anti-Doping Policy survived the defendants' Motion to Dismiss. While this may have been the sole issue all along, in hindsight, the RICO violations, fraud and battery claims seemed to be a "kitchen sink" approach to filing a lawsuit. From the outset, the court noted that the allegations were thin and more had to be pled to survive dismissal. Yet, the amendment and supplement to the lawsuit did not provide the requisite facts to satisfy the court.

With respect to the tort claim of battery on the part of Lesnar, the court made clear that the actions were dependent on the *Avila* case in determining whether the actions were outside the scope of the sport. *Avila* makes the case that it's based on the traditional methods of the game (i.e., "intentionally hitting a batter" is within the ambit of the sport). The court used the example for MMA of Lesnar doing something beyond the scope of the sport such as throwing Hunt out of the Octagon or packing his gloves with an illegal substance. But Hunt does not bring up any type of scenario beyond the fact that Lesnar used a banned substance during the time of their fight. While we had posited the question of whether taking a banned substance was "reckless," and deserved the right to survive past the pleading stage, it did not.

But it would appear that the appropriate decision would be to make the determination on the recklessness of taking the banned substance rather than the movements within the Octagon.

Wanderlei Silva Is Sued by UFC for Defamation

Wanderlei Silva fought for the UFC in the early days of the organization but made his name in Japan fighting for the PRIDE promotion. There, he won the middleweight title and, despite being a Brazilian jiu jitsu black belt, was known for his brawling style.

In 2014, he was set to fight Chael Sonnen in a featured matchup between the two bitter rivals on July 5th as part of UFC 175. Due to their personal animosity, which included trash talking and an actual brawl that needed to be broken up, fans were anticipating this matchup.

But, Silva evaded a random drug test administered by the Nevada Athletic Commission which caused him to be removed from the card. According to a report from a Nevada Athletic Commission representative, he attempted to take a random sample collection from Silva on May 24, 2014.[43] Silva was not present at his home and the representative was directed by NAC Executive Director Bob Bennett to see if he was at his gym. He did find Silva, but after indicating he would be with him in a moment, Silva exited the gym without telling the representative where he was going. Silva had conveniently evaded the blood and urine tests that the NAC sought to administer that day. The representative contacted Silva's wife, who gave him vague details about Silva's whereabouts. He was not found and the commission determined that he had knowingly evaded the testing.

As a result of his failure to submit to the random drug test, he was disciplined. It was later discovered that he had used diuretics, a prohibited drug pursuant to NAC 467.850(2)(f). At the Nevada Athletic Commission hearing on September 23, 2014, at which Silva failed to appear, the commission issued him a lifetime ban and a $70,000 fine.[44] Silva sought judicial review of the commission's unprecedented penalty by filing a lawsuit in Clark County (Nevada) Superior Court.[45] In the state of Nevada, the appeal process from an administrative hearing is to file a lawsuit in superior court. At about the same time, Silva voiced his criticism against the UFC. In a series of social media posts on twitter and YouTube, he claimed that the UFC fixed fights and he had proof.

In response, the UFC sued Silva for Defamation Per Se and Business Disparagement in Clark County Superior Court.[46] The lawsuit claimed that Silva's allegations of fight fixing were "even more heinous" since then-owners Lorenzo and Frank Fertitta were linked to Nevada's gaming industry.

To prove a claim for defamation, one has to show that a statement, either spoken or written, injures someone's reputation and is false. Silva posted his thoughts about the UFC on his Facebook page. Bringing into question the credibility of a sport in which people place bets is a huge issue. It is also clear that these types of statements, especially coming from a former UFC fighter, would damage the reputation of the company.

Defenses to defamation include truth and/or privilege. In the defense of truth, if Silva could show that the fights were fixed, then he would not be liable for defamation. For the purported injury to a company's business, there must be an injurious statement that must be publicized that would discourage people from dealing with the business. From the optics, it would look like that Silva's statement would fall into this category.

Then again, Silva claimed that "fixing fights" may have a different connotation than one who predetermines the outcome of a fight. Silva claimed that the "fight fixing" comments were in good faith and broadly encompassing matters like "asking an injured athlete to compete or ignoring drug test results."[47] Thus, the connotation is different and would not be damaging for a business. Silva's attorneys also claimed that his English proficiency was limited which may have had an impact on the wording of his statements.

Silva's attorneys brought a Motion to Dismiss the UFC's case against the fighter seeking to end the case before discovery.[48] Silva's attorneys argued that the UFC's lawsuit was a violation of Nevada's Anti-SLAPP statute which precludes lawsuits that seek to chill free speech on matters of public concern.

Silva's lawyers argued that the UFC could not show damages from his comments or disprove the comments were false. It also argued that the UFC's claim of Defamation Per Se relates to individuals and not entities. They also claimed that Silva's statements were precluded under the "litigation privilege" citing that communications "made in the course of judicial proceedings [even if known to be false] are absolutely privileged." Silva's lawyers argued that the broad swath of the privilege would be applied to his "fight fixing" comments. Silva cites that the comments made on social media were related to the "NSAC Case" and the "Class Action" lawsuit filed by several former UFC fighters which we talk about in a later chapter.

Another argument Silva claimed was that the lawsuit should be dismissed since it violated Nevada's Anti-SLAPP Statute. SLAPP, which stands for strategic lawsuit against public participation, allows those sued in defamation or libel cases the opportunity to get those types of claims thrown out early unless the plaintiff can show a probability of prevailing. The law, which is a creature of state law, is a method of protecting free speech regarding an issue of public concern. The Anti-SLAPP statute allows a party to file a motion to dismiss the complaint under the law and treats it as a motion for summary judgment.[49] Thus, the defendant can dismiss the lawsuit without an opportunity for the plaintiff to amend the lawsuit. It's an expedited way to dismiss lawsuits that were brought with the intent to harass or punish those from speaking out. The expedited motion under the Anti-SLAPP statute ensures that the defendant need not deal with the expense of a lawsuit which is mainly used to silence a party.

Notably, the motion to dismiss should focus on the best arguments for dismissal instead of the more salacious arguments. First, the UFC complaint lacked specificity; they could not prove damages as a result of Silva's remarks and the state Anti-SLAPP statute. It appeared that the UFC's complaint against Silva lacked the proximate cause needed to show the link between Silva's comments and damages. It is also worthy to note that the "litigation privilege" is not absolute in Nevada. Statements made to the media during litigation are not protected and can form the basis for a defamation claim according to a recent case. In *Jacobs v. Adelson*, the Nevada Supreme Court noted that the purpose of the litigation privilege is to allow parties to speak freely and openly during litigation without the threat of being sued.[50] But, it only applies during judicial proceedings to statements that relate to the litigation. While Silva's statements may not have gone directly to the media, there is the implication from the case that defamatory comments made to outside observers of a lawsuit can potentially form the basis for a defamation claim.

Upon a Motion to Dismiss the lawsuit by Silva, the Court dismissed the UFC's claim for Business Defamation Per Se, but upheld the parties claim for business disparagement. The parties decided to settle the lawsuit short of going to trial.

Silva's case presents an interesting scenario since he was involved in the NSAC case but was not a party to the Antitrust lawsuit. While his lawyers inferred that he may become a party and had knowledge of the case, he was not an existing part of the action. Moreover, the statements Silva made that are at issue in the lawsuit occurred at a time when he was not a part of any active lawsuit (the NSAC case was being remanded at the time and he was sued prior to the appeal to the Nevada State Supreme Court).

So, the question was whether the "litigation privilege" extends to statements made outside of a lawsuit *and* when you are not a party. This question still remains uncertain in light of the case.

The Anti-SLAPP claim was a viable claim brought by Silva's attorneys. Notably, some states have brought the statute into question as a violation of the constitutional right of due process in that it negates the opportunity for a fair trial due (Washington State struck down a similar law). However, Nevada's law is still in use, although lawmakers sought to amend it, concerned with a similar challenge to the constitutionality of the law. Silva would have to convince a judge that the statements at issue were "a good faith communication" directly connected with a matter of public concern. Sure, one can argue that fighters' rights may be a matter of public concern but were the statements "a good faith communication"? Here, the court noted that Silva's case was not directly connected to public matters.

Silva was released from the UFC and signed on with rival promotion Bellator MMA. In late 2016, Sonnen signed on with the Viacom-owned promotion as well. The two finally squared off against each other in Bellator in June 2017. Sonnen won a very mediocre match that did not emit the fire and passion their initial matchup promised.

Silva Versus Nevada State Athletic Commission

Notwithstanding the UFC dismissing Silva's lawsuit, there was still the issue of Silva's judicial review of his lifetime ban in Nevada.

In the lawsuit filed in Clark County, Nevada, Silva claimed that the commission had no jurisdiction over him because he had not applied for his fighter's license.[51] As a result, his attorney claimed that there could be no punishment for an individual that was not subject to drug testing. He also claimed that the lifetime ban and the $70,000 fine were "arbitrary and capricious" as the punishment was not supported by the substantial evidence in the record.

District Court Judge Kerry Earley held that the Commission properly exercised jurisdiction over Silva. It determined that Silva was an "unarmed combatant" under the terms of the Nevada Athletic Commission despite the argument that Silva was not licensed by the state and therefore should not be considered. Under NAC 467.850(5), he "shall submit to urinalysis or chemical tests at the direction of the Commission or its representatives."[52]

However, the court determined that the record from the Commission's hearing on the matter was not supported by the substantial evidence in the record. Judge Earley noted that the Commission had its own concerns that the sanction was "arbitrary and not supported by any type of sentencing guidelines, or within standard norms."[53]

The court thus denied the judicial review in part as the issue of jurisdiction was decided in favor of the Commission while Judge Earley overturned the punishment with the order that there be a rehearing on the issue.

Prior to the remand, Silva, upset with the court decision that he was subject to the jurisdiction, filed an appeal with the state Supreme Court of Nevada.[54] The brief argues that since Silva was not licensed, he could not be disciplined for a violation of NRS Chapter 467 (the chapter which promulgates authority for the commission). As cited by Silva's attorney, the Chapter only applies to licensees of Nevada citing NAC 467.885.

However, the state Supreme Court noted a "potential jurisdictional defect" as the trial court ordered a remand to the Commission for further ruling of the punishment. The problem was that the Superior Court had issued an order sending back the case to the Commission to recalibrate Silva's penalty. This order proved to be the reason for dismissal of the appeal since it remanded the case for further substantive proceedings (i.e., remand to Commission to determine appropriate punishment for Silva). Thus, the appellate court could not rule on the issue.

It appears that Silva's hurdle was that it could not appeal an issue to the appellate court since the trial court did not determine a punishment for Silva. Rather, the court decided to remand it back down to the Commission. It would appear that Silva wanted to avoid another punishment from the Commission, and in line with its contention that he was not under the jurisdiction of the Commission. This is probably the reason that Silva chose to appeal the court decision rather than await the Commission re-hearing.

The Wanderlei Silva lawsuit brings to light a unique question of law which seemingly remained unanswered by the legal proceedings. Can an athletic commission exercise jurisdiction over a fighter not licensed within the state? Silva did not have a license to fight in Nevada although it was expected that he would apply and eventually obtain one prior to his scheduled fight. But, the rules promulgated by the state of Nevada refer to the disciplining of licensed fighters. This issue was brought to light by Silva's attorney in his brief to the state Supreme Court of Nevada.[55] In his brief, he argued that the Nevada Athletic Commission wrongly sanctioned Silva since he had not applied for a license nor was licensed to fight in Nevada. Silva argued his only activity related to his upcoming fight was attending a press conference within the state. The trial court stated that regardless of Silva's license status, he was within the jurisdiction of the Commission

As indicated, the state Supreme Court did not rule on the merits of the argument due to the procedural issue. Thus, the question remains open. Despite the District Court asserting that the Commission correctly had jurisdiction over Silva, the arguments against jurisdiction were artful, persuasive and valid as they revealed a defect in the rules of Nevada.

Georges St-Pierre's Return—"A pretty nice form of slavery"

After an absence of three years, Georges St-Pierre sought to return to the UFC in 2016. The former UFC welterweight champion proclaimed that he was a free agent after the UFC breached its contract. The promotion thought otherwise. According to GSP's legal counsel, the contract he signed with the UFC in 2011 was terminated due to the lack of fights given to St-Pierre. GSP argued that he was not given an actual bout agreement prior to the tolling of the end of his contract. He was offered a fight with Robbie Lawler, although there was only talk about the fight occurring and not an actual agreement offered.

According to GSP's lawyer, Jim Quinn, who was practicing at Weil, Gotschal and Manges in New York at the time of the dispute, they gave the UFC 10 days to offer St-Pierre a bout agreement but was given Lawler's name as an option in a letter on the last day that the offer was open. The communication from the UFC did not come with a fight date, venue, or the number of rounds in a potential fight. Furthermore, it was unclear whether Lawler had accepted or was in condition to fight. At about that time in October 2016, Lawler had withdrawn from an upcoming bout due to injury.

In reviewing the UFC contract, Quinn was "blown away by how restrictive it is."[56] In an interview, Quinn stated, "They're basically tying him up for life. They have no rights and they own all of his licensing and all the other things. It's unheard of in the other professional sports. And they won't get away with it forever."[57] Quinn, an attorney who specializes in sports law, indicated the UFC's present contract was "something out of the 1940s."[58] He sarcastically described the contract as "a pretty nice form of slavery."[59]

The UFC argued that he remained under contract with Zuffa, LLC as his promoter. The unique situation for GSP, who took a prolonged time away from the sport, was how the promotion had changed. No longer was the company as small as it was when he signed the agreement. Moreover, the business practices had matured. GSP was not subject to the UFC anti-doping policy implemented by the promoter or the Reebok clothing deal which dictated the sponsors allowed by the company. GSP had a sponsorship deal with rival clothing company Under Armour when he left the UFC. He also had other lucrative sponsorships which added to his overall earnings. The UFC was now much more restrictive on sponsors not aligned with the UFC. The UFC eliminated fight week sponsorships, which were a source of revenue for fighters in addition to their fight purses. For some fighters, this additional revenue stream made up for the purse money, which remained flat.

Notably, at about the time, GSP was involved in an organization that sought to better the financial conditions of UFC athletes. The Mixed Martial Arts Athletes Association (MMAAA) was made up of UFC fighters and a Board that sought to increase fighters' purses fivefold to fifty percent of all revenues generated by the UFC as well as other financial improvements and benefits for the UFC-contracted fighters. While his association with MMAAA did not seemingly hurt the negotiation with the UFC, it had to upset the organization.

The contract dispute calls into question the reach the UFC may have over a retiring athlete. GSP's last fight in the UFC was in November 2013 and he was seeking to return in 2016. GSP claimed that he was not given a bout agreement for a fight and, as a result, believed that the contract was breached which would make him a free agent. The UFC believed that offering a fight, regardless of whether a bout agreement was made, constituted grounds for satisfying the terms of the contract.

There are obvious blanks that cannot be filled here without knowing the position of the two sides. At the time of his departure in 2013, the UFC was caught off guard, as it did not know that GSP would be taking time off. He was a top fan draw and losing GSP was a blow to their business. It is not known how long GSP was looking to return and it's not clear when his intentions to the UFC were conveyed.

The contract dispute may have been a ploy for St-Pierre to receive more money or a legitimate disagreement with the UFC due to the lack of opponents offered by the company.

In the end, St-Pierre and the UFC came to terms on a bout agreement and a new deal. Notably, St-Pierre fought in November 2016, but had yet to return to the Octagon as of January 2019, after the fight in which he won the UFC Middleweight Title from Michael Bisping.

However, Quinn's warnings about the UFC contract may be foreshadowing an upcoming fight in the UFC—not one in the Octagon, but one within the courtroom as the UFC's contract is placed under scrutiny.

10

The UFC Antitrust Lawsuit

Introduction

It might be the biggest legal development in mixed martial arts in its sports history as ex–UFC fighters filed a lawsuit against the company in December 2014 citing violations of antitrust law. Specifically, the plaintiffs claimed that the UFC is an illegal monopoly under Sherman Antirust Section 1 and 2.

The lawsuit sought to expose the alleged predatory practices of the UFC which allowed the company to benefit from the business while suppressing the wages of its independent contractor athletes. The plaintiffs claimed that the UFC held a monopsony and a monopoly over the relevant markets for fighters. The UFC has attempted to dismiss the lawsuit citing issues with the fighters' definition of the markets among other defenses.

Still undetermined, the lawsuit exposed what many within the industry knew about the business of MMA: Zuffa took a financial gamble on a sport, it paid off and its fighters were now wishing to be paid and treated in accordance with their own contributions. But the UFC believes that it is not in violation of antitrust laws and chalks up its acquisition of rival organization to superior business acumen and investment in its promotion.

The Sherman Antitrust Act

The Sherman Antitrust Act is one of the rules of law that governs antitrust law in the United States. It was enacted to protect trade and commerce against unlawful restraints and monopolies. Its application mainly focuses on protection of consumers and not competitors.

Section 1 of the Sherman Act addresses the nature of constraining interstate commerce. Violations of Section 1 of the Sherman Act are considered "per se" violations. A "per se" violation requires no further inquiry into the practice's actual effect on the market or the intentions of those individuals who engaged in the practice. According to 15 USC §1 "Every contract, combination in the form of trust or otherwise, or conspiracy, in restraint of trade or commerce among the several States, or within foreign nations, is declared to be illegal."

In general, these types of restraint on trade agreed to between competitors, even indirectly, with pricing are per se illegal. A combination or conspiracy is established by proof of "a conscious commitment to a common scheme designed to achieve an unlawful objective."[1] Market power is the ability of a market participant to increase prices above levels that would be charged in a competitive market.[2]

Section 2 of the Sherman Act makes it unlawful for any person to "monopolize, or attempt to monopolize, or conspire with any other person or persons, to monopolize any part of the trade or commerce among the several States, or with foreign nations." This section of the Sherman Act establishes three offenses commonly termed "monopolization," "attempted monopolization," and "conspiracy to monopolize."

Monopolization requires (1) monopoly power and (2) the willful acquisition or maintenance of that power as distinguished from growth or development as a consequence of a superior product, business acumen, or historic accident.[3]

The plaintiffs claim that the UFC's practices stifle competition from other MMA leagues. As a result, it is able to suppress fighter salaries and impose harsh restrictions in its contracts which include such things as exclusivity, automatically extending contractual rights if a fighter becomes a champion and signing over the fighter's intellectual property rights.

In its contracts, UFC fighters agree to several clauses which the fighters believe are oppressive. There is a "champion's clause" which triggers an automatic extension of a fighter's contract if he or she becomes champion and a "right to match" clause which allows the UFC the opportunity to match any contract offer made by a rival organization in order to retain fighters. The UFC contracts also grant the promotion certain intellectual property rights over the athletes. Other chapters in this book go into these contract clauses in depth but these are just three of the examples which the former fighters claim in their lawsuit.

The Lawsuit

The plaintiffs are comprised of ex–UFC fighters claiming that the UFC holds a monopoly and a monopsony over contracted UFC fighters. On December 16, 2014, former UFC fighters filed a lawsuit against Zuffa (operating as the Ultimate Fighting Championships). The lawsuit claimed that the UFC pursued an aggressive strategy of depriving key inputs to potential rival promoters or merging with them to maintain its monopoly position. It also stated that the UFC implemented an "exclusionary scheme" to impair and foreclose competition, whereby the UFC deprives potential competitors in the fight promotion market access to elite MMA fighters, premium live event venues and sponsors.

Among the chief complaints from the fighters was that the UFC was able to suppress compensation of its contracted fighters. The lawsuit alleged that fighters were paid "approximately 10–17% of total UFC revenues generated from bouts." It also called into question several clauses in the standard UFC fighter contracts including the "Champion's Clause" (allowing UFC to extend a champion's contract for as long as they are champion), the "Right to Match Clause," (allowing the company to match another promotion's offer of services and thereby retaining the fighter), an "Ancillary Rights Clause" (granting the UFC exclusive and perpetual worldwide identity rights of contracted athletes) and the "Sponsorship and Endorsement Clause" (allows UFC sole discretion on approving sponsors and endorsement of fighters).

The plaintiffs claim that they suffered from the lack of a union and/or association like other leagues which looks out for the rights of the players and has the opportunity to collectively bargain on behalf of the players. As a result, there is not collective bargaining or another unified attempt by the contracted fighters to address issues with the promoter. This has proved to be an issue as such promotion-wide policies such as the implementation of the Reebok outfitting policy, which eliminated athletes from obtaining their own sponsors in favor of a payment-tier based upon the number of fights, has been criticized by the fighters.

The UFC is structured as a "single entity." They are a wholly owned company and, as such, they are not subject to Section 1 of the Sherman Antitrust Act which regulates competitors.

The plaintiffs claim that the UFC has foreclosed competition establishing monopoly power and monopsony power over "Elite Professional MMA Fighters." In its lawsuit, the plaintiffs define an "Elite Professional MMA Fighter." This definition was an attempt to differentiate the class of fighter over other professional MMA fighters. Zuffa has questioned this definition, claiming that the plaintiffs created the term for its own advantage.

A monopoly is the exclusive possession or control of the supply or trade in a service. Monopsony power is a market situation in which there is only one buyer. The plaintiffs argue that the UFC has exclusive control over the "Elite Professional MMA Fighter" market. It forces out other rival promotions and is able to do things such as limit fighter earnings and control their intellectual property rights. As the plaintiffs argue, since Zuffa is the only buyer in the market, the UFC is able to demand its fighters submit to oppressive contract terms.

Sherman Antitrust Section 2 makes it unlawful for any person to "monopolize, or attempt to monopolize, or combine or conspire with any other person or persons, to monopolize any part of the trade or commerce...."

The requirement for monopolization under Section 2 is "(1) the possession of monopoly power in the relevant market and (2) the willful acquisition or maintenance of that power as distinguished from growth or development as a consequence of a superior product, business acumen, or historical accident."[4]

The plaintiffs argued in its lawsuit that the UFC had acquired the "Relevant Output Market" by exclusionary tactics which included buying rival organizations and leveraging its market share to "block actual or potential rivals from accessing inputs necessary to compete in the market for promoting live Elite Professional MMA bouts."

The plaintiffs defined the relevant markets to show that the UFC obtained monopoly and monopsony power illegally. The Relevant Output Market is the promotion of live Elite Professional MMA bouts according to the plaintiffs. It defined the Relevant Geographic Market as the United States or, in the alternative, North America. The Relevant Input Market is the market for Elite Professional MMA Fighter services. The plaintiffs maintained that the UFC obtained the markets for each illegally.

The Plaintiffs' Complaint included boasts from UFC president Dana White stating he had killed rival organizations. It also embedded a photo in the lawsuit in which White is shown holding up a fake tombstone with the names of extinct organizations due, in part, to the UFC. The bragging about defeating rivals may have shown a flex of business muscle. But, the plaintiffs used this to show that the UFC forced out competitors—a central theme in its lawsuit.

The UFC argued that the plaintiffs had failed to plausibly allege that its exclusive dealing agreements with fighters were anticompetitive. In legal filings to dismiss the lawsuit, Zuffa argued, "Plaintiffs' claim boils down to no more than a complaint that they believe they contracted away too many rights for too little compensation because Zuffa allegedly possesses a monopoly."[5]

Moreover, the UFC alleged that the plaintiffs failed to properly define relevant product markets. The UFC accused the plaintiffs of manufacturing a term "not used in the industry" and created for the lawsuit. They point to the term "Elite" fighters and how it is distinguishable from other fighters.

From a pragmatic view, the fighters voluntarily signed contracts to fight in the UFC. Also, the UFC just did a better job in the industry and as a reflection of its business acumen, it became the most successful. Despite the moniker that it ran other promotions out of business, it was really a superior product, rather than predatory maneuvers, that gave the company the advantage.

The Federal Trade Commission investigated Zuffa's purchase of Strikeforce, World Fighting Alliance and other MMA organizations in 2011 and 2012. It did not pursue the matter further. The matter was reopened in May 2015, several months after the antitrust lawsuit was filed. However, there was nothing substantive that came of the reopening of the investigation.

Zuffa's Motion to Dismiss

As one may have expected, Zuffa did not agree with the portrayal of its business practices by its former fighters. Zuffa filed a Motion to Dismiss citing deficiencies with the fighters' lawsuit including lack of defining a correct market and alleging that its business practices are not anticompetitive. In an official statement supporting its legal filing, it stated that it contests the "plaintiffs' characterization of the facts…. [E]ven with that high legal standard, UFC's motion demonstrates that UFC competed in lawful ways that helped fighters and built UFC into a premiere organization in the sport of Mixed Martial Arts." The statement went on, "[t]he UFC treats its fighters well, compensates them fairly, competes against other MMA promoters, and produces a product that is enjoyed by millions of fans around the world."

However, the Court denied the motion.

As it was Zuffa's burden to prove that the plaintiffs had no case, the promotion failed to prove to the judge that the plaintiffs lacked a cognizable legal theory or that it had insufficient facts for stating a cognizable claim.

The Court addressed four key points argued in the Motion to Dismiss:

1. Strong Competition v. Antitrust Violation

This argument was quickly dismissed by the court. Zuffa argued that its business practices are examples of "strong competition" whereas the plaintiffs argue that Zuffa's conduct "has foreclosed competition and thereby enhanced and maintained the UFC's monopoly power in the Relevant Output Market and monopsony power in the Relevant Input Market."[6] The promotion's claim was centered on its business acumen and, despite the claims made by the former fighters, its alleged business moves were done to bolster the company and not done with the intent to suppress the wages of its independent contractors. The court did not find its argument viable. For purposes of meeting the threshold to satisfy a motion to dismiss, the Court sided with the plaintiffs.

2. Properly Defined Relevant Markets

The court looked at whether the plaintiffs properly defined a "relevant market." The plaintiffs identified two relevant markets: (1) live Elite Professional MMA bouts (referred to as the "Relevant Output Market"), and the live Elite Professional MMA Fighter services (referred to as the "Relevant Input Market"). Zuffa claimed that these definitions were made solely for the purpose of litigation and that they were vague and subjective.

However, the court sided with the plaintiffs for purposes of this motion to dismiss. The court noted that the validity of the "relevant market" is typically a factually element and not a legal element. The court is looking at whether the lawsuit can be dismissed as a matter of law. As the court notes the market may survive an initial scrutiny under the motion to dismiss but may not under a motion for summary judgment or at trial. But, the court found that the plaintiffs' relevant market is sufficient for "Section 2" antitrust purposes and could not be thrown out at this initial stage of the lawsuit.

3. Specificity of Anticompetitive Conduct

Zuffa argued that exclusive dealing arrangements are common, procompetitive and a part of sports and entertainment, the plaintiffs failed to allege specific facts showing that the exclusive arrangements foreclosed competition in either the input or output market and the UFC has no duty to deal with competitors.

The court did not address the last argument (dealing with competitors) as it did not construe the complaint that it had to deal with competitors. The court did side with the plaintiffs in finding that its allegations that exclusive dealing arrangements are a part of the anticompetitive scheme. It also dismissed the argument that the plaintiffs' claims are a "monopoly broth"—the term given to the use of various allegations to satisfy an antitrust scheme.

4. Ancillary Rights and Reduced Competition

The court looked at the rights issue related to fighters signing off on their likenesses for purposes of Zuffa using them for things such as video games. In this claim, the plaintiffs argued that they were forced by Zuffa to adhere; the court utilized the same analysis as it did with the exclusive dealing contracts in finding that the plaintiffs pled sufficient facts to show an anticompetitive scheme. Once again, the court did not rule on the actual evidence, but whether the complaint states a sufficient amount of facts to survive a motion to dismiss.

The denial of Zuffa's Motion to Dismiss meant that this fight would go longer than the promotion had hoped. Unlike other lawsuits Zuffa had engaged in, this lawsuit had the possibility of destroying its business. Moreover, the discovery process could lead to the revealing of information about the company and confirm rumors of the strong-arm, cutthroat tactics of the UFC. This would not only cause a shift in business, but a public relations issue with many of the intended fans.

Discovery Disputes in Lawsuit

As one might expect, the discovery in this case was contentious and included disputes over information provided. There were several key revelations in discovery although an overall fight over the sealing of documents emerged as Zuffa filed its Motion for Summary Judgment to dismiss the case.

This case presented several issues related to the withholding, sealing or redacting of documents due to their commercial sensitivity and being deemed a trade secret. In fact discovery, the parties do not have to disclose information that they deem to be trade secrets or confidential. A party seeking to withhold a document must include it on a privilege log and submit it to the opposing party. The opposing party has an opportunity to challenge the withheld document. In addition, if a party were to request that a portion of its brief be redacted, the opposing party may challenge the redaction.

In one skirmish, Zuffa was required to produce six documents previously marked as privileged. In an Emergency Motion to Compel Production of Documents withheld on Privilege Grounds and for Other Relief, the court could not comply with the request but required Zuffa to produce 25 percent of Dana White's documents withheld on the basis of privilege for "in camera" (reviewed by the court) review. Due to the voluminous number of documents, the court requested a sliver of the documents. Of 86 total documents reviewed, six were deemed not privileged. As one might understand, there were an inordinate number of documents that would need to be sifted through by the court to determine the nature of the documents. The court's time and resources would be wasted on what would amount to a "fishing expedition" for the truth. Clearly, one side or the other could conceal information it thought might harm their case and risk getting caught. Lawyers are bound by a code of ethics which would preclude such practice. Thus, the checks of the privilege log make this process important.

In general, documents that are cited as Attorney-Client privilege are those which ask an attorney for its legal impression, opinion or are asking for legal advice.

The Order below details the documents. Briefly, they are:

1. An August 16, 2011 press release which UFC claimed was reviewed by legal counsel. The release was about an agreement reached with Fox. Likely, the news of the rights agreement with the network.
2. An October 3, 2006 email chain between Kirk Hendrick (UFC legal counsel) and Lorenzo Fertitta which appeared to be about a bonus for MMA fighter Mirko CroCop for signing a contract.
3. An October 8, 2007 email chain regarding a "Joe Hand Update." Hand is the PPV distributor for the UFC. It appeared to be negotiations between the two sides related to a new deal.
4. A May 23, 2003 email which claims to be providing legal advice regarding broadcasting agreements. It is an email from Hendrick to Lorenzo Fertitta and Dana White regarding "iN Demand and

DirecTV paying for Lindell (sic) vs. Ortiz"? According to the Order it requests, "input from the recipients about Mr. Hendricks's proposal for 'aggressively'" telling Zuffa's PPV partners to reduce their fees for major fights. The last paragraph of the email does include legal advice which the Court will require Zuffa to redact prior to disclosing.

5. A September 29, 2008 email from Hendrick to Lorenzo Fertitta, Dana White, Lawrence Epstein and John Mulkey regarding "our final draft" of an agreement with Affliction. It relates to an agreement "Zuffa believes it reached with Affliction." Based on the description of the document it is difficult to discern whether the acquisition was related to the clothing brand or short-lived fight promotion or something else.

6. An October 10, 2005 email chain which discusses the dollar amount of a media buy Zuffa will purchase from DirecTV. There were portions of the chain that were produced but an email between Bonnie Werth of the UFC and Hendrick were not disclosed. The court determined that Werth did not ask for legal advice from Hendrick and privilege does not apply. Werth discussed Zuffa's evaluation of DirecTV net revenue from 2003 to 2005 without UFC media buys and provides the media buys Zuffa is willing to purchase.

Other Promotions Caught in Crosshairs of Lawsuit

As part of the litigation, third parties were contacted about providing the parties information requested by the plaintiffs and defendants in the case.

Bellator, AXS TV, Top Rank Boxing, ONE FC and Zinkin Entertainment were among the parties pulled into the lawsuit as either the plaintiffs and Zuffa requested company financial documents to be produced.

Bellator, the UFC's main competitor in MMA, brought a legal action in attempt to halt the UFC from obtaining contractual information about its fighters. The lawsuit, originally filed in federal court in Los Angeles attempted to quash the subpoena issued to the Viacom-owned company.[7] In court filings, it indicated it already had produced in "excess of two thousand pages of responsive documents."[8] Still, the UFC indicated that it needed more information including actual fighter contracts, payouts for Bellator fighters and company financial information.

Despite the fact that Bellator's corporate offices are located in Newport Beach, California, the federal court in Los Angeles decided that the dispute should be sent to the federal court in Las Vegas to determine the dispute.

The federal district court in Los Angeles cited to the Las Vegas court's familiarity with the dispute as one of the central reasons why it transferred the case to the trial court in Las Vegas.

The federal magistrate in Las Vegas determined the discovery dispute by issuing the following:

Bellator was ordered to produce[9]:

1. A random sample of at least 20 percent of fighters under contract with Bellator between January 1, 2010 and the present. This will include any "amendments, modifications, side letters, or extensions that may exist with respect to any contract that is produced...."
2. "Anonymized contracts" with a unique identifier although identifying information "may be redacted."
3. The contracts "shall include the fighter's gender, weight class, number of fights during term of agreements and any compensation to be paid."
4. The court limited and modified Bellator's request for production to the following:
   a. A list of all MMA events it promoted or co-promoted from January 1, 2010 through the present.
   b. An unaudited profit and loss statement through the quarter ending March 31, 2017 which will include Revenue, Expenses, Operating Income and Net Income.

Similarly, ONE FC's executive, Matt Hume was subpoenaed in Washington State where Hume resides. The plaintiffs requested documents from OneFC and Hume's deposition as it relates to the antitrust lawsuit. Hume had provided a written declaration in which he stated that "One Championship is not a minor league or feeder league for the UFC" and it "competes with Zuffa to sign professional MMA fighters." The plaintiffs wanted documents supporting Hume's statement and also to depose him. Hume's Washington State attorneys objected to the deposition and document requests citing that it was an attempt to make an end around from requesting documents from the Singapore-based company.[10] It also argued that Hume did not have access to the documents requested. The federal court judge determined that the complexity of the case and the familiarity with the subject matter were defining reasons why the case should be transferred to Nevada. Hume filed a motion to quash a subpoena and objected to document requests by the plaintiffs in the UFC lawsuit. In response, the plaintiffs filed a motion to compel and requested attorney fees in excess of $21,000.[11]

The federal court in Washington State decided not to intervene in a nonparty discovery dispute despite the fact that Hume resides in Washington. Essentially, the court forced Hume to defend his case in Nevada. For Hume, it may seem unduly burdensome for an individual to retain counsel in Nevada to defend his lawsuit. The plaintiffs would contend that moving the case to Nevada would ensure the discovery dispute would be fairly resolved by a court familiar with the issues.

Obtaining documents from third-parties is a challenging process especially when it involves procuring business information it may deem confidential or trade secrets. Similarly, the parties in the antitrust lawsuit received business records from a sports agency that represents MMA fighters and Top Rank Boxing. In the Bellator example, the request for documents was argued to be overbroad and unduly burdensome. According to Bellator, it would "force Bellator to disclose a wide array of its most sensitive and confidential commercial information to its largest competitor and to the athletes with whom it negotiates." They claimed that the requests would require Bellator to disclose a trade secret or confidential research, development, or commercial information.

Experts Enter the Lawsuit Introducing Unique Theories

As part of the antitrust lawsuit, there were a hefty amount of expert reports processed by the parties in February 2018. Each sought to opine on their assertions for their side of the antitrust lawsuit. The expert reports would be heavily used at the time of trial if the case gets to that point. They also would be used in support when Zuffa filed its Motion for Summary Judgment. While there are several experts retained by both sides, the most salient experts are two of the plaintiffs' experts regarding fighter economics and the rebuttal expert from Zuffa.

From the plaintiffs' position, it introduced economic expert Dr. Andrew Zimbalist, who provided an opinion on the anticipated damages of UFC athletes as a result of Zuffa's actions. Dr. Zimbalist's report is heavily redacted and some information could not be deciphered due to the redactions, but Dr. Zimbalist predicted the representative plaintiffs' damages to be $1.6 billion. This is an astronomical amount in damages. But considering the company sold at the time for $4 billion dollars and the lawsuit could have the potential to include hundreds of fighters, the alleged damages were not out of the question.

Dr. Zimbalist reviewed the payment of athletes in the NBA, NHL, NFL, MLB and boxing in comparison to the fighters in the UFC. He utilized player share of the company's revenue rather than the actual pay levels of the players. The complete evaluation detailing the estimate for damages was redacted in the report made available to the public.

As he noted:

> For each sport that I use as a benchmark, I apply the athlete compensation share of revenue to the reported Zuffa bout revenues to arrive at what Zuffa's fighters would have been paid if they received the same share as the athletes in these other sports

where competitive labor markets prevail. I then take the mean of these but-for compensation levels from the different sports and compare it to the total event-related fighter compensation paid out of Zuffa's athletes. The difference is the basis for my estimate of the total amount members of the bout class were underpaid due to the challenged conduct.[12]

The "yardstick method" is at issue here as Dr. Zimbalist comes to the conclusion that the UFC used anticompetitive conduct which would lead to anticompetitive effects for a firm with monopoly and/or monopsony power. He also believes that the rationale given for the conduct are not procompetitive, are invalid, do not theoretically apply to MMA and are therefore less restrictive conduct in its labor market. Utilizing the "Big 4" sports and boxing to come up with a comparable estimation for damages is contested by Zuffa as they make the assertion that the 4 sports leagues have unions which facilitate athlete compensation. But, UFC fighters do not. The data used from boxing is based on 2.5 years from Golden Boy Boxing so the argument there is that the analysis is incomplete as it originates from just one promoter and is extrapolated from a short span of time.

The plaintiffs also retained Hal Singer as an expert in support of its claims.[13] Dr. Singer has a Ph.D in Economics and has served as an expert in antitrust cases in the past. His role was to opine on whether Zuffa possessed monopoly or monopsony power (or both) and whether the alleged conduct foreclosed competition and generated anticompetitive effects. He was also asked to determine the "aggregate amount of undercompensation to members of each Class" attributable to Zuffa's conduct. Dr. Singer indicated in his report that he interviewed plaintiffs Cung Le, Nate Quarry, Javier Vazquez, Jon Fitch and Kyle Kingsbury in preparing his findings. Dr. Singer's findings were heavily redacted for the public since much of the conclusions were based on Zuffa's confidential business information.

Dr. Singer's report is dedicated to how the UFC foreclosed competition. The report went into great detail of how the UFC put competitors out of business and locked-in fighters to long-term contracts. The report was substantially redacted due to the confidentiality of the things that were discussed. In one example, according to the report, Dana White had threatened fighters not to associate with the International Fight League or he would never work with them, as they were competitors. UFC pulled its sponsorship deal with Affliction clothing when it learned that it was attempting to start its own MMA promotion. It also controlled fighter contracts and, based on evidence, the report suggests that Zuffa had the ability to control the timing of a fighter's matchups, who they fought and where they fought on the card (i.e., whether they fought on preliminary bouts or on pay-per-view). Presumably, these details would affect payment of a fighter. In deposition testimony from Dana White used in Dr. Singer's report, White testified that Joe Silva, the company matchmaker of fights was "mean" and it would not be wise to say to no to any fight he asked a fighter to participate in. This goes to the belief that the contracted employee had no real choice in the fights.

In addition, Dr. Singer took an extensive look at the fighters under contract and their ranking in coming up with a determination that Zuffa could exercise monopsony power over "headliners" or as the plaintiffs defined them, "Championship-Caliber" fighters. He notes that the top fighters comprised nearly 80 percent of Zuffa events between 2010 and 2016. This sort of monopsony power foreclosed competition of rival promoters. It was exclusionary and harmed competition.

Dr. Singer took a wage share analysis of whether Zuffa had the ability to suppress fighter pay below norms. Here, fighter compensation is based on a measure of a share of event revenues. Based on this application, Dr. Singer concluded that it was able to pay its fighters a lower share of its event revenues. He also suggested that despite the dip in fighter pay, the athletes did not leave to go to other promotions. This inferred that once a fighter's contract was up or was offered a renewal, the fighter decided to re-sign with the UFC despite the drop in wage level compared to the success of the company.

Contrary to Dr. Zimbalist's opinion, Zuffa countered with its own expert to opine on the subject. Dr. Roger Blair argued on behalf of Zuffa that Dr. Zimbalist's measure of damages was "fundamentally flawed and unreliable."[14] Dr. Blair advocated for a "wage level" analysis which would reveal that athlete salaries increased over time. There would be no damages as a result since it would not factor in the proportionate share of Zuffa revenue.

One of the most notable passages from Blair's extensive report rebutting Dr. Zimbalist is the assertion that the reason why fighter's revenue share comparison is so low is because they were not represented by a union. By itself, the statement makes some sense. Dr. Zimbalist is making an observation rather than an opinion. But it was picked up by the plaintiffs as an admission. The next sentence of Dr. Blair's report seems to explain. "As a result, one likely cannot compare compensation between unionized and non-unionized athletes in a yardstick analysis because the compensation outcomes would differ regardless of the differences in competition between the yardstick and target firm."[15] In his report, he dedicates some time to the argument that the four major sports leagues (i.e., NBA, NFL, NHL and MLB) have been affected due to their athlete unions.

Blair also attacks the tracking of the plaintiffs losses due to a wage share analysis. Blair refers to this as a pay-to-revenue ratio. In his report, he argues that using this type of ratio is not reliable and not generally accepted. Furthermore, the report argues that the model for determining the damages is flawed. Dr. Blair advocates for a "wage level" analysis which essentially looks at the actual wages of the UFC athletes over time. As is evident through the information, wages of UFC fighters have gone up throughout the years. Thus, Dr. Blair sees no monetary damages suffered by the plaintiffs. The question is whether the rise in UFC fighter wages is proportionate to the revenues made by Zuffa. With the success of the company over time, did fighter wages increase over the same period in correlation with the overall revenues of the company? It appeared that this did not happen.

Blair argues against the "yardstick method" for damages used by Dr. Zimbalist.[16] The damages method that Dr. Zimbalist advocates in his report is "fatally flawed" according to Blair. The "yardstick method" measures damages by obtaining a "but-for price" from a market that closely approximates the market in which the violation occurred. Per this method, the "but-for price" is a measure of what the price of the product would be if the wrongful behavior had not occurred. A "yardstick" may vary and can come from a different but related product market in the same or similar geographic market, or from a different but related geographic market in which the same product or products are sold. The argument against utilizing this comparable method according to the UFC expert is the inability to find a comparable market. Here, Dr. Blair argues that Dr. Zimbalist says he used the "yardstick approach" but only used data available to him from the four sports leagues and some data from boxing. It was clear Dr. Blair questions the validity of his methodology in debunking his report that Zuffa's business methods foreclosed competition based on his comparative data. He also suggests that Dr. Zimbalist does not understand the "yardstick" method considering his failure to use it adequately.

Dr. Blair indicates that the comparison used by Dr. Zimbalist were not an accurate comparison due to uncommon variables (e.g., unions and team sports). Boxing's inclusion is only from one promotion and is over a small period of time. Thus, Dr. Blair points that there was a lack of variability over the course of the short time span.

While the plaintiffs filed rebuttals to Dr. Blair's report, Zuffa filed motions to exclude the testimony of Dr. Singer and Dr. Zimbalist, citing that they did not qualify under the evidentiary standard for admissibility in Court. Known as the "Daubert test" after the famous case that came to the decision, the court will decide based on whether the reasoning or methodology of the expert is scientifically valid, and if so, then whether that reasoning or methodology could be applied to the facts of the present case. In this capacity, the court acts as a "gatekeeper" for the admissibility of evidence. The hearing and ruling occur prior to the time of trial and so a ruling that excludes expert testimony could prove fatal to a party's case if an expert's opinion is successfully precluded from testimony.

At the time of this writing, the court had not decided on whether the plaintiffs' experts would be excluded from testimony. The battle of the experts is an important part of these types of cases as it provides evidence of the harm caused and provides a roadmap for the type of damage sustained and the amount that the plaintiffs might recover. On the other side, experts can debunk the plaintiffs' claims and give an analysis as to why the claims must be denied.

Class Certification Key to Antitrust Lawsuit

A central part to the plaintiffs' case is to obtain class certification so that the lawsuit can become a class action lawsuit where other UFC athletes similarly situated to those that filed the complaint could join.

Under Federal Rule of Civil Procedure 23, four elements are required to show class action status is viable: Numerosity, Commonality, Typicality and Adequacy.

The Numerosity requirement calls for the class to "be so numerous that joinder of all members is impracticable." The plaintiffs stated that the proposed Bout and Identity Classes each contain over 1,200 members.

The Commonality requirement refers to there being only a single significant issue of law or fact common to a class. According to the plaintiffs, the common issues include (1) whether Zuffa violated antitrust laws; (2) whether Zuffa possessed market power; (3) whether Zuffa's scheme had anti-competitive effects; (4) what injunctive relief, if any, is appropriate; and (5) the aggregate amount of damages caused by Zuffa's unlawful scheme.

The Typicality requirement is that typical claims generally arise from the same events and the same legal arguments. The plaintiffs argue that their claims are typical because "they stem from the same event, practice, or course of conduct that forms the basis of the claims of the class and are based on the same legal or remedial theory."[17] Here, the claims arise from the allegation of Zuffa's monopsonization of the market for professional MMA Fighter Services.

The Adequacy requirement relates to the counsel representing the party bringing the lawsuit. They must not have interests in conflict with those of the Classes regarding the litigation and are represented by qualified counsel competent to pursue the interests of the Classes.

In the motion for class certification, the plaintiffs highlighted that common issues predominate the case overall and for each component of the claim. They also argued that class action status would be superior to individual actions brought by each fighter with similar allegations against Zuffa. In its motion, it argued that Zuffa's "main criticism" of the plaintiffs' analyses of the allegations are that the economic experts' analyses are wrong.[18] This refers to the measure of Wage Share as opposed to Wage Levels.[19] The plaintiffs argue that the correct way to measure how much Zuffa would pay its fighters in a competitive market is in proportion to its Event Revenues. As such, the more revenues events generate, the more compensation the fighters in those events would receive.

As one might expect, Zuffa opposed the plaintiffs' Motion for Class Certification. As the plaintiffs went through the four requirements to approve class certification, Zuffa had its own view of whether or not the plaintiffs passed these requirements.

In direct contradiction to the plaintiffs' motion, it argues that class certification is "not routine" in actions involving the type of claims made by the fighters. It argued in its opposing brief that "no court has granted class certification in a Sherman Act Section 2 monopsonization case involving allegations based on unilateral conduct."

Zuffa utilizes declarations from fighters to argue that the alleged 1,200 athletes in the proposed Bout Class differ.[20] Their opposition to the motion includes quotes from fighters which give their own personal reasons for signing with the UFC. From this, it argues that the purported anticompetitive terms in the contracts made with fighters "have been central to Zuffa's ability to succeed and grow the sport of MMA."[21]

They claim unique defenses against certain plaintiffs which would go against the requisite "Typicality" requirement. Zuffa also argues that the plaintiffs are not adequate since all are former UFC fighters and are not representative of the class required to bring forth a class action lawsuit. They argue that the "commonality" of claims differs since the allegation of "coerced" contracts were individually negotiated. Thus, there would have to be "mini-trials for each plaintiff and class member as to whether they voluntarily entered into their contracts."

The theory of Wage Share versus Wage Level analysis is argued here again, as Zuffa attacks the expert report submitted by the plaintiffs which suggests that the fighters were paid less as Zuffa revenues increased. Zuffa argues that since the plaintiffs' evidence cannot support damages caused by its claims, class certification must be denied.

One of the more surprising assertions made by Zuffa is that there is no testimony that promoters could not obtain MMA athletes during the class period. Zuffa argues that promoters have not testified to having a problem with this thus negating the argument that other promotions were foreclosed from obtaining MMA fighters from the UFC. It also dents the argument that Zuffa closed down other promotions due to its market share.

Parties File Motions for Summary Judgment

As anticipated, Zuffa filed for a Motion for Summary Judgment in late July.[22] The Motion for Summary Judgment sought to prove that, despite the extensive discovery process, depositions and expert reports, the plaintiffs failed to show that there was factual evidence to support their antitrust claims. As a result, it was asking the court to dismiss the case.

Once again, in its motion, Zuffa argues that the expert reports of the plaintiffs should be excluded, and if not, they do not set forth evidence to establish a market, examine the correct wage comparison exhibiting losses and establish causal injury.

Zuffa argues that the plaintiffs have identified the wrong market for its antitrust claim. This is due to the assertion that they define the market by the athletes in the market and not the MMA Promoters which compete in it. This argument was buttressed by the testimony of competing promoters which denied any hindrance with their business when it came to obtaining fighters or sponsors. Moreover, they believed that Zuffa's success would help their own business. Again, this testimony differs from the plaintiffs' theory that Zuffa foreclosed competition. For example, Zuffa indicates in its brief that it has been outbid by other promoters for fighter services. This would be contrary to the allegation that Zuffa could be the only purchaser of "Elite MMA Fighter services."

The motion leans on the January 2017 ruling which dismissed Golden Boy Boxing's antitrust lawsuit against promoter Al Haymon.[23] In that case, the Court determined on summary judgment that "without a properly-defined market, it is impossible to accurately determine Defendant's market share."

Zuffa argued that the "properly defined market" is the available MMA promoters and not the fighters. It asserted "[t]he accepted test for market definition is whether "a significant number" of customers (or athletes in the input market) would turn to other sellers (or buyers/MMA promoters in the input market) in the event of a small but significant non-transitory increase [or decrease in the input market) in price [SSNIP, or SSNDP] by a hypothetical monopolist."[24]

In September 2018, the plaintiffs filed their Opposition to the Motion for Summary Judgment.[25] The 47-page rebuttal included over 100 exhibits with many sealed or portions redacted. The main argument in the plaintiffs' opposition is that the UFC is the "major league" of MMA and it has done so through predatory means. Only a "critical mass" of elite fighters would make it necessary for any to compete with it. But, Zuffa's scheme of foreclosing opposition has done away with this opportunity.

Zuffa identified elite fighters in order to lock them into exclusive contracts, making it difficult for athletes to move to other organizations. The plaintiffs contend that this tactic usually occurred during the peak years of a fighter's career. The plaintiffs argued that Zuffa used its market leverage to extend exclusivity over its fighters through coercion, intimidation and other means of forcible persuasion.

The plaintiffs highlighted four ways it did this.[26] First, they would move fighters to unfavorable placement on the fight card of an event. This could mean being on at the beginning of a card where there are less fans and the fight is not aired during the "main card" that is televised or on PPV. Second, Zuffa would control the timing of the bout. According to some of the fighters deposed in this case, the company would refuse to offer fights to them despite their willingness to fight. Thus, they would have to spend multiple months awaiting a chance to fight. This would harm the athlete's earning potential since, due to exclusivity, there would be no other place they could fight. Third, Zuffa would delay a fighter's opportunity for starting with another organization by using its "Right to Match" and "Exclusive Negotiation" clauses in its contract. These clauses allow Zuffa a time period for which they have the opportunity to contemplate making an attempt to retain an athlete. However, the plaintiffs argue that Zuffa has used it to prevent the athlete from competing in the other promotion. Finally, the plaintiffs claim that athletes were deprived of title opportunities. Despite a rankings system, the UFC has entertained fights based on "what the fans want." There were examples of athletes whose fight style may have been less appealing to fighters that were jumped over for a title shot.

The opposition brief points out other promoters cited in Zuffa's motion that indicated that they could compete "are not credible and are disputed."[27] In fact, the plaintiffs show why Bellator, OneFC and PFL's statements indicating that they are on par with the UFC are false. Also, noted in a footnote to the motion, Absolute Championship Berkut, also recognized as a direct competitor, noted the cancellation of three events due to "organizational and financial problems."

The plaintiffs cite Dr. Singer's expert report regarding the input and output markets and its showing how Zuffa has suppressed fighters' wages, restricted the output of fighter services and excluded rivals. The plaintiffs also argue that the acquisitions of other organizations by the UFC stifled competition and restricted fighter mobility.

Depositions and Sealing of Documents

The lawsuit has produced a voluminous amount of testimony, including depositions from key UFC officials Dana White and Lorenzo Fertitta, as well as Bellator MMA head Scott Coker. The testimony provided some interesting backstory to the lawsuit. But, the parties sought to seal certain documents for confidentiality. Most of the documents that they sought to seal were by Zuffa which claimed that much of the testimony and documents included confidential business strategy which would be harmful to the commercial nature of their company if disclosed. A Protective Order, a document which give the rules for the handling of confidential and private documents, was issued at the outset of this case. In the fall of 2018, the plaintiffs opposed Zuffa's motion to seal documents in its Motion for Summary Judgment citing that they did not meet the standards for sealing documents.

In September 2018, the plaintiffs opposed attempts by Zuffa to seal documents it would use in support of its Motion for Summary Judgment. It also sought to seal parts of the plaintiffs' opposition papers. It included portions of the deposition of Dana White which took place in August 2017. The deposition went over a number of issues in what was included in the filing. Notably, the deposition took place a couple weeks before the UFC's Conor McGregor went up against Floyd Mayweather, and there was some discussion about White's foray into co-promoting the boxing event.

White's testimony reflects the fact that he is a promoter at heart. In one exchange, he noted that he was a "fight genius" and "promotion genius" but did not know the ins and outs of the company's finances.[28] He also spoke about rival promotions including OneFC. He thought the Singapore-based promotion to be a grassroots MMA organization but it has grown into a juggernaut in Asia. With the UFC attempting to gain traction in other markets, White indicated that when in Asia, he would be asked if the UFC was like OneFC.[29]

Ironically, in October 2011, an email surfaced through the discovery process that then OneFC president Victor Cui emailed Mark Fischer indicating that "One FC was not intent on competing with UFC...." In October 2018, the UFC and OneFC were involved in a "trade" of contracts of two its fighters.

Similarly, Lorenzo Fertitta was deposed regarding the lawsuit. In his testimony he discussed the acquisition of other promotions as well as negotiations with athletes. In particular, text messages were read into the record between himself and Dana White. In one exchange, White complimented Fertitta on "cut throat nasty business like you see in movies," regarding negotiations with Gilbert Melendez. Other passages were redacted due to the claim that they covered confidential business strategy.

UFC matchmaker Joe Silva was deposed in June 2017 for the lawsuit. The limited portions that were disclosed reveal his role with the company. He was asked to discuss several texts and messages he sent to various managers with respect to how he handled the fight roster. In some instances, he told athlete representatives that the UFC could not accommodate their request to fight on certain cards because there was not enough room or that they already had enough fighters in a weight division already on a show. Silva explained the importance of not having too many people on the roster at the same time in order to fill contractual obligations. He also discussed the grounds in which he would or would not release a fighter. The testimony also poked criticism at Bellator when it signed two former UFC fighters to its roster.

In addition to the UFC officers, there were other parties that were deposed in the lawsuit, including Bellator head Scott Coker, World Series of

Fighting President Carlos Silva and other smaller promoters who testified about their respective organizations. Perhaps in a surprise, the testimony from Coker and Silva did not cast blame on the UFC for any issues and neither claimed that the company hurt their promotion's ability to obtain or retain athletes.

Sealing of Confidential Materials

As stated, the plaintiffs have brought up the issue of Zuffa's sealing of documents. The plaintiffs argue that, "Zuffa fails to show that its alleged interest in confidentiality outweighs the presumed right of access of the named Plaintiffs, the Class members, the public, and the press."[30] Zuffa argues that the information they seek to keep private is sensitive to their business strategy. They provided detailed information on why each document should be sealed. According to the plaintiffs, there are "well over 1,000 individual documents or redactions." They rebut that Zuffa does not provide the reasons why each document and redaction must occur and how they will be harmed by disclosure. The "detailed information" was cursory in nature per the plaintiffs, as they were provided a brief snippet of why it was privileged.

Similarly, in the Mark Hunt lawsuit, the trial court in the lawsuit originally denied Zuffa's Motion to Seal certain documents in that case. The documents included Hunt's Bout Agreements. The court denied the motion citing that the public has a right to inspect and copy judicial records. But, Zuffa renewed its motion to seal in that case and the court granted the motion. Without much rationale provided in its ruling, the court determined that the original request to seal documents should be granted.

The sudden reversal in the Hunt case without much explanation for the change seemed to buttress Zuffa's arguments that in the antitrust case, it had met its burden of proving why the documents it had targeted to be sealed were confidential and/or trade secrets.

The plaintiffs argued that Zuffa did not meet its legal burden. Furthermore, the plaintiffs argued the request to seal documents was done strategically as the information helped the plaintiffs' claims and/or painted the company in a bad light. Conversely, Zuffa released information that would make the company look good. The plaintiffs also argued that the contract information for the UFC was previously made public and there would be no reason to seal certain documents related to contractual information. They also argued that certain pieces of information Zuffa had identified were old. While the information may have been confidential or a trade secret at a certain point, it no longer was since the information was dated or had been placed in the public domain.

Among the items that Zuffa attempted to seal were "large sections" of the report of the plaintiffs' expert Hal Singer as the promotion claimed that his report included detailed analysis of Zuffa revenue and contractual information, which included individual contract information. Zuffa claimed that this information provided detailed information on the Zuffa business model. The plaintiffs contend that the swath of information Zuffa wanted to seal did not contain this but contained "aggregated information about Zuffa's market dominance, it's use of market dominance to maintain market power, and the effect of that dominance on fighter pay."[31]

The plaintiffs assert that the legal standard has not been met by Zuffa. The legal standard, states, "The party seeking to prevent access to judicial records must 'articulate compelling reasons supported by specific factual findings,' providing 'articulable facts' that identify the interests favoring secrecy and showing how those interests outweigh the presumption of public access to judicial records."[32] The plaintiffs claim that Zuffa falls short of this. Even with the expert report, the plaintiffs cite case law which indicates Zuffa had not made a showing how the disclosure of the information would harm the company.

It's clear that the plaintiffs contend that Zuffa is attempting to hide information from the public. It is interesting to note a couple of recent rulings decided by other courts around the time in which this issue arose were decided in favor of disclosure.

In *Nevro Crop v. Boston Scientific Corporation*, the U.S. District Court for the Northern District of California determined that a law firm should be sanctioned for a frivolous request to seal documents. The court noted that attorneys, especially those that represent corporate clients, "are under great pressure to file motions to seal information that their clients would prefer to keep secret, even if there is no legitimate basis to keep the information secret." The court issued an order which required the law firm that filed a frivolous request to pay $500 per every lawyer involved in the filing which resulted in a $2,500 fine. The court added that lawyers should, "explain to their clients that litigation is a public process, and that the public has the right to know what the litigation is about, subject only to very limited exceptions. Mere embarrassment to a corporation is not one of those exceptions."[33]

In a lawsuit involving a sports agent and his former agency, a Missouri federal court denied a request by the sports agency to seal an arbitration award and supporting documents filed with the court. The sport agency cited a confidentiality provision in the former employee's employment agreement. However, the Court determined that whether or not the arbitration itself, or the award and supporting documents were confidential did not matter due to the presumption of public access to litigation in the Courts. The opinion is noteworthy for the incredulousness of the court that the agency did not cite any law favoring its position.[34] It opined that the only reason that it wanted to seal the documents in the case was to avoid media attention.[35]

It would seem as though the presumption for public access would override the request to seal information. Comparing the two opinions from the court siding with the preference for transparency versus the reversal by the Mark Hunt court to seal documents makes the request in this case an interesting decision.

Conclusion

The result of the antitrust lawsuit could determine the future of the structure of the UFC. Even if the parties to the lawsuit decide to settle the case prior to a dispositive resolution, it would mean a concession made which would change the way that the UFC has done business. If the UFC prevails, the promotion will have validated its business practice. If the plaintiffs prevail, it would show that the company that was purchased for $2 million and was sold for $4 billion did things that went beyond normal business practices. Its success was made through savvy business acumen, but also through cutthroat tactics which established market power to siphon off rivals and its own contracted athletes to establish compliance and appreciation for depressed wages.

Regardless of the outcome, the lawsuit brought to light the disparity between fighters and founders. Familiar with gambling and games of risk, the UFC owners doubled and tripled down on their initial investment not knowing whether or not it would pay off. The company eventually dug out of debt and gained traction with the mainstream and became a money maker. But, the product it sold, the fighters, believed that they were not properly compensated. There is still fear in some contracted fighters about speaking out against the organization, but the lawsuit exemplifies the perceived inequality with management and its labor force.

11

The MMA Startup—
Problems Abound
in the World Series
of Fighting

Introduction

The World Series of Fighting (WSOF) was formed in 2012. It became an alternative to the UFC and Bellator for fighters and fans. In order to garner visibility, the WSOF signed a broadcast deal with NBC Sports Network. The promotion did not post strong ratings if compared with the telecasts of Bellator or UFC on other cable networks but was able to grasp a narrow foothold in MMA relevancy as it was constant in pushing out events on the cable network. Yet, the façade of the startup MMA organization did not reveal the fissures behind it.

The company's business suffered from mismanagement and infighting. Lawsuits were filed and it was eventually sold to a group of more experienced investors and emerged as the Professional Fighters League in 2018. This chapter will look at the lawsuits that arose out of what appears to be a power struggle between business partners that reflected a lack of foresight, business acumen and strategy. In a span of a year and a half, there were several lawsuits filed by WSOF officers against the organization, individuals and entities. These lawsuits involved the assignment of rights, loans which attempted to keep the World Series of Fighting afloat and expanding international presence. Court documents reveal a power struggle between owners of the company and an alleged cover-up regarding the misuse of company funds, self-dealing and an issue relating to one of WSOF's matchmakers being a promoter of fights and a manager which would be a violation of athletic commission rules.

The center of these lawsuits revolves around founder Shawn Lampman. In a separate legal issue, Lampman was sentenced to 10 months in prison for failing to pay taxes and was ordered to pay $2.5 million in restitution to the IRS. A real estate investor prior to being founder of WSOF, Lampman tried to fund the World Series of Fighting through a series of transactions. Based on the string of lawsuits discussed below, attempts were made to put together a company on a shoestring budget. But the officers operating the organization did not have the best interests of the company in mind.

WSOF Sues Former Officer of Company

In September 2015, the World Series of Fighting sued Shawn Wright, a former officer and fiduciary of WSOF.[1] The company claimed that Wright was guilty of self-dealing against the company's interests.

Specifically, according to the lawsuit, Wright gave a $250,000 promissory note to a company by the name of Bamboo, LLC.[2] Wright had a management interest in the company. The transaction included giving other companies in which Wright had an ownership interest, security in the WSOF promissory note. The transaction saw Wright on both sides and WSOF claimed that he violated his fiduciary obligation to the promotion. The transaction was a "win-win" for Wright since he had a stake in WSOF but also a security interest in the note he agreed to on behalf of the promotion. But if the promotion would default on the loan, Wright had a stake in the companies with security interests.

Also, WSOF claimed that Wright interfered in a possible deal with the UFC. In the late summer of 2015, WSOF and UFC were engaged in negotiations for WSOF content to air on UFC's digital subscription service, Fight Pass. According to the lawsuit, a lucrative offer was made to WSOF, but when Wright heard of the negotiations, he interfered to the point that the UFC decided to rescind its offer. This drew the ire of the upstart promotion since Wright's representations created a perception that it did not know how to conduct business.

Wright responded by denying any wrongdoing and presenting his own counterclaims in the lawsuit which named Bruce Deifik and a family partnership including Deifik's wife as a third-party defendant to the lawsuit.[3] Wright's counterclaims presented a much murkier picture as to the debt that WSOF allowed itself to get in. His allegations against the promotion indicated that he was approached by WSOF about loaning the company money.

Unlike the lawsuit filed by WSOF, the counterclaim presents another story in which in October 2012, Wright was approached by Shawn Lampman about loaning WSOF $700,000. In October of 2012, WSOF was still in development. While there was some hesitation, Tropyx, the company that Wright had an ownership interest in, loaned $700,000 to WSOF.[4] According to the lawsuit's counterclaims, Lampman, through a trust named ACAK Trust, borrowed $700,000 from Tropyx with the funds going to MMAWC (doing business as World Series of Fighting). In addition, Lampman offered to provide Wright's company with exclusive licensing rights for WSOF as well as a "nondilutable equity ownership interest" in MMAWC. Additionally, Wright's company Bamboo loaned MMAWC a total of approximately $480,000 in three different disbursements, with two occurring in November 2014 and another in April 2015. In May 2015, $273,589.03 were still due from MMAWC as a result of a loan from Zion Wood OB Wan Trust, a trust in which Wright was the trustee. Wright claimed that the loans were defaulted upon for lack of payment.

In an attempt to collect on the debt Wright's company notified MMAWC of the default and demanded that he turn over the ACAK's 26 percent equity interest in MMAWC to Tropyx. In addition, Tropyx named Bruce Deifik and his associated trust in the lawsuit citing that he was given shares of MMAWC when they were actually pledged to Tropyx as collateral from loans from Zion to MMAWC. Deifik allegedly attempted to influence the board of MMAWC and disregard the purported ownership interests of MMAWC.

As a result of the allegations, Wright and his company, Tropyx, claimed that MMAWC breached its contract with it and that Deifik usurped control over MMAWC. The lawsuit ended in a Settlement Agreement between the companies but that would not be the end of this tale of assignment, loans and corporate disputes.

WSOF Asia Sues MMAWC

Vincent Hesser, a member of WSOF, attempted to expand the reach of the new product by trying to forge deals overseas. This lawsuit is a result of a dispute over the use of the name of the promotion. In October 2015, an entity named WSOF Asia filed a lawsuit against MMAWC (doing business as World Series of Fighting) and a host of other individuals alleged to have an ownership and/or managerial interest in citing that it had breached a licensing agreement for the company's use of its trademark and licensing rights outside the United States.[5] The lawsuit alleges that the World Series of Fighting was in dire need of cash for operations and on the cusp of shutting down.

There was an agreement between MMAWC and Hesser on behalf of WSOF Asia that gave the latter the rights to use the WSOF mark. Hesser had "pre-existing relations" with a number of contacts in Asia which, according to the court-filed document, would likely lead to a potential business opportunity for the World Series of Fighting. The belief was that the expansion of the company in Asia and other parts of the world would bring in revenue for the company.

Tropyx, the company that was owned by Shawn Wright as mentioned in the previous litigation, assigned its rights it obtained from WSOF to an entity named Royal Union Trust. The assignment was executed by Shawn Lampman on behalf of WSOF. Royal Union Trust in turn assigned its rights obtained from Tropyx to the entity known as WSOF Asia Holdings, Limited. Hesser indicated that he expended $200,000 in out-of-pocket funds in trying to expand the WSOF brand overseas.[6]

In the First Amended Complaint filed by WSOF Asia, it explained a "rift" between Hesser and Bruce Deifik. Hesser and Deifik were members of WSOF and clashed over "critical management and finance issues." The lawsuit claimed that Deifik agreed to provide immediate short-term capital infusions and then would not perform in accordance with the terms and provisions of the loans. He then bought out Lampman's share of MMAWC and secured a controlling interest in the company. As a result, per the Complaint, he was able to exercise "undue dominion over the board [of directors] and employees and usurped and undermined the authority of the duly appointed officers."[7]

It also stated that he became aware of "certain improprieties" by the company's then Chief Operating Officer, Keith Evans. Allegedly Evans claimed expenses in excess of his actual expenses when traveling. He also utilized fight footage from World Series of Fighting and "surreptitiously obtained and rebroadcast WSOF's fight library footage for personal profit."[8] This was done without consent from the company. When Hesser discovered this, he obtained board approval to terminate Evans from his position. However, Deifik, according to Hesser, ensured that Evans was retained.

Then there was the allegation that WSOF employed Ali Abdelaziz as matchmaker despite the fact he managed fighters. Abdelaziz managed a stable of fighters for Dominance, LLC. It was claimed that Abdelaziz did not act in the best interests of the company as he attempted to set matches that favored his fighters and did not look to arrange fights for fighters that he did not manage. There was also an incident in which a corporate sponsor cancelled its sponsorship because its commercials were not run during an event because Abdelaziz had allegedly requested it change its commercials because it conflicted with one of his fighters' sponsors.

WSOF Sues Former Officers for Use of Trademark

The WSOF Asia lawsuit dovetailed into another lawsuit in which the World Series of Fighting sued Vincent Hesser, WSOF Asia and Shawn Wright. The case, originally filed in Clark County District Court in Nevada was removed to federal court in the state. This lawsuit addressed trademark infringement with respect to the WSOF name.[9]

This lawsuit struck back at Wright and Hesser, claiming that while as officers the two engaged in self-dealing which took the form of Hesser using his authority to grant security interests to Wright-associated entities that made loans to WSOF. This would seem to differ from Wright and Hesser's accounting of the situation in which they claimed that the promotion sought their help in obtaining loans.

In a bit of irony, WSOF claimed that Hesser improperly incurred expenses from international trips. This likely was from his work in attempting to expand the WSOF brand. However, the charges that he made were likely questioned. The accusation was similar to the one lodged against company Chief Operating Officer Keith Evans.

In addition, WSOF claimed that Hesser, acting as the authority for the promotion, signed a deal with a Japanese corporation to act as WSOF's representative at events in Japan and paid monthly retainer fees and a split of profits. Unbeknownst to WSOF executives, Hesser purportedly had an ownership stake in the company. He also engaged in a joint venture with a company in which Wright and Hesser had an ownership interest.

Finally, the WSOF lawsuit also claims that Wright and Hesser utilized the WSOF Global name to solicit networks for a television deal in breach of the company's existing contract with NBC Sports Network.

WSOF claimed that Wright and Hesser infringed the company trademark in using the WSOF Global name to create confusion between companies. The lawsuit claimed that Hesser was not allowed to use the WSOF mark and even if it was allowed a license to do so, he was not allowed to alter it in any way. The lawsuit brought up instances where Hesser used the WSOF name and added Global to it in operating as an "alternative" mark and not in conjunction with the WSOF promotion. It also secured domain names which were similar to the WSOF mark but were not authorized by the company.

Although WSOF filed for a Motion for Preliminary Injunction which attempted to preclude Wright and Hesser from using the alleged WSOF Global mark, the parties agreed to dismiss the lawsuit. But the litigation did not end.

In addition to the above lawsuits, WSOF found itself in trouble with other promotions. In February 2018, A Canadian mixed martial arts regional promotion sued WSOF. The company, Aggression Fighting Championship ("AFC"), claimed that WSOF wanted to purchase its company in a purported plan to expand into Canada. The lawsuit alleged that WSOF misrepresented that they had a network deal with NBC and "substantial money behind the company." AFC believed that it would be a franchised entity of WSOF. It signed a 5-year licensing agreement but never received information on the financials or requisite documents needed to be a franchise. It essentially paid WSOF for costs and expenses in holding events but was met with a company embroiled in internal fighting due to money troubles.

A Settlement Agreement?

A Settlement Agreement was brokered on February 19, 2016, between the WSOF, its officers, Wright, Hesser and WSOF Asia and Global. The settlement sought to quash the lawsuits between the parties up to that date. The hope was that it would bring an end to the onset of lawsuits between the officers and parties.

The key parts to the Settlement Agreement included Zion's membership interest being reduced to 4.5 percent of the "total outstanding ownership units in WSOF." The promotion also agreed to satisfy the promissory notes which amounted to $900,482.26 including interest for $750,000 in full satisfaction of the debt.

It appeared that the stream of litigation which started just a couple years into the existence of WSOF was over. But, with a new owner, came another lawsuit.

New Owners, New Lawsuit

In April 2017, WSOF was sold to the successor company, the Professional Fighters League ("PFL") for $15 million according to a press release announcing the transaction. MMAX Investment Partners purchased WSOF's assets and operates as the PFL. The group was led by Washington, D.C., area businesspeople with knowledge of the sports business. This included the former chair of the bid for the 2024 Olympics in Washington, D.C., the owner of the Washington Capitals, Mystics and Wizards and the Chief Financial Officer of the Los Angeles Dodgers.[10] WSOF Global and the trust in which Shawn Wright was trustee filed a lawsuit against the World Series of Fighting, the new investors and individual officers of the company.[11] They claimed that it did not have an opportunity to purchase the sale of the assets which implies it had a right of first refusal. Moreover, it was not made privy to the name change to PFL. This made the license and use of the WSOF trademark useless.

The lawsuit claims that the Zion Wood Obi Wan Trust ("Zion") had made "extensive loans" to the company to allow for it to continue operating but they had refused to pay back the loans. It also claimed that when WSOF was in need of office space in 2013, it allowed the company to use space Zion rented. However, WSOF did not pay rent for use of the space according to the lawsuit. Zion also claimed that WSOF had diluted Zion's ownership stake in the company despite agreements that it could not. In the aforementioned February 2016 Settlement Agreement, the sides had agreed, per Zion, that it had a 4.5 percent stake in WSOF. Zion claims that WSOF denied that Zion had any interest in the PFL and believed this to be a breach of their Settlement Agreement. As a result, Zion demanded that it should have a 4.5 percent stake in the PFL.

One of the more interesting parts of this particular lawsuit is its claim that WSOF's New Year's Eve event on December 31, 2016, reported $0 income from broadcasting right to New York State.[12] An internal report sent to Zion revealed that it actually had $190,000 in broadcasting revenue from NBC for the event. The event featured the top WSOF fighters on the roster, including former UFC fighters Jon Fitch and Jake Shields. It also had future UFC lightweight Justin Gaethje. The event did draw record television ratings with 951,000 viewers tuning in on NBC Sports Network to watch on New Year's Eve. But the alleged $0 income from broadcasting brought into question the bookkeeping of the organization.

As in a previous lawsuit, it took aim at Vice President of Matchmaking Ali Abdelaziz. Abdelaziz continued to manage a stable of fighters while holding a position with WSOF. This dual role is in direct conflict of interest and against regulations within the state of Nevada. The complaint filed by Zion claimed that Abdelaziz was in the United States illegally. It also claimed that Abdelaziz had connections with Islamic terrorism against U.S. citizens. Notwithstanding this allegation, it was claimed that Abdelaziz was "skimming money" from sponsor payments and remit partial funds to WSOF.

The primary argument was that Wright and Hesser had invested in the WSOF Global license and now the brand would be obsolete since it was now rebranding as the Professional Fighters League. The company was taken over by outside investors not within the incestuous realm that pervaded the loans and lawsuits of the first several years of the organization.

One might infer that some of the factual assertions made in the lawsuit were lashing out at WSOF, including some irrelevant accusations against Abdelaziz and the information regarding the 2016 New Year's Event. It might be seen as the officers of WSOF attempting to settle its claims and outstanding debt with Zion and WSOF Global prior to seeking a buyer for the company. If it knew before or after the settlement would have been an interesting question.

Whether or not Zion and WSOF Global had a right to know of the sale of the company was an issue, although one would assume that a vote to sell the company may have overridden any interest it may have had. The legal issue for Zion was whether the sale and name change were in violation of a previous settlement agreement of a lawsuit in which it had sued the promotion for not paying off money it was loaned. Also, whether that settlement agreement granted Zion the right with respect to its ownership stake, to have an opportunity to bid for the company when it came up for sale and whether a subsequent sale would have eliminated its "non-dilutable" shares.

As of 2018, the case was moved to arbitration by the company formerly known as MMAWC d/b/a World Series of Fighting. However, an appeal was pending in attempt to litigate the case in court.

Conclusion

The panoply of lawsuits around the promotion reflects the dysfunction of the company in the beginning. The overarching theme was that there was a need for capital to continue with the promotion. Without a major corporate backer, the company relied on short-term loans and unique relationships to obtain cash. But, when these loans were not satisfied, there were immediate lawsuits. One needed a scorecard to count the number of shell companies created to house loans and funding for the organization. The startup included a lot of family members involved in the shell companies based on the court filings, the individuals sought personal loans to help fund the promotion. The trail of litigation in this case is a reason for the need of institutional investors and venture capital. The lawsuits showed how individuals attempted to cobble together enough capital to ensure it stayed afloat.

The inability of this startup organization to address money issues reflects that not all organizations could be as successful as the UFC. It also shows that the officers of an organization must maintain a commitment to the organization and its mission. Refraining from self-dealing, side deals and conflicts of interest are keys to successful corporate governance.

12

MMA and IP

Introduction

Pay-per-view is one of the primary revenue drivers of the Ultimate Fighting Championships. While the UFC has built up a robust media package and has forged lucrative media deals with Fox in 2011 and ESPN starting in 2019, the company still relies on PPV revenue. Through its business model, the UFC is dependent on the success of these events, which occur on a monthly basis. The PPVs require consumers to purchase them online or through a cable or satellite provider. Dependent on the main event, fighters on the card or any number of certain variables, PPVs have produced robust revenues for the company. The Standard & Poor's Ratings Service included PPV sales in its evaluation of the financial stability of the company. At times, PPV revenues have been a disappointment. While there are risks with PPV events such as athlete injuries taking key matchups off of the card, fan malaise and saturation, the PPV business is still vital to the success of the company.

As a result of the importance of PPV to its business, the UFC has taken an aggressive stance on protecting its copyright and trademarks. Even when short online videos on YouTube are used by fans or pictures on web sites, the UFC has issued "cease and desist" letters and/or takedown notices.

Notably, the UFC, in conjunction with the National Football League, issued a takedown notice of the twitter account of the website Deadspin, alleging copyright violations. Also, prior to an event in November 2015 featuring Ronda Rousey, it issued a release warning of copyright violations if the fight ended via stoppage. The short duration of Rousey fights made it easier for pirates to post the videos. It also has obtained personal information of individuals using a website showing UFC PPVs illegally and then threatened to sue the end-user for going to the site to watch the PPV for free. These are just some of the strategies that the UFC implements in protecting its intellectual property.

Prior to the start of each PPV broadcast, the UFC has a black screen which warns the viewer that the unauthorized use of the program is a crime. This reminder enforces the belief that piracy is not a victimless crime. Yet, the PPV price, which has risen from $45 to $55 to $65, has caused many casual fans to seek alternative ways to watch the fights.

UFC fans are some of the most loyal fans in sport and have dedicated pictures, blogs and videos featuring the promotion. A lot of fans have used UFC videos online to make their own hype videos and have used photos to produce their own posters for upcoming events. Yet, some feel betrayed by the company when they are issued cease and desist letters or takedown notices for their work. There have been calls for a relaxing of the intellectual property defense by the UFC to allow its fans to aid with promoting the brand. But, the UFC has not yielded and is one of the strictest enforcers of its brand ownership.

This chapter will look at the reasons for the strict protection of its intellectual property and any defenses for use without consent.

"Pirates are going to jail"

With the ferocity that made him a shrewd businessman, Dana White was in favor of expending the legal costs to go after end users that he felt stole the UFC's PPV. He stated that he wanted to see these pirates in jail. While jail might be a heavy price for accessing PPVs without purchasing, White's sentiment reflected the company's stance on those who attempted to infringe on their copyrights and trademarks.

In December 2009, UFC CEO Lorenzo Fertitta testified at a hearing of the U.S. House Judiciary Committee to let lawmakers know that the UFC was losing millions to online piracy.[1] The former UFC owner took aim at websites like Justin.tv and Greenfeedz that allowed illegal streams to be carried on their websites.

"The piracy of live sporting events is illegal; it kills jobs, and threatens the expansion of U.S.-based companies," told Fertitta before a House Judiciary Committee.[2] He indicated that they were the largest PPV provider in the world since 2006, "with over 22 million residential transactions." Fertitta testified that the UFC has a "team of in-house technicians" policing websites and chatrooms for pirated content. Yet, it's clear that the "user generated" video content uploaded on to sites like Justin.tv and Greenfeedz includes UFC PPV. Fertitta noted that "watching a live pee wee football game will not generate" much interest. He also claimed that "those that aid and abet copyright infringement are no less culpable than the direct infringers."[3]

Despite attempting to work with Justin.tv to find ways to combat piracy, the UFC sued Justin.tv and other websites for copyright infringement. They also obtained subpoenas for websites in order to gain the IP addresses of people who illegally downloaded and aired UFC events. While the UFC recognized that the legal costs for this exercise would likely outweigh the financial benefit, the company believed it was the right thing to do to protect its content.

Zuffa Seeks Help Through DMCA

The overarching law that Zuffa uses in protecting its PPV is copyright law. It protects original works of authorship "fixed in a tangible medium of expression."[4] Audiovisual works are considered works of authorship. Since Zuffa produces a live audiovisual product that is simultaneously fixed upon transmission, Zuffa events are protected under copyright law.

The Digital Millennium Copyright Act ("DMCA") was passed in 1998 to balance the rights and interests of copyright holders and the protection of Internet service providers ("ISP"), and to enable copyright law to keep pace with the expansion of the Internet.

Under the DMCA, a copyright holder has the ability to inform a service provider of any infringing content that appears on that service provider's website by issuing a "takedown notice." The DMCA requires that a takedown notice contain the copyright holder's physical or electronic signature, the exact location of the infringing work, the work it allegedly infringes, and a statement that the copyright holder has a reasonable belief that the allegedly infringing work is actually infringing.[5]

In exchange for the ISP's compliance with removing or blocking the infringing content, the DMCA allows for a "safe harbor," freeing it from liability from monetary, injunctive or equitable relief if sued by the owner of the copyright for contributory or vicarious copyright infringement.[6] The service provider must not have actual knowledge that its hosted content is infringing, nor can the service provider be aware of facts or circumstances from which infringement would be apparent.

Can Fair Use Be a Defense?

Some users that have received "cease and desist" letters and/or takedown notices have argued the doctrine of "Fair Use" as a defense to use copyrighted content without permission. Fair Use permits limited use of copyrighted material without acquiring permission from the rights holder. It is one of the limitations and exceptions to the exclusive rights Copyright Law grants to the author of a creative work.

Under the Copyright Act, the fair use factors include

1. The purpose and character of the use, including whether such use is a commercial nature or is for nonprofit educational purposes;

2. The nature of the copyrighted work;
3. The amount and substantiality of the portion used in relation to the copyrighted work as a whole; and
4. The effect of the use upon the potential market for or value of the copyrighted work.

Fair use is a popular defense but the doctrine is constantly evolving, which makes it hard to determine an outcome.

Many people tend to focus on factor number 3, the actual amount of time they use the copyrighted work. It might be a plausible argument to suggest that a 30-second clip should be considered fair use. However, courts consider the "substantiality" of the portion used to determine the amount used.[7] So, a short clip showing the finish of a UFC fight or a key technique in the fight might be weighed much more than the fact it was only a very brief use of the copyrighted material.

Of course, one of the more famous cases asserting the defense of fair use was the 2 Live Crew case.[8] If you recall, the lawsuit was based on a parody of the Roy Orbison song, "Oh, Pretty Woman," which was retooled by the Miami rap group; 2 Live Crew established that its song was a commercial parody of the Orbison song and qualified as fair use. It prevailed.

More recent fair use cases take us down different paths. In 2015, a federal judge in New York deemed an Off Broadway Play named "3C," which was a dark version of the 1970–80s sitcom *Three's Company* did not violate copyright laws as it was a "highly transformative parody of the television series."[9] Despite having the same characters and appropriating a substantial amount of material from the original ABC show, the judge found the play posed "little risk to the market for the original."

In another noteworthy case regarding the fair use doctrine, Universal Music Corporation on behalf of recording artist Prince filed a takedown notice to YouTube citing Stephanie Lenz for posting a 29 second clip of her baby dancing to his song, "Let's Go Crazy."[10] Lenz claimed fair use and requested that the video be reposted. She sued Universal. After a lengthy court battle the U.S. Court of Appeals for the Ninth Circuit determined that copyright holders must consider fair use in good faith before issuing a takedown notice for content posted on the internet.

The noteworthy thing in the *Three's Company* and Prince cases was that the parties sued by the copyright holders received pro bono (i.e., free) legal assistance. It's clear that a legal fight is costly and if it were not for the legal teams that were willing to work for free (aside from the notoriety they would obtain from winning), there would not be a case. Instead, in all likelihood, the copyright holder would win.

While the three cases discussed here (2 Live Crew, *Three's Company* and the Prince case) all revolve around parody, a legal theory not claimed by many in the MMA-copyright issue world, the cases show the broad depth and interpretation of the law.

The Preemptive Strike

The UFC implemented a strategy in which it sues its fans directly for piracy of its PPVs.[11] It obtained all of the email addresses, usernames and IP addresses of users who had illegally streamed a UFC PPV with the intent to file lawsuits against the end-users who used a particular website that streamed the events. This legal strategy was reminiscent of the "Napster"-era when individuals would be able to digitally download music for free without a license.

In 2012, the UFC's Chief Legal Counsel, Lawrence Epstein, had strong words for PPV pirates. "We love our fans, and we've got some of the greatest fans in the world, and all the success we've had with the UFC is directly attributable to those fans. But people that steal our stuff—they're not our fans."[12]

The UFC used the Digital Millennium Copyright Act as a way to police its intellectual property rights online. Passed in October 1998, the law extends the reach of copyright, while limiting the liability of the providers of online services for copyright infringement by end users.

The DMCA has prevented fans of the UFC from posting video highlights of UFC content. Certain websites and YouTube channels used UFC content to outline technical breakdowns of fighting styles. Or, they would create websites to mash together their own promotional videos of favorite fighters or upcoming events. However, the UFC cracked down on these videos, making claims for copyright infringement. The UFC utilized automated crawlers to detect uses of its material online.

While fair use might be a defense, the ever-changing use and interpretation of this theory likely shifts the UFC's strategy in combatting piracy claims.

Zuffa has gone after individuals and sports bars that do not license its PPVs for use. They have claimed copyright violations as a result of the unauthorized use of obtaining their PPV. In many instances, Zuffa attorneys obtain default judgments from some of these defendants, which may or may not end in monetary judgments against the pirates. The strategy leads to successful judgments which may shut down individual pirates and websites, but once one pirate is taken down, another pops out for the company to pursue.

UFC Takes Down Site That Allowed Free Access to PPVs

In 2014, the UFC took down and seized the records of website www.cagewatcher.eu, which illegally streamed two UFC pay-per-view events. It did the same with www.greenfeedz.com. As a portion of the takedown, it obtained details of the streaming site's user base, including email addresses, IP addresses, user names and information pertaining to individuals who watched pirated UFC events.

While some might have believed that the news of the UFC obtaining the information of end users in order to file a lawsuit against them was a scare tactic, the company went through with filing lawsuits against those that used the websites to watch illegal streams. In one instance, a judgment was obtained against an individual who did not respond to a lawsuit. As a result, the attorneys representing the UFC filed a default and obtained a judgment in excess of $11,000.

Even though the UFC has a judgment against the individual, it was up to the UFC to determine if it would want to collect the money from the individual. For practical reasons, having a judgment against you is a bad thing. It affects your credit and the ability to purchase real estate and the entity that has the judgment can garnish your wages or put a lien on real estate. So, even if the UFC decided not to collect on a judgment, it still goes on the individual record of the person.

Justin.tv Case

In January 2011, the UFC filed a lawsuit against Justin.tv for copyright and trademark infringement for repeated and ongoing failure to meaningfully address the rampant and illegal uploading of video of live PPV events by members and users of the Justin.tv website.[13]

The Justin.tv website enabled anyone with an internet connection to broadcast live streaming video to an unlimited audience. Although purportedly developed to bring user-generated content to a large, live audience, the Justin.tv website is routinely exploited by users to broadcast illegally uploaded content, including UFC events.

The UFC alleged in its lawsuit that Justin.tv profits from showing UFC PPVs on its website by "embedding" or pairing the sites with video and other advertisements.[14] It claimed that Justin.tv did not engage in efforts to protect copyrighted material and encouraged users to engage in "massive copyright infringement." The lawsuit indicated that Zuffa made attempts to notify Justin.tv of copyright infringement but it did nothing to "prevent or reduce the blatant copyright and trademark infringement," of a UFC PPV. The UFC determined, through the use of a third-party contractor, that 50,000 viewers watched illegal streams on the Justin.tv website of UFC 121.[15]

In its motion to dismiss the lawsuit, Justin.tv argued that the lawsuit was "wholly without merit" due to the fact that the DMCA provides statutory immunity to service providers.[16] It argued that it complied with the statute and should be entitled to its protection. Notwithstanding this, it argued that it went "above and beyond" to address Zuffa's concerns.

Zuffa amended the lawsuit to include additional causes of action of the Communications Act. The company claimed that Justin.tv and its members and users received UFC PPVs without paying. It claimed that Justin.tv allowed for users to post UFC PPVs for "private financial gain," as it received advertising revenue from its websites, according to the promotion. Under the Communications Act, Zuffa would be entitled to the maximum statutory damages or actual damages.

However, the UFC overreached in its claims against Justin.tv as a court dismissed eight of the claims that did not arise under the Copyright Act.[17] Although Justin.tv did not believe that the Copyright claims had merit, it focused on dismissing other portions of the lawsuit. The parties eventually settled the lawsuit and stipulated to dismiss the lawsuit.

One of the interesting questions brought by Justin.tv was whether it was immune to being sued due to section 230 of the Communications Decency Act. The section provides broad immunity from suit to providers of "interactive computer services" for content posted by "another information content provider." Justin.tv claimed that since its users were the ones that posted the content, it should be immune from liability for copyright infringement. The Court noted that there had not been any case cited where section 230 has been asserted as a defense against Communications Act claims.[18] But, since Zuffa failed to state claims under the Cable Communications Act, it would not address the issue.

The Justin.tv case was an example of the UFC stretching a legal premise to enforce its intellectual property. In pragmatic terms, the UFC's legal theory attempted to find Justin.tv liable on the idea that it knew or should have known that its end users were infringing its copyright by streaming PPVs without paying. Additionally, it was slow to act when notified of copyright infringement and a tool Justin.tv provided to the UFC to takedown copyright pirates did not work. Justin.tv argued that the DMCA's safe harbor provisions applied in this instance which immunized it from copyright infringement.

Nick Diaz Backstage Conversation Gets to YouTube and Taken Down

Can the UFC have YouTube take down a video of a backstage conversation between a fighter and a UFC official? The answer came before Diaz's big fight against Georges St-Pierre in March 2013. The short answer is yes.

In preparation for one of the biggest fights of 2013, a video surfaced of UFC fighter Nick Diaz being told by a UFC official that the Quebec Athletic Commission would grant the fighters a 0.9-pound allowance of the mandatory 170-pound weight limit. This contradicted the usual case in which the fighters for a championship fight were not granted an allowance. Revelation of the video would cause a stir. The UFC's decision to make a copyright claim to YouTube of UFC Senior Vice President of Business and Legal Affairs and Assistant General Counsel Michael Mersch talking to Diaz sparked controversy as many questioned whether it was legal to take it down.

Many of the reporters covering the event took issue with the UFC's copyright claim stating that the conversation took place right before UFC weigh-ins in a relatively empty stadium.[19] There were no UFC logos or signage which would distinguish it. Further, the individual filming the conversation on their phone was not a UFC official and therefore they should not have a valid right to block the public viewing of the footage.

But the issue is not the substance of the video but where the video was taken. It was taken backstage at the weigh-ins. In order to get there, one must obtain access from the UFC. And while we do not have definitive information on this, it's likely that the UFC made each person sign something and/or wear a pass to get to the back. We also assume that the UFC limits its liability as well as has language which states that it owns rights to videos, images, sounds, etc., for those entering the backstage area. It's not a public area although we might think it is. Certainly, we all would want to hang out before weigh-ins if we could. But we cannot. Why? We don't have the necessary access.

If we may infer from the UFC fighter contracts, the UFC has contemplated the control of pre- and post-bout access. One can look to the Eddie Alvarez contract which was produced in the Bellator litigation to take note that pre- and post-bout happenings are covered by the UFC.

The Alvarez Promotional and Ancillary Rights Agreement is a section entitled Ancillary Rights. The section provides an exhaustive list of rights that the fighter agrees to grant Zuffa. Among the rights is Section 2.3(b) which states:

> All media, including, but not limited to, motion picture, radio, television (which term whenever referred to herein shall include, without limitation, live or delayed, interactive, home or theater, over-the-air broadcast, pay, pay-per-view, satellite, closed circuit, cable, subscription, Video On Demand, Near Video On Demand, Subscription Video On Demand, multi-point, master antenna, or other), telephone, wireless, computer, CD-ROM, DVD, any and all Internet applications (including, without limitation, netcasting, podcasting, direct download, streamed webcasting, internet channels (e.g., Youtube) or any other form of digital media download or web syndication), films and tapes for exhibition in any and all media and all gauges, including but not limited to video and audio cassettes and disks, home video and computer games, arcade video games, hand-held versions of video games, video slot machines, photographs (including raw footage, out-takes and negatives), merchandising and program rights, in connection with or based upon the UFC brand, the

Bouts or activities pertaining to the Bouts, including but not limited to, training, interviews, press conferences, weigh-ins and behind-the-scenes footage for the Bouts (the "Pre-Bout Events"), post-fight interviews and press conferences (the "Post Bout Events") and any parts thereof on a commercial, sustaining, theatrical or other basis, and by any and all means, methods and devices whatsoever, now existing or hereafter devised.

An interesting note about the ancillary rights that Zuffa will retain from the fighter: it lasts in perpetuity—even after the fighter dies. It's repetitive but emphasizes that Zuffa owns the rights forever. This was one of the issues that led to the former UFC fighters to sue, due to the ownership of their identity rights being held forever.[20]

Based on this particular language, it means that someone like Nick Diaz probably signed over his rights to any "Pre-Bout Events" such as a "behind-the-scenes footage." Even if the video was shot by someone else, it still features a UFC official and Diaz talking backstage at a UFC weigh-in. Thus, the UFC could make the copyright claim.

There are steps that an individual can do to reclaim their video. The first is to send a counter-notification.

Via YouTube re: counter-notification[21]:

A counter notification is a legal request for YouTube to reinstate a video that has been removed for alleged copyright infringement. The process may only be pursued in instances where the upload was removed or disabled as a result of a mistake or misidentification of the material to be removed or disabled, such fair use. It should not be pursued under any other circumstances.

In this instance, there was a counter-notification filed by the maker of the video. As of this writing, the video no longer appears on YouTube, as the parties may have settled the matter short of the UFC filing a lawsuit.

The DMCA is at the center of this controversy. As one can see, it is a confusing law as to what rights an individual may have to upload videos to sites like YouTube.

The issue of a spectator's rights at a sporting event came up with NASCAR in 2013 when a crash occurred during one of its races and fans posted their view of it on YouTube.[22] NASCAR has flipped on its stance on the reasons for taking down spectator videos of the crash but the fact remains that NASCAR had licensed its rights to the images. Journalism advocates argued whether NASCAR had a legitimate claim to take down a video of the crash.[23] One of the arguments made is that facts cannot be copyrighted. Some advocate that the case of *NBA v. Motorola*,[24] which found in favor of a pager service that would provide live scores and stats of NBA games, would allow for factual information to be free from copyright protection. The court held that while the official recordings of the NBA may be protected by copyright law, actual athletic events are not copyrightable. The holding in the case was premised on the logic that the NBA could assert protections over its official recordings, but not over every recording in the arena. Therefore, the argument to allow the recording to remain on YouTube would be based on the fact that the discussion was factual information communicated between two individuals and not an official recording from the UFC. Moreover, there would be the argument that the substance of the conversations was between a UFC employee and a contracted fighter in the arena about the practices of a third party, the Quebec Athletic Commission. Notwithstanding hearsay issues, this would be one of the best arguments for including the information online.

Yet, the contractual issue probably would hold the day. If Diaz and other contracted UFC fighters in the video signed Zuffa fight contracts, they likely signed over their ancillary rights as well. Thus, the UFC would have a strong case to stake its claim to have YouTube take down the video.

However, with the prevalence of social media the issue of ownership of cellular phone videos is an ongoing question. There is a balance between copyright ownership and an individual's right to film events. There is a difference between some of the blatant examples of taking advantage of copyright versus a fan shooting a video for their own use. But, the difference sometimes can get blurred. The Diaz example reflects the subtle issues surrounding the need for the UFC to protect its intellectual property versus an overreach of its rights to quash the use of videos.

In the case of fans using copyrighted material such as UFC fights and posting them on social media such as YouTube, there is a viable right by the copyright holder to assert their intellectual property right to take down videos. But, in such "gray areas" like the Diaz footage, it's hard to state with certainty that a backstage conversation is under official UFC copyright. Rather, if anything, a contractual bar would be the asserted right rather than an intellectual property one.

The Argument Against Blanket Enforcement

While it is within the right of the UFC to monitor their trademarks and copyrights, many question whether the strategy is worth the number of individuals it may alienate. While the UFC might argue that people who attempt to steal their PPV broadcasts are not really fans, there are a set of the company's followers that would sour on its attempts to threaten, and even take legal action against them.

In a recent 2018 incident, a UFC employee had a social media account shut down of a fan of the promotion after the individual tweeted out pictures of a UFC athlete.[25] However, it was a case of mistaken identity, since the athlete was not in the UFC and the company did not own the image. Yet, the fan had her twitter account suspended due to the reporting. This alienated the fan and raised the ire of many already upset with the company for its strict enforcement of its intellectual property rights. However, this highlights the competing interests on this issue. In a December 2018 post, one of the athletic teams that trains many UFC athletes had their Instagram account disabled for posting UFC content.[26] Despite promoting the UFC and its fighters, it's clear the suspension was a challenge to using unauthorized UFC content.

The UFC's youthful demographic are early adopters when it comes to technology. They were the first to become fans of a sport that was on the fringe of the mainstream. Their interest in the sport is so much that they would like to watch the big events. Most younger fans are social media and technologically savvy. They understand how to put together videos of their favorite moves or fights and can push them out on their social media platforms. The problem is that many of these same fans do not have the financial capability to pay for the PPVs. Or, there is just one fight on a PPV card that interests them. Rather than not watch, they attempt to watch via illegal streaming.

While this might not be a sound argument for watching an illegal stream without paying, the legal threats may backfire in the future when the younger demo has money to spend. Thoughts of being hounded as a youth by the UFC may hinder a future fan relationship.

The UFC admitted that the cost of fighting unauthorized access would cost more than any losses it might have from the illegal streaming. Yet, the UFC still went down the path of enforcing its copyright. Was this a smart business move? The UFC brand is important for the company. One might make the argument that the fighters are interchangeable, the brand is not. As a result, protecting the brand, literally, is paramount at all costs.

Preemptive Warnings

Aside from the piracy of PPVs, the streaming of highlights of a UFC broadcast is another obstacle that the promotion has dealt with in the age of the internet. Highlights of endings to UFC bouts have popped up all over the internet. The overarching issue is that these short (or even longer) snippets of UFC copyrighted content would deter potential PPV purchasers and/or UFC viewers from watching the product as the posted video would reveal the most important part or ending of the fight.

Ronda Rousey, one of the company's top stars and PPV draws, garnered a reputation for producing short fights. Three of her UFC fights lasted under 35 seconds and prior to her November 2015 fight against Holly Holm, the UFC issued a press advisory noting not to post any highlights from the event until the UFC said so. The notice referred to 17 U.S.C. section 411, which is an advance notice of potential copyright infringement.

The notice stated, "As we expect greater than normal interest for this event, we remind you [media member] that unless otherwise provided by Zuffa, LLC, no highlights are authorized for distribution until we distribute the approved guidelines." It went on to indicate that the UFC "will be monitoring compliance." While not specific in the notice, it was clear that the warning was aimed at potential copyright violators and about Ronda Rousey's fight, which the UFC anticipated might last less than a minute, based on her prior fights. Due to the short duration, the complete fights could be encapsulated in a single "vine," the short-form video hosting service that was popular in the mid–2010s. Airing of the fight would circumvent paying the requisite PPV price. Additionally, the airing of copyrighted content without consent would hinder the working relationships the UFC had with its broadcast partners. While the UFC sent out notice of potential copyright violators, it also allowed its broadcast partners and preferred media outlets access to the video footage.

The warning to the media members sought to prevent someone with a robust social media following from posting the fight. This would detract PPV purchasers, as one could just wait until the fight was posted online.

Ironically, Rousey lost her fight with Holly Holm via knockout in the second round of the championship fight.

The preemptive request by the UFC was twofold. First, it put media on notice that it should not release finishes to any fights, especially that of Rousey. Secondly, it allowed control of the intellectual property by Zuffa to send it to its favored media outlets for use. Over time, Zuffa has allowed its television partners access to these clips. Through the use of the control of the access, social media users see their television partners clip and will "click" on their link and look to either their site or the UFC site to know further details.

Similar to fan discontent over the unauthorized use of Zuffa fights and/or copyrights, the protection of short, streamed videos was and still is a point of contention. The argument that showing the clip would not harm the UFC, but rather promote the company, is a viable one. Fans tend to argue that Zuffa chases away its most die-hard fans as it punishes those wishing to share its content. But, Zuffa would not have control over the individual user and may not want the endorsement with an individual with an unsavory past or someone looking to monetize content for their own interests. Moreover, it's the lack of control and ownership right of Zuffa that is key. It has a right to protect its intellectual property, and allowing short clips of their fights on social media raises the concern that it will get out of control.

The Future of Protecting IP in MMA

Intellectual property is one of the more misunderstood and confusing issues in mixed martial arts. It is misunderstood because there is a backlash against the company for going after its fans for posting content online. It is confusing due to the practical implication that the content shared by fans is unauthorized, yet seems to promote the product considering it is presumably sharing it with others, albeit without authorization. The problem, as discussed in this chapter, is the intellectual property rights of the owner. It must be defended and exercised even if there are good intentions occurring with the infringement. Many fans like to clip together videos and online tutorials on some of the moves performed by the athletes. One of the unique aspects of the sport of mixed martial arts, is that there are so many students of martial arts that they enjoy "breaking down" the techniques implored by the fighters. For those practitioners, they become training points they can take back to their martial arts schools and/or training partners. Yet, the fights themselves are the intellectual property of Zuffa. Likely ingrained in your brain from years of watching professional sports, whether you know or not, you cannot replay or redistribute a game without the "express written consent" of the league. You could almost guarantee that this does not happen without the league requesting a licensing fee.

New technologies on mobile applications that are able to live-stream videos and immediately show them online will be a key question that intellectual property owners will need to address. Many users may claim First Amendment or Fair Use with the unauthorized use of the videos. This argument may not have much traction, based on the information provided in this chapter.

An under-the-radar issue that comes with videos related to content is the use of such information for purposes of sports betting. The U.S. Supreme Court struck down the relevant law that prohibited sports betting in most parts of the nation.[27] With the repeal, the states can independently determine whether sports betting is legal within their state. Thus far, a handful of states have granted the right to bet on sports. The connectivity of many with their cell phones has allowed the ease of relaying information to sports books easier than before. Although not a concern now, if sportsbooks were to have in-game betting and proposition betting (a bet based on the occurrence or non-occurrence of an event within a game), this may impact the use of Wi-Fi if there is any time delay. The incentive for real-time scoring and updating will be imperative for sportsbooks and they must police any attempts to circumvent this by "courtsiders." The coined term was based on individuals at tennis matches who would relay information to their accomplices at sportsbooks, allowing them to place wagers prior to the information reaching the sportsbook. This issue has yet to be addressed, but will be something to look for as more states introduce sports gambling.

13

The Fight to Promote Fights

Introduction

In this chapter, we take a look at lawsuits involving Zuffa and other promotions. The legal disputes arise from the battle over the MMA industry. Due to the emerging industry and competition between companies, the fight to promote fights led to lawsuits between rivals. It also became a fight over resources and fighters. As discussed in this chapter, we take a look at a rivalry between the International Fight League and the UFC. The International Fight League was a brainchild of MMA fans and utilized their own resources to fund a promotion. It went up against the UFC in a bitter dispute over former employees. In another lawsuit, Pride Fighting Championships was a big promotion in Japan. It was known for its unique matches and dedicated fan base. But in the mid–2000s, its quest to expand to the United States coincided with an effort by Zuffa to acquire the organization. What was thought to be a collaborative deal in which Zuffa would operate Pride autonomously turned into the UFC shutting down the popular company. Finally, we take a look at former UFC champion Randy Couture as he attempted to resign from the UFC and sign on with Mark Cuban's HDNet Fights. The dispute looked into the terms of the UFC contract and the possible length and duration it had over its fighters. In this chapter we review one of the first big lawsuits involving a promotion and a fighter as the UFC sued its former heavyweight champion Randy Couture.

UFC-IFL Fight Over Trade Secrets

The International Fight League ("IFL") was the brain child of Kurt Otto and Gareb Shamus. The two were fans of the sport and wanted to create the first mixed martial arts league with fighters competing on a team. Unlike other organizations that paid fighters a purse, the IFL paid a salary and health benefits to train and fight. Unlike other promotions, it envisioned itself as similar to that of traditional sports, with MMA athletes comprising teams and representing regions. The league came into conflict with another startup at the time—UFC. The two companies exchanged lawsuits over the fight to be the dominant promotion in North America.

Notably, the IFL was acquired by real estate developer Richard J. Kurtz. Through the acquisition, it was made a publically traded company. The market capitalization of the IFL in 2006 was around $150 million. While the founders and stockholders had high hopes for the IFL, its prospectus noted factors which were possible risks for the company. It incurred losses, had capital and stockholders' deficits and limited cash to fund operations. It received loans from Kurtz to fund MMA operations and sold stock in order to repay some of the debt.

The tenuous nature of the IFL business rested on securing a television deal. If it could not obtain a television deal, it would likely not survive as a company. The need for visibility to draw fans, sponsors and revenues was based on landing a spot with a network. If it could not obtain a deal, it would likely fail. Thus, when a potential deal with Fox Sports was put on hold due to perceived interference by Zuffa, the IFL sued.

The IFL filed a lawsuit against the UFC on February 2006.[1] The IFL believed it secured a deal with the Fox Sports Network ("FSN") to air its league on the network. However, at the last minute, IFL claimed that the UFC threatened FSN with litigation against the network, which caused FSN to put the deal with the IFL on hold. The threats were related to claims that the IFL illegally hired away two former Zuffa employees. Through this they gained "unauthorized" access into UFC television production trailers and "stolen" UFC confidential information, including business and marketing plans. The UFC, according to the IFL's lawsuit, threatened FSN with a lawsuit if it entered into a television contract with the IFL. The IFL alleged that the UFC made threats against its business and those it did business with as retribution.

The IFL claimed that the UFC's actions were improper and caused financial losses and damage to its business relationships. Clearly, this would be the case if the UFC had interfered with a potential contractual relationship the IFL's chance to obtain a television contract. The allegations inferred that the UFC threatened Fox Sports and any other parties that it would work with in helping the IFL with a lawsuit.

As a result, the IFL sought an injunction to stop the UFC from interfering in its business relations and its prospective deal with Fox Sports Network. IFL claimed that Dana White and other UFC representatives contacted FSN to relay that IFL had "illegally hired" two former Zuffa employees away from the company.[2] In addition, they had "stolen" confidential and proprietary information from Zuffa, which included business and marketing plans. The two former Zuffa execs had also gained access to "inner television trailer production workings of a UFC-sponsored fight." IFL alleged that the accusations made by the UFC were false and the company's representations to FSN were deliberately misleading for the sole purpose of interfering with the IFL's opportunity to pursue a network television contract.

The IFL also stated that the two former Zuffa employees were legally hired and did not have any contractual obligations with their previous employer. Additionally, the IFL claimed that the UFC reached out to fight managers stating that if they worked with IFL, their fighters would find it hard to receive fights in the UFC.

The IFL sued on the grounds of interference with business relations and prospective business opportunities, unfair competition and business disparagement.

Zuffa Files Its Own Lawsuit Against IFL, Request Case to Be Heard in Vegas

On February 2, 2006, the UFC filed a lawsuit against the IFL, its owners and its former employees.[3] The promotion depicted Keith Evans and Steven Tomabene as long-time company employees who used their status with Zuffa to illegally procure company trade secrets for use with the upstart IFL. In turn, the IFL knowingly and willingly utilized the information for its benefit. According to their lawsuit, Evans worked for owners Lorenzo and Frank Fertitta's Fertitta Enterprises for 11 years and when Zuffa was purchased, began to work for it. Evans had no prior experience or training in the mixed martial arts industry, which infers all that he knew of the industry was from his time in Zuffa. Tomabene worked for Zuffa for four years and was Vice President of Production, and was responsible for production aspects of UFC live and taped television programming.

The UFC accused the IFL of conspiring with Evans and Tomabene to "convert, remove and misappropriate significant amounts of Zuffa's Confidential information and Trade Secrets."[4] This included Evans copying confidential and proprietary documents from Zuffa's office while still an employee of the promotion. According to the complaint, Evans copied records dating back to 2001, which included Zuffa's confidential and proprietary pay-per-view records, market research that included information on demographics, and results of commissioned surveys by Zuffa. He also took copies of Zuffa's merchandise sales histories, merchandising agreements, sponsorship and pricing information. Evans also took his "rolodex" of contact information used to conduct Zuffa business.

As part of their allegations, Zuffa claimed that Tomabene obtained "all-access" credentials for IFL owners Shamus and Otto to gain unauthorized access to Zuffa's production office and facilities during UFC 55, an event on

October 7, 2005. The allegation infers that this would help the IFL with its prospective television production.

Tomabene and Zuffa parted ways in November 2005. The two parties entered into a Separation Agreement. Although not disclosed, the agreement had a non-compete clause styled as a "separation period" where Tomabene was paid for not taking a position with another company competing with Zuffa. The agreement also included a clause that Tomabene would not disclose or make use of Zuffa's Confidential Information and Trade Secrets. But, Zuffa claims that Tomabene had a relationship with the owners of the IFL prior to leaving the UFC, unbeknownst to Zuffa.

While Zuffa had requested and received all of Zuffa's Confidential Information and Trade Secrets from the defendants, Zuffa believed that they had retained copies with the intent of using them against the company.

The lawsuit, filed in Clark County Nevada, brought causes of action for violation of trade secrets, intentional interference with business relationships/prospective economic advantage, breach of fiduciary duty against Evans and Tomabene, breach of implied duty of good faith and fair dealing against Tomabene based on his separation agreement, and conspiracy, unjust enrichment, conversion and injunctive relief.

Although a Delaware corporation, the IFL operated out of a New York office and established a Las Vegas office to presumably compete with Zuffa as well as focus on events in the city. Since the UFC operated out of Las Vegas, it sought to move the lawsuit filed by the IFL to Las Vegas. As the party that filed its lawsuit first, Zuffa argued that the IFL could have filed its counterclaims in Nevada, but decided to file a completely different lawsuit in New York federal court.

The UFC requested an injunction to prevent the use of its confidential information allegedly obtained by the IFL. It also requested that the IFL refrain from interfering with the UFC's current and prospective business relationships or contacting its current or future employees. Essentially, the UFC and IFL lawsuits mirror one another in certain ways.

The legal dispute between the UFC and IFL shows the competitive nature of rival organizations. The bad blood started here with the hiring of UFC employees and continued with the allegations that the IFL gained access to confidential information from its rival. The UFC, according to the IFL, sought retribution for the hiring of its former executives and wanted to ensure that it would be unable to compete. IFL claimed the UFC interfered with a potential network deal that could have been a game changer for the company. The UFC also interfered with managers who gave counsel to prospective fighters. The IFL alleged that the UFC made threats to managers to not work with the IFL as a way to block the promotion from garnering talent.

Zuffa brought a Motion for Preliminary Injunction against the defendants. On March 2, 2006, less than a month after the company filed its lawsuit against the IFL, et al., the court heard oral arguments.[5] Notably, the court indicated a question with respect to what the UFC deemed to be a trade secret. The court took issue with what the company considered a trade secret and whether the information it claimed the IFL and its former employees had was confidential at all. The judge, who admitted on the record that he had watched MMA, stated that when his law clerk asked him about one of the purported trade secrets on demographics, he knew the information by guessing. "We're not talking about the secret ingredient in Pepsi," the judge quipped.[6] He noted that a lot of the information claimed by Zuffa was "fairly obvious." The judge stated that while he was fine with protecting the confidential trade secrets of Zuffa, that right had to be balanced against things that anyone could figure out or was already in the public domain. The attorney for the IFL brought to light one of the central issues of an attempt to enforce an injunction: "what do you enjoin when somebody says I don't have it, and I'm not using it?"

While the lawyer for the IFL sought to find a narrow order to protect the promotion's interest, to ensure it would not have the stigma with any prospective business partner that it may be in violation of some injunction, the overarching concern was attempting to limit knowledge of former employees when their experience may be the source of the ideas versus confidential information. The Zuffa lawyer, Lawrence Epstein, agreed to a narrow order but maintained the information that the company sought to protect was not in the public domain. Epstein brought up the example of budgetary information.

The parties initially agreed to the order. Yet, the initial hearing showed the hard chore it would be for Zuffa to prove that the former employees were using confidential trade secrets to aid the IFL. The fact that certain information could be inferred from following the industry and was in the public domain as well as the work experience of Evans and Tomarene would make it hard for Zuffa to prove a violation unless it was explicit.

While the preliminary injunction was heard in Las Vegas, the IFL's lawsuit was still in New York. The UFC sought to transfer the IFL case to Nevada. As the IFL lawsuit was filed in federal court in New York, the UFC argued that it had no jurisdiction and even if it did, the more convenient forum would be in Nevada. Since the IFL had an office there, the UFC argued it could not be harmed.

The lawsuit was sent to Nevada where the IFL opposed a Preliminary Injunction by the UFC and included a Motion to Dismiss the UFC's lawsuit. The court denied each. But despite these procedural issues, the parties were able to come together and resolve their dispute short of trial and further litigation.

The newness of the industry gave rise to the protection of its business practices. As we see with the IFL case, the concern of hiring away executives from one organization to another caused concern about stealing trade secrets. In almost every industry, there are situations where individuals move from one organization to another. In so doing, the company from which they leave may be concerned with the shuttling of trade secrets. Some companies require a "non-compete" agreement be signed which would preclude an individual from immediately joining a rival. However, with labor laws varying from state to state this clause cannot be relied upon. Moreover, having someone sit out a number of months prior to working with a competitor does not mean they did not obtain "trade secret" information from their previous company.

Japanese Promotion Sues Zuffa After Acquisition

Pride Fighting Championships ("Pride") was a Japanese mixed martial arts promotion company founded in October 1997 in Tokyo, Japan. The company was the popular predecessor of the UFC and many of the modern-day MMA fighters began their career or had a tour of time with Pride. For early adopting fans of MMA, they look back at the days of Pride with reverence and nostalgia. The rules were different in Pride. There were 3 rounds with the first round lasting 10 minutes with the other two another 5. The combatants fought in a ring instead of a cage which led to many moments where fighters fell outside through the ropes. Most notorious of the rules that differed from modern day UFC, soccer kicks to the face, stomps, and knees to the head of an opponent on the ground were allowed. In the UFC and most promotions in MMA, the rules prohibit these strikes. There were also one-night tournaments where athletes fought and if they won, they would advance through the night with the possibility of fighting two or three times. There were some technology experiments in Pride as referees wore cameras so that viewers could see the fighting first hand. In March 2007, Dream State Entertainment ("DSE"), the owners of Pride, sold the promotion to Lorenzo and Frank Fertitta. Depending upon which side you believed, the acquisition agreement by the two entities was supposed to have the Fertittas running Pride independent of the UFC. However, that did not happen.

In October 2007, Pride's Japanese staff was laid off and the promotion was closed down. According to Zuffa, this was due to the failure of Pride's former ownership to cooperate with background checks as required by the agreements between the companies. Zuffa claimed that Nobuyuki Sakakibara in particular was hesitant to provide the most basic of information and evaded investigators. It was believed that there were inherent conflicts of interest within the company which led to the attempts to conceal certain information.

Also, there were claims of ties to organized crime in Japan. Zuffa filed a lawsuit against DSE due to a breach of the contract in the purchase of Pride. In return, DSE filed a lawsuit against Zuffa alleging a breach of the Asset Purchase Agreement and a Consulting Agreement.[7] They also claimed damages for fraudulent and negligent misrepresentation and breach of the covenant of good faith and fair dealing.

DSE Claims Against Zuffa

DSE claimed that there were numerous "suitors" for Pride, but chose Zuffa because of a promise by the promotion to keep the Pride brand and have it remain on the same level as the UFC. Prior to the sale Pride was "aggressively cultivating the U.S. market." In its lawsuit, Pride owners claimed that they were aggressively pursued by Zuffa, which made promises to them that they would keep the promotion and back it as much as it did the UFC. However, this was a ruse by Zuffa, according to the complaint.

Without Pride owners knowing, the UFC were negotiating with several of its fighters about jumping to the UFC. Only months after Pride was acquired by Zuffa, all of its employees were fired and the offices in Japan closed down. There were no efforts by Zuffa to hold a Pride show in Japan after it was acquired. Zuffa claimed that this was due to the failure to comply with the asset and purchase agreements. But, DSE believed that this was due to incomplete and inaccurate information obtained by Zuffa from its hired investigators.

There were two documents that were at the center of the court filing. DSE claimed a breach of a consulting agreement that Sakakibara entered into with Zuffa on behalf of Pride. The purpose of the consulting agreement was to provide the purchasers with business and marketing strategies. DSE alleged that initial payments were made but were not paid in full. Zuffa claimed that Sakakibara did not complete a background check. DSE argued that one was not necessary according to the rules in Nevada. Sakakibara asserted that he applied for and received a promoter's license from the Nevada State Athletic Commission.

This federal case filed by Sakakibara was stayed as Zuffa had filed a lawsuit in state court in Clark County, Nevada, prior to the case in the United States District Court of Nevada.

Sakakibara filed a lawsuit against the companies that were retained to conduct background investigations on Sakakibara in April 2007 in relation to the purchase by the Fertittas. He claimed that the companies committed violations of the Fair Credit Reporting Act. Sakakibara claimed that the investigating companies used consumer reports for impermissible purposes, failing to follow reasonable procedures to assure maximum possible accuracy, failing to conduct mandatory reinvestigation and failing to correct inaccurate or incomplete information.[8] This allegation related to the claim that Sakakibara's lawyers requested the investigation firm that the information it had was incomplete and not accurate yet ignored requests to correct the information.

Sakakibara also claimed defamation and negligence claims. The allegations claimed that the investigators knew or should have known that the information in the reports were "incomplete, inaccurate or false."[9] They also breached a duty to perform the investigation in a professional manner which Sakakibara claims they did not do. Sakakibara's lawsuit claimed damages in excess of $5 million dollars in addition to punitive damages.

Zuffa Finds Sellers Uncooperative

In response to Sakakibara's federal court lawsuit, Zuffa filed a motion to dismiss citing deficiencies in his pleading and remarking that he never attached the contracts at issue to his lawsuit due to the fact that it would reveal the problems with his claims. Zuffa's investigation into the company it acquired was rife with problems. The investigators claimed that Sakakibara was one of the main individuals that delayed or refused to cooperate with providing background checks. According to Zuffa, as part of the asset purchase agreement the background checks were a necessity in order for the business transaction to go through. The checks against Sakakibara revealed conflicts of interests as he personally had ownership stakes in some of the vendors that were contracted with Pride. They discovered other issues with the company as many executives were uncooperative and/or failed to produce business records requested by investigators.

The parties eventually settled their lawsuit short of trial in August 2010.

The End of Pride

The lawsuits related to the acquisition by Zuffa of Pride was a boon for the company as it was able to obtain a major asset in efforts to expand the company. The lawsuits were the price of doing business. The rumors of Pride being tied to organized crime in Japan was a major hindrance and if Zuffa's goal was to try to legitimize the sport of mixed martial arts, it had to make sure that the transaction was legal with knowledge and background checks of everyone involved. Despite Sakakibara's claim that Zuffa's hired investigators did not comply with rules and reported information inaccurately, the concerns over the background of Pride were not readily known. In fact, the investigators noted that some of the background information from Pride executives were incomplete or were not provided.[10] There was stalling and a lack of cooperation. Even with Sakakibara filing a lawsuit claiming that the investigation process was not done properly, questions had to come up with why basic business information could not be provided. While Zuffa went on to complete the purchase of Pride and the former owner's reprise of the Japanese promotion fizzled out with most of its major stars signing on with the UFC, the fan base that enjoyed the early days of the promotion has to look to the UFC's digital library to relive those times.

Randy Couture and UFC Tangle in Court

Former UFC Light Heavyweight and Heavyweight Champion Randy Couture was a popular figure in MMA in the late 1990s and 2000s. A former amateur wrestling great and U.S. Army veteran, he had won the titles on a number of occasions within the promotion. However, a schism was evident. After a successful stint with the company which gained him notoriety, fame and financial stability, Couture took a step back from fighting in the Octagon. "The Natural" as he was nicknamed, invested in several businesses, including an MMA gym where aspiring fighters trained. In addition, in 2007, he found a job as an ambassador of sorts for the sport with the UFC. He signed a three-year contract and was paid $200,000 per year in commissions, to meet with fans and to promote the sport on behalf of the UFC. Not even a year into his duties outside of the octagon, Couture wanted to return to fighting. The UFC obliged with a four-fight contract with the company. On October 11, 2007, Couture resigned from the UFC. A lawsuit was filed by Zuffa against Couture for allegedly devising a plan in which he claimed that the UFC lied to him. As a result, Zuffa argued that based on these misrepresentations, Couture had a pretext to breach his contract with the promotion and sign with another MMA promotion.

In February 2008, HDNet, a cable company owned by Mark Cuban, filed a lawsuit against Zuffa seeking interpretation of its contract with Couture.[11] HDNet sought to add Couture to its upstart MMA organization. Couture stated that he would wait to fight in another organization until his Zuffa contract expired. Zuffa attempted to block this from happening as it claimed that Couture was still under contract with the UFC.

Although Couture believed that his resignation was valid, Zuffa invoked the contractual right to "suspend" his contract in the case he decided to return to active fighting. Couture believed that he would be free of all contractual obligations so that by October 2008 he could enter into a new promotional agreement with another promoter.[12] The promotion believed that Couture stepping away from the octagon meant that his contract was on pause and would restart when and if he came back to fight. Still, HDNet signed Couture to a fight contract upon the date he believed he was free from his previous contract.

The purpose of the HDNet lawsuit was for an order determining the promotion's rights under its contract with Couture. "A key technique utilized by Zuffa to maintain their iron grip on the MMA industry is litigation and intimidation," wrote HDNet's lawyers in its legal filing seeking a declaratory judgment.[13] They indicated that reviewing court filings, Zuffa is not afraid to "tie their opponents down with expensive and lengthy court battles regardless of merits."[14]

In response to Couture's resignation, UFC President Dana White indicated that per its contract it was suspending the terms of the written agreement. According to HDNet, the UFC portrayed Couture's departure as a retirement rather than a resignation. This put Couture in legal limbo since he wanted to wait out the term of Zuffa's contract in order to sign with another promotion. HDNet did not want to breach Zuffa's contract but believed that the position they took in its interpretation of Couture's contract was unconscionable as it would tie up Couture from fighting until he conceded to the terms dictated by Zuffa.

The court case moved to Nevada state court in Clark County where Zuffa filed for a Preliminary Injunction and Couture opposed.

The dispute between Couture and Zuffa grew. While there was the issue of HDNet, Zuffa believed that Couture was working with another rival, the IFL, which it believed was in violation of the terms of its employment agreement with Couture. In his opposition to Zuffa's Motion for Preliminary Injunction, Couture explained the allegations that he was working with the IFL in purported breach of his contract with the UFC.

Zuffa claimed that Couture breached his Employment Agreement as he allowed the use of his name and likeness to be used by the IFL to promote an upcoming event by that fight promotion. This would be in direct conflict with a clause in his Employment Agreement that stated he could not use his name or likeness in an unarmed combat event for a one-year period following the expiration of his Zuffa deal.

According to Zuffa's motion, the company gave Couture a job with the UFC where he was a commentator for UFC fights, interacted with athletic commissions and regulatory officials and served as an overall ambassador for the UFC. The UFC paid Couture $200,000 per year for a three-year deal as well as incentive compensation. The Employment Agreement also included a "Duty of Loyalty" which prohibited the disclosure of Zuffa's confidential business information. The Employment Agreement had a 3-year term. The Agreement lasted ten months. Couture wanted to come out of retirement to fight once again. In early 2007, he entered into an Exclusive Promotional Rights and Ancillary Rights Agreement with the UFC.

On February 1, 2008, Zuffa filed a preliminary injunction in Clark County, Nevada District Court seeking to enforce an Employment Agreement between Zuffa and Couture.[15] Zuffa claimed that Couture violated terms of his employment agreement as the promotion claimed that Couture helped promote an IFL event. The allegation was that Couture's MMA gym, Xtreme

Couture, and his picture were featured in IFL promotional material which would be in direct conflict with his Employment Agreement.

According to Couture, he did not lend his likeness to the IFL, as he explained that it was a mistake posted by the company and his photo was published without his authorization. He did not provide permission or authorization to use his name or likeness for the promotion and was never contacted about consent. In his opposition to the preliminary injunction, declarations were attached from the IFL stating that Couture's name and likeness were mistakenly posted to promote an upcoming event.[16] The mistake originated when it was believed that Couture was the coach of the Xtreme Couture team that was competing at the IFL event. Couture further argued that under his Employment Agreement, he was allowed to market his MMA school, Xtreme Couture, which trains fighters, provided he did not get involved with any promoter. Couture argued that the UFC did not object to his training facility and whether his fighters could fight in various promotions outside the UFC. He also noted that there was no objection from the UFC that Xtreme Couture could sponsor his athletes. Substantively, Couture argued that Xtreme Couture was not a party to the Employment Agreement since Couture's gym was a separately owned legal entity.

Couture claimed that during negotiations of his Employment Agreement, he indicated to the UFC that he would also be involved in other business ventures including selling a clothing and nutritional supplement line, working with an MMA gym in Los Angeles, working with a Canadian television network and establishing and operating Xtreme Couture Mixed Martial Arts schools. The former heavyweight champion claimed that under the Employment Agreement with Zuffa, there was a "carve-out exception" which allowed Couture to establish and operate the Couture MMA & Fitness schools under the name Xtreme Couture.

It was believed by Couture that the reason for the enforcement of the Engagement Agreement at this time as opposed to previous use of the Xtreme Couture name was due to the fact that Couture was under contract with Zuffa and the UFC. But, after he resigned, Couture claimed that the preliminary injunction was a result of his resignation from his Employment Agreement and fight contract. Zuffa claimed that the crux of the matter was his promoting and sponsoring the IFL website in violation of his non-compete clause with Zuffa. The two sides argued this point in a Clark County courtroom and it was determined that the non-compete was reasonable.

The Court granted Zuffa's Motion for Preliminary Injunction, but it was limited in nature and was not punitive against Couture, but, rather, instructive.[17] It did instruct that Couture could not use the name of his MMA gym, Xtreme Couture, to promote an upcoming IFL event. It ordered Zuffa to post a bond in the amount of $10,000 to obtain the preliminary injunction.

In addition to this legal issue, the lawsuit between Couture and Zuffa included the fighter's departure from the UFC. Although Couture claimed to have resigned from his UFC contract with two fights left on his Promotional Agreement with the company, Zuffa claimed that Couture's resignation was a retirement. Based on Zuffa's interpretation, it designated Couture's contract as on hold and not over. Thus, the promotion exercised its right to Couture's services as a fighter if he were to ever come back to MMA. UFC president Dana White sent Couture a letter advising as much.

In response, Zuffa claimed that Couture signed an agreement to fight for HDNet and claimed to wait out the term of his contract with the UFC. They also claimed that Couture made inflammatory statements about his contract with the UFC as to how he was being precluded from working with other promotions. Couture referred to the non-compete agreement as a "restrictive covenant" as a point of emphasis, asserting that the contract term was not enforceable as it was overbroad in scope and did not offer a reasonable need of protection for Zuffa.

Notwithstanding the preliminary injunction over the restrictive covenant clause, the overarching issue was whether Couture could resign from a contract he willingly entered into with Zuffa. It's clear that Couture decided to leave the UFC with there being no real clear grievance leading to his departure. Couture was paid approximately $3 million within two years, according to the UFC. Yet, Couture did not want to fulfill the last two fights of his deal.

The exclusivity of the contract is something that Zuffa believes is vital in promoting its events. As it argued more than 10 years later, the restriction for its athletes to compete in the UFC and nowhere else is important, as the company invests financially in the marketing and promotion of the athletes. If a fighter saw a better contract in another promotion and could simply resign, it would not appear fair for the promotion. Conversely, if an athlete felt he or she was treated unfairly and no longer wanted to compete for the company, they should have some sort of relief rather than being forced to stay under the terms of the contract. This case differs from a normal athlete who makes a modest salary. Couture was one of the highest paid athletes on the UFC roster. According to the UFC, he made $3 million in the short timeframe of this lawsuit. After he retired, he was given a job with the company with a starting salary of $200,000. He had other business opportunities that most athletes would not have. Thus, when Couture resigned from the UFC, there was likely animosity between the two companies, which set off the lawsuit.

Couture's attempt to release himself from the contract likely meant that the UFC would not allow him out of it. In fact, Zuffa categorized Couture's resignation letter as a retirement and suspended, not voided, his contract.

This would prevent him from going to any other promotion without fulfilling the terms of his deal with the UFC. While HDNet's attempt to obtain a ruling in the matter was warranted, it was clear that based on the contract, Couture could not break his deal.

Another aspect of the dispute was the aggressive stance Zuffa took with Couture. Certainly, Zuffa could have filed defamation claims against Couture for his purported statements about the company to the MMA media. Yet, its enforcement of his deal, along with the preliminary injunction, seem like strong statements made against Couture, and let other athletes know the exclusivity of the contracts should not be taken lightly.

The parties ended up settling this case and despite the animosity, Couture returned to the UFC in November 2008 to defend his UFC Heavyweight Championship. He lost to Brock Lesnar in the second round of that fight.

14

Odds and Ends

Introduction

There are several lawsuits that did not fit into any of the preceding chapters. They are unique, peculiar and have their own set of specific facts which make them stand out. Three of them involve Conor McGregor and antics outside of the ring. Another includes a lawsuit with an employment pact gone wrong involving Bellator. These lawsuits exemplify combat sports. They are outlandish lawsuits that make one cringe when reading about them. While you cannot justify stating that these types of lawsuits are specific to MMA, they have certain characteristics that make one believe that MMA is the only sport that could have such colorful characters.

Conor McGregor Throws Can During Press Conference

Known for his brashness, Conor McGregor is the top draw in the UFC. He's known for trash-talk and getting into the heads of his opponents. Based on the next three cases, you could also argue he's known for reckless behavior outside of the octagon.

In August 2016, William Pegg was inside the Copperfield Theater at the MGM Resort & Casino during a pre-fight press conference to promote McGregor's rematch against Nate Diaz. Diaz defeated McGregor earlier in the year in something of an upset. The rematch guaranteed to be contentious inside and outside of the octagon. For the pre-fight press conference, McGregor did not show up at the scheduled start, while Diaz was on stage, with other fighters ready. It was not until 10 to 15 minutes into the press conference that McGregor showed up to take his place on the stage. Immediately after McGregor sat down, Diaz stood up and left the stage and exited through the crowd.

Words (and gestures) were made between McGregor and Diaz as well as people within both fight camps. It was at that point that objects were thrown between the groups including water bottles and cans. Pegg was hit in the back by a can thrown by McGregor.

Pegg sued McGregor for damages related to the injury he received from the can. He stated that McGregor was guilty of negligence and battery for hurling the can into the crowd and hitting Pegg. The lawsuit, which was filed in state court in Nevada, claimed that McGregor breached his duty to "act as a reasonable and prudent person" when he threw cans at Diaz.[1] The lawsuit read McGregor "intended to cause a harmful or offensive contact with a person" by throwing the cans. There was also a cause of action for Unjust Enrichment, which claims that McGregor profited from the wrongdoing. This is to say that due to the altercation, McGregor made money from the incident.

Pegg's lawsuit was a basic personal injury case in which one injures another. Here, McGregor threw a can into a crowd seeking to hit Diaz but missed and hit another, causing injury. The altercation may have increased the number of fans willing to buy a ticket or purchase the PPV to see the fight. In most combat sports, animosity between the combatants increases interest. The melee caused by McGregor and Diaz drew news and was something that the casual fan would check out online. Due to the bad blood, one might purchase the PPV to see the fight. Thus, the claim for Unjust Enrichment is plausible.

There seem to be some critical issues with the lawsuit. First, McGregor (and his sports and entertainment company) were the only defendants in this case. While it was McGregor who hit Pegg, there were others that might be at fault, such as the UFC for conducting the event without proper security or a plan in the event of such an altercation. Similarly, the MGM might be a possible defendant. Although it rented the space to the UFC, it still had a duty to ensure that there was security for its premises. There is Diaz who may be someone who contributed to the altercation by leaving the stage and inciting McGregor. One would assume that there would be insurance policies that would cover such an incident. Yet, the plaintiff did not pursue this route by suing either the promotion or the venue, which may have carried coverage for the property damage and physical injury.

Secondly, the lawsuit was filed in state court with the knowledge that McGregor was not a citizen of Nevada. The UFC champ frequents Las Vegas for fights and training but does not have a residence in the state. Moreover, his company, which Pegg sued, was located in California. Although Pegg was a Nevada resident, it faced a venue issue. Also, there was the case that the plaintiff was asking for monetary relief that exceeded the threshold amount of $75,000. The plaintiff filed an Offer of Judgment for $90,000 to McGregor.[2] The offer allowed for McGregor to accept the judgment offer in order to resolve the case short of further expense.

Instead of accepting the offer, McGregor's legal team removed the case to federal court.[3] It cited the Offer of Judgment as evidence that the amount in controversy exceeded $75,000. The defendants also argued that McGregor was not a citizen of Nevada and his company's place of business was in California. The plaintiff argued that the removal was not made in a timely fashion, but the defendants indicated that they made their move to send the case to federal court upon receipt of the Offer of Judgment. The differences between federal court and state court vary, but federal court tends to be strict with its rules, which would favor the defendants.

Pegg's attorneys could not adapt to the change in forums, as the federal court denied a motion to compel the deposition of McGregor and documents. The order from the court indicated that due to the fact that the plaintiff's motion to compel lacked legal analysis, the motions should be denied.[4] The ruling was based on the lack of stylistic form of the motion, which failed to follow the rules.

The plaintiff argued that its motion to compel was not heard in state court due to the fact that McGregor's attorneys had removed the case to federal court. Thus, the motion, which was slated to be heard, was nixed due to the removal. Under the federal rules, once a party moves the case to federal court based on jurisdiction issues, it is allowed to move the case subject to a potential remand. Here, the court determined that the rightful place for the case was in federal court.

The plaintiff attempted to compel the deposition of Conor McGregor as well as obtain a plethora of financial information including W-2s, tax returns and UFC contracts indicating that they were needed to ascertain whether McGregor had the money to cover a potential damage claim. McGregor's attorney indicated that the documents were confidential and not discoverable. He also stated that McGregor would not be available for deposition in Las Vegas prior to his scheduled fight with Khabib Nurmogomedov on October 6, 2018. According to McGregor's attorney, his time in Las Vegas was solely scheduled for fighting and there was no time for his deposition. They did offer McGregor for a deposition in his home in Dublin, Ireland.

It was a power move by McGregor's attorney since it is clear that they could compromise on availing their client for his deposition while in Las Vegas. Even after the fight, there was the possibility that he could stay to be deposed. But, the underlying purpose of providing a date of deposition that is out of the way for the plaintiff is to make it difficult for the plaintiff. Since McGregor is not a citizen of the state of Nevada, he has no obligation to be deposed in the state. However, it would seem as though it would be helpful to litigate the lawsuit if he were to do it while he was in Las Vegas. That is not the case. Instead, the plaintiff would have had to travel to Ireland to depose McGregor unless another arrangement could be made.

The federal magistrate denied both the plaintiff's motions on the grounds that it did not follow the rules of the court. Specifically, it did not include a legal analysis section.[5] This was an embarrassing mistake made by the plaintiff's counsel, as it was an elementary protocol. The court determined that since the motion did not have the proper form, it should be denied without assessing the merits—a harsh ruling, but a correct one. Thus, without an appeal, the plaintiff would be without the deposition of McGregor and pertinent documents that may relate to a damage claim.

While McGregor's attorney berated the plaintiff's attorney for not knowing the rules in federal court, it was McGregor's legal representatives who found themselves at the end of not following procedure. In response to a failure to respond to a deposition notice, the plaintiff filed a Motion for an Order Striking defendant, Conor McGregor's Answer.[6] The sanction is indicated in the rules and would seem an extreme one but a possibility. The plaintiff argued that McGregor willfully and in bad faith refused to attend his deposition. Notably, the plaintiff stated in its written motion that McGregor had his deposition scheduled for April 6, 2018. "However, McGregor did not appear for his deposition. Instead, on the night of April 5, 2018, he was throwing metal barriers and other objects at the UFC 223 [sic], at which he was not scheduled to appear."[7]

McGregor's attorneys previously indicated that he would not show up for his deposition. In most litigation, the parties attempt to make efforts to find a reasonably amicable time to schedule a deposition. If that is not the case, it is the responsibility of the plaintiff to ensure that the deposition is taken or that a motion to compel is filed to preserve the rights of the plaintiff. McGregor's attorney had offered his client to be deposed in Dublin after his October fight with the knowledge that it would be costly for the plaintiff's attorney to travel.

Instead, the plaintiff set the deposition for September 18, 2018, a couple of weeks prior to McGregor's fight on October 6, 2018. As expected, McGregor did not appear since this notice was unilaterally scheduled by the plaintiffs. Yet, with a looming discovery deadline, the plaintiff's attorney likely felt the need to schedule it. Or, it could have been a strategic opportunity with the knowledge that McGregor was deep in training. One might infer the latter considering the contentious battle between the sides stemming from Pegg's initial claim. Notwithstanding the veracity of the claims, with the possibility of a court striking McGregor's effort, which would pave the way for a default, the plaintiff sought to press the strategy.

The court denied the defendants' Motion for Protective Order, as the defendants failed to properly comply with the rules to indicate the reasons why the topic of the discovery was improper.[8] The denial is ironic in that McGregor's attorneys made fun of the plaintiff's counsel for its lack of knowledge in filing in federal court. Yet, in this instance, the court chided McGregor's attorneys due to their failure to provide the basic information on why they objected to certain discovery requests.[9] While the requests may seem outlandish and speak for themselves, that is not good enough and the attorney must be familiar with the rules. Without spending the additional cost to refile a protective order, McGregor decided to settle with Pegg and the court received a Notice of Settlement on October 29, 2018.[10]

Conor McGregor Throws a Dolly into a Bus

Conor McGregor's sparring partner and teammate Artem Lobov was scheduled to face Alex Caceres on April 7, 2018, at UFC 223 at the Barclay's Center in New York. During fight week, Lobov was involved in an altercation with Khabib Nurmagomedov at a hotel in Brooklyn, New York. Nurmagomedov, a rival of McGregor, got into a heated exchange with Lobov with the men almost coming to blows.

Two days later Conor McGregor appeared with several other members of his team in an attempt to confront Khabib. McGregor and a dozen or so of his teammates were given access to the UFC media day at the Barclay's Center. As a bus with Khabib and other UFC fighters on board was leaving, McGregor attempted to stop the bus. When it did not stop, Conor threw a hand truck into the window, causing glass to shatter and injure at least two fighters.

McGregor and a fellow teammate faced 12 criminal charges including assault and felony charges. McGregor turned himself into the New York City Police Department. Initially, he faced two felony charges for criminal mischief. The crime of criminal mischief relates to intentionally damaging or defacing others' property. The severity of the punishment is based on the amount of damages caused. Based on his hurling the object through the window of the bus, McGregor faced one felony charge for causing more than $1,500 in damage and a lower-level felony charge for causing more than $250 in damage. While the charge of causing more than $1,500 in damage carried a heavy-handed seven-year sentence, it would be an unlikely scenario considering the actions were his first criminal offense.

The one issue that may have been skirted was the immigration status of McGregor. During the time of the incident, the United States was undergoing a national debate on immigration and the enhanced crackdown by the Trump Administration. Certain kinds of criminal offenses have led to deportation under new immigration policies adopted by President Trump. Despite the criminal charges, in the end McGregor's immigration status was not affected.

A plea deal was brokered by the prosecutor and McGregor and his teammate Cian Cowley in July 2018 without much legal wrangling. He pleaded guilty to disorderly conduct and was handed community service. The district attorney dropped two felony counts of criminal mischief in exchange for pleading guilty to the misdemeanor.

McGregor had to pay damages for the bus attack, perform five days of community service and take anger management classes. His teammate, Cowley, received a similar sentence except he was given only three days of community service.

Dana White, who was initially furious with McGregor, later softened his stance and while one might think that such an act may deserve a fine or suspension by the UFC it did not happen.

In the end, McGregor's antics did not lead to a criminal conviction, jail time or even a criminal record, as his record was cleared as part of the plea deal. It did disrupt three fights on the UFC card as two fighters on the bus were unable to fight due to injuries from the glass. Also, Lobov's fight was cancelled as a disciplinary measure. In fact, the friction between Nurmogomedov and McGregor made their eventual fight in October 2018 the second-highest grossing attended event in the UFC and the biggest PPV in company history.

With only Lobov losing out on a payday, McGregor escaped criminal prosecution without having to serve jail time and was not suspended, fined or even banished from the UFC. Yet, the promotion needed McGregor. Of the nine PPVs that have topped over 1 million buys since Zuffa took over ownership, McGregor has headlined five of them. As its top draw, the UFC allowed McGregor to take a sabbatical from the UFC to pursue a boxing match, cause an altercation at a pre-fight press conference for which he was sued, and be arrested for criminal mischief for throwing a hand dolly through a bus. Despite McGregor's actions outside of the octagon, his drawing power led the UFC to grant him this much latitude in his actions.

Fighter Sues McGregor for Missing Fight After Bus Attack

Michael Chiesa, one of the fighters on the bus at which McGregor threw the dolly, sued McGregor as a result of damages sustained from the bus attack. Chiesa had to pull out of his fight with Anthony Pettis due to cuts he received when glass shattered in his face. Chiesa sued McGregor for assault, battery, negligent infliction of emotional distress and intentional infliction of emotional distress.[11]

In addition to McGregor, Chiesa sued the Barclay's Center for negligence, as the incident occurred at the venue. Chiesa's decision to sue Barclay's was expected to trigger insurance from the venue. Thus, there may be insurance that Chiesa may recoup.

The lawsuit was inevitable considering Chiesa's injury and cancelled fight. It was McGregor's actions which caused Chiesa's injury. Regardless of how severe the injury might be, it's undeniable that Chiesa had to withdraw from his fight because of it. Aside from the anticipated insurance proceeds, it was believed that Chiesa would argue that Barclay's neglected to have sufficient security to ensure someone would not commit such an attack.

In December 2018, McGregor's legal team filed a motion for summary judgment on the issues of negligence and negligent and intentional infliction of emotional distress.[12] While the two emotional distress claims may be viable based on

Chiesa's initial complaint, since McGregor alleges that there was no factual information on the fighter's alleged emotional injuries, he would need to amend his complaint to provide more of a detailed statement on how he suffered negligent and intentional infliction of emotional distress. On the negligence claim, McGregor's actions of picking up an object and throwing it at a bus would lead one to believe that he had breached a duty of care. Also, he would be liable for anyone he may have injured in the bus, regardless of whether he targeted Chiesa or not.

Chiesa amended his complaint which included additional facts related to his emotional distress claims, as well as a claim that McGregor should not benefit from his wrongdoing.[13] According to the amended complaint filed on December 20, 2018, Chiesa was to be offered the opening spot against headliner Khabib Nurmogomedov but for his injury sustained in the bus attack spurred by McGregor. Chiesa claimed that when Max Holloway was unable to fight, a UFC executive texted him about the possibility. It's presumed that the text was sent prior to knowledge that his injuries would keep him from fighting. The "Son of Sam" law in New York was made to prevent criminals from profiting from the publicity of their crimes.[14] The law was made after serial killer David Berkowitz, known as the "Son of Sam," gained fame in the mid–1970s for his crimes.

McGregor was charged with multiple crimes and, while he was acquitted of the charges, Chiesa claims that the law would apply since it relates to those charged with crimes. The UFC had used the footage of McGregor throwing the hand truck into the bus as marketing for his fight against Nurmogomedov for October 2018's UFC 231. The footage was used to show the bitter rivalry between the two fighters. McGregor also bragged about the incident and stated that he meant to do harm to Nurmogomedov when he traveled from Ireland to New York. At about the same time as the promotion of UFC 231, McGregor unveiled a new whiskey manufacturing company known as Proper No. 12. He promoted his new whiskey at the UFC 231 press conference and the brand name was sponsoring the event as it had a logo on the canvas. Chiesa claimed that McGregor "staged and engaged" in criminal acts to create publicity with the intent to profit from it.

In July 2019, the court heard McGregor's motion for a partial dismissal of certain claims in response to Chiesa's new amendments to his lawsuit. This lawsuit is interesting from the perspective that Chiesa has a viable claim for personal injuries which should be settled. However, his claim under the "Son of Sam" law creates an interesting wrinkle in the lawsuit. McGregor's attorneys will claim that he received a dismissal of all of his criminal charges and therefore the law does not apply. Chiesa's attorney will claim that it is the actual charging of the crime and McGregor's intent to profit from it that is important. Notably, UFC head Dana White said that the footage of McGregor throwing the hand truck at the bus was a part of the story leading up to the fight and was necessary. Inadvertently, White may have helped Chiesa's case.

Former Bellator Employee Sues Company

In one of the more salacious lawsuits of this compilation, a former Bellator employee sued Bellator for wrongful termination.[15] Zachery Light claimed that Bellator head Scott Coker and matchmaker Rich Chou attempted to influence Light not to press issues related to the falsification of forging medical information for fighters. Light also claimed that an MMA manager was hired by Bellator in an executive capacity, while managing fighters at the same time. This would be considered a conflict of interest and not legal per California state rules. In turn, Bellator sued Light, claiming that he was loaned money by the company but failed to pay it back

Light was terminated as a result of what he claimed was stress from the job. He was granted a leave from work but was fired upon return. Bellator filed a cross complaint against Light claiming conversion, theft and breach of a written contract which stemmed from a loan given to him by the company.[16]

Bellator claimed that Light requested a loan from the company and was given $9,403 and that it entered into a written agreement with Light that made him pay back the money on an agreed schedule. But, he never paid back the loan according to the company. Bellator also states in its cross-complaint that Light did not return "thousands of dollars in VIP ticket sales." Light denied the allegations in the Cross-Complaint.

The lawsuits were filed in Los Angeles Superior Court.

Light was hired by former Bellator president Bjorn Rebney as the promotion's Talent Development Manager. He was soon promoted to Talent Development Director and received praise for his work and "received the highest ranking on his annual reviews," according to Light.

In September 2015, Light claims he became aware of instances where Bellator "failed to observe and knowingly disobeyed laws enacted to protect the health and safety" of MMA fighters. He claims that certain medical forms were forged for fighters so they could participate in matches. He also stated that some fighters at an event in San Diego, California, submitted state-required medical forms from a physician by the name of Adam Rendon—but Rendon was not a licensed physician and submission of the medical forms would be in violation of California law.[17]

Allegedly, when Coker was informed about Light's questioning of the medical clearances, Coker asked him whether he wanted to keep his job.

Since he was in Talent Development, he was asked to arrange fights that were represented by a certain manager Coker did not like, and to put together fights which would ensure that those fighters would lose. According to the plaintiff, this was "tantamount to fight fixing."

Under the Sarbanes-Oxley Act whistleblower provisions, employees in privately held subsidiaries of publicly traded companies who assist in an investigation into an employer's violation are protected from employer retaliation.[18] Under the California Business and Professions Code, there is a similar provision claimed by Light.[19]

Light also indicates that in "late 2014 and early 2015," Mike Kogan was hired by Bellator in an executive capacity. Kogan, who Light alleges is a "close friend" of Coker, claims that Kogan was "paid management commissions for fighters he represented in bouts that occurred with defendant Bellator." This would be a "serious conflict of interest" and violation of California law.

The lawsuit states that due to stress related to Coker and Chou refusing to follow laws and regulations and "requiring plaintiff to engage in illegal practices as a condition of keeping his job," Light suffered an anxiety attack. The health scare occurred on April 10, 2015, after Bellator 136 on the campus of UC Irvine. He was taken to the emergency room and diagnosed with severe depression and anxiety. Light had to take an extended medical leave. He was cleared to return to work without restrictions on March 10, 2016, but was terminated on March 17, 2017, via a letter. He was advised that "his job was no longer available."

Similar to the lawsuits filed in the World Series of Fighting legal drama, this case had all the indications that it could possibly tear down Bellator. Light's claims were serious in nature since they indicated Bellator forged and falsified medical clearances for fighters, engaged in a form of fight fixing and intimidated employees from reporting problems. Such issues could deal a public relations blow to Bellator. Yet, Bellator defended itself from Light's lawsuit by bringing up counterclaims of its own.

Bellator claimed that Light stole $4,600 in cash and failed to repay a loan the company had provided him. The allegations painted Light in a poor light as someone that had financial problems. This was done to sink his credibility.

The change in management at the top of Bellator may have caused the dispute. In June 2014, Bjorn Rebney left the company and was replaced by Scott Coker as CEO. Light testified to seeing a change in management style after Rebney left, indicating a loose management style which included "a disregard for well established [sic] business protocols in the accounting for consignment tickets and income from events." The opinion of Light might be seen as an employee that does not like new management. It also may be the opinion of an individual who truly believes that new management has a disregard for the laws and regulations.

Whistleblower lawsuits like Light's are contentious by nature, since they deal with the severing of ties between parties. Here, Light claimed business practices which may harm the promotion. One had to think that the allegations of putting together matchups to ensure that one fighter had an advantage to win over another would be looked at as "fight fixing," assuming that it was the intent to place a fighter in a match where the skills of the opponent were superior to that of the fighter. The employee does not want to be a part of a business practice that might implicate him in the future since he was advised to do things on the company's behalf. What might be more damaging is the disregard for the commission with respect to the claim that Bellator falsified records to allow fighters to participate. As the regulating body, the commission serves as an independent third party that verifies the fights and ensures the health and safety of the fighters. A part of this is making sure that the fighters provide valid medical information. If the allegation that Bellator was falsifying records and submitting physician signatures from non-physicians was true, it could be disastrous for their reputation and relationship with the commission and other commissions across the nation.

From Bellator's perspective, it saw a disgruntled employee who did not pay back a loan that was now seeking his revenge. The allegations were serious since it addressed Bellator business practices as well as the validity of its fights. Bellator could not allow Light to make these allegations without answering. The counterclaims addressed Light's allegations as a former employer that could not handle his job and was not able to repay a loan.

Yet, Bellator indicated that it loaned Light money that he did not repay. For a Viacom-owned company, this seemed odd. Loaning money to an employee is a bad policy with bad implications. According to a document produced by Bellator, they loaned Light $6,974.57 and charged him interest on his repayments. The company then accused Light of stealing VIP tickets he was selling. They claimed that Light stole $4,600 worth of VIP tickets. The facts seem unconventional considering the amount of money Light was allowed to handle. Moreover, the loan and interest charged for it would also make the employer a creditor if the employee defaulted.

So, was Light's case an attempt to expose a wrong within an organization, or a disgruntled employee attempting to extricate himself from employment and having to repay a loan? We may never know since the case settled. This is one of the cases where it is hard to decipher which side was telling the truth.

15

Emerging Legal Issues

The sport of mixed martial arts continues to grow as it enters its second decade of mainstream awareness. While many believe it to be a sideshow and barbaric, the sport has gained traction with casual viewers, marketers and networks looking for content to fill its programming. With the evolution of the sport, there are future legal consequences to consider beyond the scope of contractual bickering or outside of sports torts from Conor McGregor. Here, we discuss the legal future of MMA.

Will Lawmakers Pass the Expansion to the Ali Act?

Introduced by a Republican congressman from Oklahoma, the expansion of the Ali Act is sure to face tension along party lines. While there are Republicans and Democrats supporting the bill, the issue of regulation in a political climate where the trend is the opposite may cause headwinds for the legislation. The drafters of the law did not do much (if anything) in altering the language in the original Muhammad Ali Act aside from the inclusion of the term mixed martial artists. Amendment to language may seem necessary, even required, if supporters of the bill hope to see the legislation get past Congress.

The issues of health and safety may find some traction as the constant concern in sports is head injuries. Certainly, MMA, which invites head blows to win a match, would be susceptible to potential lawsuits. Setting its own footprint, MMA could set federal regulations to address the concerns for head trauma in the sport. In New York, the legalization of MMA as a sport also came with a hefty price tag for promoters that had to provide additional insurance in the case of head trauma of an athlete at the event. The additional insurance affected boxing promoters, who did not pay the insurance prior to the legalization of MMA in the state.

A federal mandate may be too altruistic for supporters of health and safety of fighters. Rather, these types of issues may be up to the states to decide. But, with the various budgets for each state, laws on head trauma safety in combat sports seem low on the list of needs.

MMA as an Investment Opportunity

Taking a concept and seeking to monetize it, Alliance MMA tried to sell itself as the "feeder leagues" for the likes of ONE Championship, Bellator and the UFC. It became the first publicly traded mixed martial arts company trading on the NASDAQ when it made its debut in October 2016. The company's business strategy seemed to be one in which it would acquire regional promotions across the country, infrastructure (such as a ticketing platform) and a sports agency with a stable of young and hungry fighters and utilize these resources to cultivate fighters. The hope was to build a partnership with the UFC and Bellator and help fighters in their regional promotions move up to the big promotion.

But the dreams of changing the face of MMA business did not go as planned. Two investor lawsuits arose out of securities issues in reporting. The stock fell from its October 2016 opening of $4.65 to somewhere below 30 cents per share as of January 2019. The Chief Executive Officer resigned and the company president was terminated, which initiated a lawsuit which was subsequently resolved. The stock never fulfilled expectations and the company has not realized the business strategy it wanted to execute. While the UFC continues to be at the top of the sport, there are many alternative promotions regionally that have strong followings hoping to gain a foothold through the use of sponsorships, ticket revenue and streaming online. The major promotions keep an eye on the regional circuit for up and coming fighters and those veterans seeking to return to prior glory.

As we've seen with the multiple lawsuits in the World Series of Fighting chapter, the business of running an MMA promotion takes capital and a dedicated organization that has funding. The Professional Fighter's League received an infusion of money several months after it was purchased by some famous investors which included comedian Kevin Hart.

The Singapore–based ONE Championship (formerly ONE FC) MMA promotion has seen an infusion of cash from institutional investors. It has used this money to expand including signing notable former UFC fighters and negotiating a television deal for its product to be seen in the United States.

Is MMA a lucrative investment opportunity? The answer likely depends on who you ask, but the trajectory points up for its expansion.

Sports Betting and Mixed Martial Arts

The striking down of the Professional and Amateur Sports Protection Act of 1992 by the U.S. Supreme Court in May 2018 allowed individual states to determine whether it would allow sports betting. Still in its infancy stages in 2019, followers of sports betting believe that the number of states that allow betting will grow as many see the business as a form of boosting its revenue for their state budgets.

Mixed martial arts would be a likely target for sports betters. The UFC has published betting lines and even announced the lines during televised fights. The seamless inclusion of who is the favorite and who is the underdog into its television broadcasts infers that there is a population of fans betting on the fight. Embracing gambling is a 180 degree turn for sports and ensuring the integrity of the sport will be vital.

A UFC fighter from Korea was indicted by Korean prosecutors for alleged match fixing. The fighter, UFC lightweight Tae Hyun Bang, was accused of taking a bribe of almost $88,000 if he lost his bout in November 2015.[1] UFC officials monitored the betting lines and saw an unusual swing in betting lines which led them to Bang. Bang, a favorite in the fight, saw a last-minute swing in odds which made him a massive underdog. In a fight he was supposed to lose, Bang changed his mind about fixing the fight and won a split decision. It was determined that his opponent, Leo Kuntz, was not involved in any fight fixing. This was not the first time that the UFC monitored potential irregularities in betting lines to investigate potential fight fixing. In the same month, at UFC 193 in November 2015, there were concerns of corruption on the card due to "irregularities." While there was no actual fight or fighters on the card identified, the announcement put people on notice about an issue.

If sports gambling will be a part of the sports culture moving forward, sports will need to be more vigilant about the potential pitfalls of betting.

Fighters versus Promoters

The UFC antitrust is the biggest threat to the current state of mixed martial arts business. While the lawsuit could be dismissed by the federal court in Nevada, the possibility that it could survive dismissal and proceed to trial is a distinct reality. If the plaintiffs were to win a jury verdict, they may be entitled to treble damages per antitrust law. This would mean that the fighters could recoup three times the damages proven at trial.

Dependent on how the case proceeds and court rulings, either party that may lose may appeal the decision. If Zuffa were to lose a huge monetary verdict, one would expect an appeal. Similarly, if the plaintiffs have its case dismissed or lose at trial, there would be a possibility of appealing a ruling. This would tie up the case in the appeals court for years to come.

Assuming that there would be no appeal, there could be a scenario where the parties attempt to settle the case short of trial to avoid a jury verdict and potentially save legal costs and public perception.

Chapter Notes

Chapter 1

1. Complaint, *Jones v. Schneiderman*, 974 F. Supp. 2d 322 (S.D.N.Y. 2012)(No. 11 Civ. 8215 KMW).

2. *Id.* at ¶238.

3. *Id.* at ¶240.

4. *Id.* at ¶242.

5. Edwin Chemerinsky, "Constitutional Law: Principles and Policies" (1997), Aspen Law & Business.

6. *Id.*

7. *Id.*

8. N.Y. Unconsol. Law § 8905-a(2).

9. N.Y. Uncconsol. Law § 8905-a(3).

10. Supra at n. 1, ¶262.

11. *Id.* at ¶268.

12. Opinion & Order, *Jones, et al. v. Schneiderman, et al.*, United States District Court S.D.N.Y., 11 Civ. 8215 (KMW), August 16, 2012.

13. *Id.* at p. 12, FN 10.

14. *Id.*

15. *Id.* at p. 15, FN 13.

16. First Amended Complaint ("FAC"), *Jon Jones, et al. v. Eric T. Schneiderman*, Case No.: 11 Civ 8215 (KMW), September 24, 2012.

17. *Id.* ¶15.

18. *Id.* ¶62.

19. Joe Palazzolo, *Wall Street Journal*, November 15, 2011, "UFC Wants to Express Itself in New York," Quote from Barry Friedman, professor at New York University School of Law and one of the attorneys of record for the Plaintiffs.

20. *Id.*, see also FAC, supra 15.

21. *Id.* at p. 11, Johnson, 491 at U.S. at 404; see also Zalewska, 316 F.3d at 319.

22. *Id.*

23. *Id.* at 11.

24. FN 6.

25. *Jones v. Schneiderman*, 1:11-cv-08215-KMW-GWG, Opinion and Order at 7.

26. *Id.*

27. *Id.*, citing Lujan, 504 U.S. at 561.

28. *Id.*, citing *Fenstermaker v. Obama*, 354 F.App'x 452, 455 n.1 (2d Cir. 2009).

29. *Id.*

30. Specifically, "deliver...kicks, punches or blows to the body of an opponent or opponents, whether or not the event consists of a professional match or exhibition, and whether or not the event or any such act, or both, is done for compensation." N.Y. Alco. Bev. Cont. Law sec. 106(6-c)(a). See also paragraph 188 of Original Complaint at n. 1.

31. Plaintiff's Memorandum of Law in Support of Its Motion for Preliminary Injunction, *Zuffa, LLC v. Schneiderman, et al.*, U.S. District for S.D.N.Y., No. 15-cv-7624, September 29, 2015.

32. Notice of Appeal to the United States Court of Appeals for the Second Circuit, 11-cv-08215(KMW)(GWG), April 21, 2015.

33. Brief for Plaintiffs-Appellants, United States Court of Appeals for the Second Circuit, 11-cv-08215(KMW)(GWG), August 4, 2015.

34. *Id.*

35. Brief for Appellees, United States Court of Appeals for the Second Circuit, 11-cv-08215(KMW)(GWG), November 3, 2015.

36. *Id.* at p. 36.

37. *Id.* at p. 65.

38. *Zacchini v. Scripps-Howard Broadcasting Co.*, 433 U.S. 562 (1977).

39. Nathan Layne, Reuters, "U.S. judge rejects World Chess bid to block websites from airing moves," http://www.reuters.com/article/us-chess-world-lawsuit-idUSKBN13600V, November 10, 2016.

40. Dan Barry, *New York Times*, "Brain-Damaged Boxer to Receive $22 Million." B12, September 11, 2017.

Chapter 2

1. UFC Anti-Doping Policy Rules re Arbitration A.4 at https://www.usada.org/wp-content/uploads/UFC-anti-doping-policy-EN.pdf.
2. UFC Anti-Doping Policy Rules, Article 3.1 at https://www.usada.org/wp-content/uploads/UFC-anti-doping-policy-EN.pdf.
3. Arbitration Award Pursuant to the UFC Arbitration Rules, *Jon Jones vs. United States Anti-Doping Agency* ("USADA") dated November 6, 2016, p. 20, https://ufc.usada.org/wp-content/uploads/Award-6-November-2016.pdf.
4. *Id.*
5. *Id.* at p. 21.
6. *Id.* at p. 28.
7. In the Matter of an Arbitration Pursuant to The Ultimate Fighting Championship Anti-Doping Policy & The UFC Arbitration Rules re Francisco Rivera, dated January 19, 2018.
8. In the Matter of an Arbitration Pursuant to The Ultimate Fighting Championship Anti-Doping Policy & The UFC Arbitration Rules re Felipe Olivieri, dated January 21, 2017.
9. In the Matter of an Arbitration Pursuant to The Ultimate Fighting Championship Anti-Doping Policy & The UFC Arbitration Rules re Josh Barnett, dated March 23, 2018.
10. Steven Marrocco, MMAJunkie.com, "Josh Barnett Doesn't Trust USADA and Won't Settle, Expects Four-year Suspension," January 15, 2018, https://mmajunkie.com/2018/01/ufc-josh-barnett-usada-settlement-four-year-suspension.
11. In the Matter of an Arbitration Pursuant to The Ultimate Fighting Championship Anti-Doping Policy & The UFC Arbitration Rules re Jon Jones, dated September 13, 2018.
12. *Id.* at ¶ 7.14.
13. *Id.* at ¶ 7.20.
14. USADA Statement on Jon Jones Sample and UFC Anti-Doping Policy, December 23, 2018, https://twitter.com/usantidoping/status/1076987333688229895.

15. "Nick Diaz Accepts Sanction for Violation of UFC Anti-Doping Policy," April 9, 2018, https://ufc.usada.org/nick-diaz-accepts-whereabouts-sanction/.
16. *Id.*
17. Shaun Al-Shatti, "Cynthia Calvillo Receives Nine-month Suspension, fine from Nevada Athletic Commission for marijuana failure," MMAFighting.com, March 13, 2018, https://www.mmafighting.com/2018/3/13/17117368/cynthia-calvillo-receives-nine-month-suspension-fine-from-nevada-athletic-commission-for-marijuana.

Chapter 3

1. Complaint, *Good v. Gaspari Nutrition, Inc., et al.*, Supreme Court of the State of New York County of New York, October 19, 2017.
2. Order, In re Lyman Good Dietary Supplements Litigation, Supreme Court of the State of New York County of New York, Case No.: 17-CV-8047, October 15, 2018.
3. *Id.*
4. Memorandum of Law in Support of Motion to Dismiss Due to Spoliation of Evidence, In re Lyman Good Dietary Supplements Litigation, Supreme Court of the State of New York County of New York, Case No.: 17-CV-8047, December 14, 2018.
5. "UFC Athlete, Romero, Accepts Sanction for Anti-Doping Policy Violation," April 4, 2016, https://ufc.usada.org/yoel-romero-accepts-sanction/.
6. https://ufc.usada.org/carlos-digeo-ferreira-accepts-doping-sanction/.
7. Plaintiff's First Amended Petition, *Carlos Diego Ferreira Neves v. Zinpro Corporation, et al.*, In the District Court of Hidalgo County, Texas 139th Judicial District, Cause No. C-1998–18-C, July 12, 2018.
8. *Id.*
9. Complaint for Damages, *Josh Barnett v. Bikor, L.L.C., et al.*, Superior Court for the State of California for County of Los Angeles, Case No.: BC701422, April 9, 2018.

Chapter 4

1. https://www.nlrb.gov/what-we-do/conduct-elections.
2. Leslie Smith Charging Letter against Zuffa, LLC dated May 2, 2018.

3. https://twitter.com/lkmiddleb/status/1012809097199177729.

4. www.nlrb.org.

5. *Id.*

6. NLRB Dismissal Letter to (Leslie Smith's attorney) Lucas K. Middlebrook, Esquire, dated September 19, 2018.

7. *Id.*

8. *Id.*

9. Appeal Acknowledgment Letter dated October 4, 2018.

10. Declaration of Leslie Smith attached to Appeal Acknowledgment Letter dated October 4, 2018.

11. *Id.*

12. Pa. Interscholastic Athletic Ass'n, 2017 BL 238231, 365 NLRB No. 10, July 11, 2017.

13. In re Velox Express, Inc. Case Number 15-CA-184–6, September 12, 2016.

14. *FedEx Home Delivery v. NLRB* 563 F3d 492 (DC 2009).

15. Minnesota Timberwolves Basketball, LP, 365 NLRB No. 124 (2017).

16. Letter from United States National Labor Relations Board to Lucas K. Middlebrook, Esq. (attorney for Leslie Smith) dated November 27, 2018.

17. Simon Samano, "Dana White: Yair Rodriguez released by UFC after Refusing to fight Zabit Magomedsharipov," MMA-Junkie.com, May 11, 2018, https://mmajunkie.com/2018/05/dana-white-yair-rodriguez-released-ufc.

Chapter 5

1. Verified Complaint, *Bellator Sport Worldwide, LLC v. Quinton "Rampage" Jackson*, Superior Court of New Jersey Chancery Division: Burlington County, Docket No.: C-025–15, March 2, 2015.

2. *Id.*

3. *Id.*

4. Jason Cruz, "NJ court grants Bellator MMA's Injunction; Rampage Off of UFC 186," MMAPayout.com, April 7, 2015 http://mmapayout.com/2015/04/nj-court-grants-bellator-mmas-injunction-rampage-off-of-ufc-186/.

5. UFC Statement on Rampage Jackson, UFC.com, April 7, 2015.

6. Order, *Bellator Sport Worldwide, LLC v. Quinton "Rampage" Jackson*, Superior Court of New Jersey Appellate Division Docket No. F-001539–14, issued April 21, 2015.

7. Complaint and Jury Demand, *Bellator Sport Worldwide, LLC v. Eddie Alvarez, et al.*, U.S. District Court for the State of New Jersey, Case 2:13-cv-00063-JLL-MAH, filed January 3, 2013.

8. Verified Answer, Affirmative Defenses and Counterclaim, *Bellator Sport Worldwide, LLC v. Eddie Alvarez, et al.*, U.S. District Court for the State of New Jersey, Case 2:13-cv-00063-JLL-MAH, filed on January 15, 2013.

9. Order, *Bellator Sport Worldwide, LLC v. Eddie Alvarez, et al.*, U.S. District Court for the State of New Jersey, Case 2:13-cv-00063-JLL-MAH, signed by U.S. District Judge Jose L. Linares dated January 25, 2013.

Chapter 6

1. Complaint, *B.J. Penn v. Zuffa, LLC, et al.*, Clark County District Court, Nevada, July 8, 2004.

2. Plaintiff's Motion for Preliminary injunction, *B.J. Penn v. Zuffa, LLC, et al.*, Clark County District Court, Nevada, August 31, 2004.

3. *Id.* at p. 16.

4. Declaration of B.J. Penn in support of Motion for Preliminary Injunction attached to Plaintiff's Motion.

5. Zuffa's Opposition to Plaintiff's Motion for Preliminary Injunction, at p. 8*B.J. Penn v. Zuffa, LLC, et al.*, September 13, 2004.

6. *Id.*

7. Appellant's Opening Brief, p. 6, *Ken Shamrock, Inc. v. Zuffa, LLC, et al.*, In the Supreme Court of the State of Nevada, Case No. 55621, Filed November 5, 2010.

8. Complaint, *Ken Shamrock, Inc. v. Zuffa, LLC, et al.*, Eighth Judicial District Court Clark County, Case No.: A561085, April 15, 2008.

9. Appellant's Opening Brief, supra at n.7, p. 5, *Ken Shamrock, Inc. v. Zuffa, LLC, et al.*, In the Supreme Court of the State of Nevada, Case No. 55621.

10. Order of Affirmance, Ken Shamrock, Inc. v. Zuffa, LLC, et al., In the Supreme Court of the State of Nevada, Case No. 55621, November 18, 2011.

11. Complaint, *Zuffa, LLC v. Randy Couture*, Clark County District Court of Nevada, Case No.: A555208, January 14, 2008.

12. Letter from Zuffa to Randy Couture

dated October 11, 2007 attached to Zuffa's Motion for Preliminary Injunction.

13. Steven Marocco, MMA Junkie, "Randy Couture Spent $500,000 Fighting UFC in Court Expects Tough Road for Georges St-Pierre, https://mmajunkie.com/2016/10/randy-couture-spent-500k-fighting-ufc-in-court-expects-tough-road-for-georges-st-pierre, October 21, 2016.

Chapter 7

1. In the Matter of the Arbitration of Contract Dispute Between Ronda Rousey and Fight Tribe Management, LLC dba Fight Tribe Management, Darin Harvey, California State Athletic Commission Decision of the Arbitrator, March 28, 2014.

2. *Id.* at p. 5.

3. *Id.*

4. Petitioner Fight Tribe Management, LLC's Notice of Petition and Petition to Compel Arbitration and to Appoint an Arbitrator, and Application to Seal Briefing, *Fight Tribe Management, LLC v. Ronda Rousey, et al.*, Los Angeles Superior Court, Case No.: BS147674, March 7, 2014.

5. Daniel Herbertson, "Alistair Overeem Splits with Golden Glory, Possibly More to Follow," September 21, 2011, MMA Fighting, https://www.mmafighting.com/2011/09/21/alistair-overeem-splits-with-golden-glory-possibly-more-to-foll.

6. MMA Payout, "Overeem Cut from Strikeforce," July 29, 2011, http://mmapayout.com/2011/07/overeem-cut-from-strikeforce/.

7. Complaint for Breach of Contract, Etc., *Knock Out Investment, et al. v. Alistair Overeem, et al.*, Clark County District Court, Case No.: A-11-653894-C, p. 7–8.

8. Complaint, Alistair Overeem v. Knockout Investments, et al., Los Angeles Superior Court, Case No.: BC 473018, November 7, 2011.

9. *Id.* at p. 5.

10. Jason Cruz, "Overeem paid in full for UFC 141," MMAPayout.com, January 4, 2012, http://mmapayout.com/2012/01/overeem-paid-in-full-for-ufc-141/.

11. Michael David Smith, "Marloes Coenen Among 3 Golden Glory Fighters Released," MMA Fighting, August 3, 2011, https://www.mmafighting.com/2011/08/03/marloes-coenen-among-3-golden-glory-fighters-released.

12. Alex Williams, "Carry a Flag for Mixed Martial Arts," *New York Times*, September 22, 2010, https://www.nytimes.com/2010/09/23/fashion/23upclose.html.

Chapter 8

1. www.ftc.gov/enforcement/statutes/muhammed-ali-boxing-reform-act.

2. H.R.44—Muhammad Ali Expansion Act.

3. H.R. 1832 (106th)—Muhammad Ali Boxing Reform Act.

4. House Hearing on Mixed Martial Arts, December 8, 2016, https://www.c-span.org/video/?419534-1/hearing-focuses-mixed-martial-arts-industry.

5. Stephen Marrocco, "Randy Couture spent $500,000 fighting UFC in court, expects tough road for Georges St-Pierre," MMAJunkie.com, October, 21, 2016, https://mmajunkie.com/2016/10/randy-couture-spent-500k-fighting-ufc-in-court-expects-tough-road-for-georges-st-pierre.

6. Perspectives on Mixed Martial Arts, November 9, 2017, https://energy-commerce.house.gov/hearings/perspectives-mixed-martial-arts/.

7. U.S. House of Representatives—Energy and Commerce Subcommittee on Digital Commerce & Consumer Protection Hearing entitled "Perspectives on Mixed Martial Arts" Written Statement of Randy Couture, November 9, 2017.

8. Jason Cruz, "Algieri situation presents problem with Ali Act," MMAPayout.com, April 14, 2016, http://mmapayout.com/2016/04/algieri-situation-presents-problem-with-ali-act/.

9. U.S. House of Representatives—Energy and Commerce Subcommittee on Commerce, Manufacturing & Trade Hearing: "Perspectives on Mixed Martial Arts" November 9, 2017, Statement of Tracey Lesetar-Smith, Esq. on behalf of Bellator MMA.

10. *Id.*

11. U.S. House of Representatives—Energy and Commerce Subcommittee on Commerce, Manufacturing & Trade Hearing: "Perspectives on Mixed Martial Arts" November 9, 2017, Letter from Jon Fitch, Professional MMA Fighter.

12. *Id.*

13. Jason Cruz, "Is the Muhammad Ali Act helping protect fighters?" *The White*

Bronco, May 2, 2016, http://thewhitebronco.com/2016/05/is-the-muhammad-ali-act-helping-protect-fighters/.

Chapter 9

1. Per USADA Athlete Test History database, accessed September 7, 2018 at https://www.usada.org/testing/results/athlete-test-history/.

2. UFC Anti-Doping Policy, https://ufc.usada.org/wp-content/uploads/UFC-anti-doping-policy-EN.pdf.

3. "Reporter says he was removed from UFC 199, 'banned for life' after reporting Brock Lesnar story," ESPN.com, June 5, 2016, http://www.espn.com/mma/story/_/id/15978217/reporter-says-was-removed-ufc-199-banned-life-reporting-brock-lesnar-story.

4. UFC Anti-Doping Policy, Article 10.9, https://ufc.usada.org/wp-content/uploads/UFC-anti-doping-policy-EN.pdf.

5. UFC Press Release, "UFC Athlete, Brock Lesnar, Receives Sanction for Anti-Doping Policy Violation," January 4, 2017, https://ufc.usada.org/brock-lesnar-receives-doping-sanction/.

6. Mike Coppinger, "Brock Lesnar to retire from UFC," February 14, 2017, *USA Today,* https://www.usatoday.com/story/sports/ufc/2017/02/14/brock-lesnar-retiring-from-ufc/97922872/.

7. Marissa Payne, "WWE Won't Punish Brock Lesnar for his Failed UFC Drug Tests Because he Works Part-time," *Washington Post,* July 27, 2016, https://www.washingtonpost.com/news/early-lead/wp/2016/07/27/wwe-wont-punish-brock-lesnar-for-his-failed-ufc-drug-tests-because-he-works-part-time/?utm_term=.a7730de8ed2e.

8. Plaintiff Mark Hunt's Complaint, et al., *Mark Hunt v. Zuffa, LLC d/b/a Ultimate Fighting Championship, Brock Lesnar and Dana White,* Case 2:17-cv-00085, January 10, 2017.

9. Mark Hunt, "If I die fighting, that's fine," PlayersVoice.com, July 4, 2017, https://www.playersvoice.com.au/mark-hunt-if-i-die-fighting-thats-fine/#ZStRid030yzJccM8.97.

10. Plaintiff Mark Hunt's First Amended Complaint ("Hunt FAC"), In the United States District Court for the District of Nevada, Case 2:17-cv-00085-JAD-CWH, June 1, 2017, at n. 2, p. 1, ¶17, p 42, ¶210–212.

11. *Id.* at 43, ¶212.

12. "In Depth: The Bertuzzi Incident: A Blow-by-Blow Account," CBC Sports, March 11, 2004, http://www.cbc.ca/sports/indepth/bertuzzi/timeline/.

13. "A Star Player goes Offside," CBC Sports Online, February 15, 2005, http://www.cbc.ca/sports/indepth/bertuzzi/.

14. *Id.*

15. "Bertuzzi receives conditional charge, probation," CBC Sports, December 24, 2004, http://www.cbc.ca/sports/hockey/bertuzzi-receives-conditional-discharge-probation-1.477217.

16. Statement of Claim, *Moore v. Bertuzzi* (Ont. Super. Ct. Feb. 14, 2006), see also, 61 Me. L. Rev. 205. Rewriting hockey's unwritten rules: MOORE V. BERTUZZI.

17. Jeff Z. Klein, "Bertuzzi Lawsuit Settled," *New York Times,* September 5, 2014, p. B12.

18. "Williams sought millions but pleased with verdict," Associated Press, March 23, 2005, https://www.playersvoice.com.au/mark-hunt-if-i-die-fighting-thats-fine/#ZStRid030yzJccM8.97.

19. *Avila v. Citrus Community College District,* 38 Cal. 4th 148 (2006).

20. John T. Wolohan, "Injured Ballplayer Strikes Out Before the Supreme Court of California," www.athleticbusiness.com, July 2006, https://www.athleticbusiness.com/injured-ballplayer-strikes-out-before-the-supreme-court-of-california.html.

21. *Id.*

22. Avila, supra at 153.

23. Supra at 163–4.

24. *Id.* at 165.

25. *Id.* at 169.

26. *Id.* at 171.

27. *Id.* at 173.

28. Avila, supra citing *Cheong v. Antablin,* 16 Cal.4th 1063, 1075 (1997).

29. *Id.* at 173.

30. *Knight v. Jewett,* 3 Cal 4th 296 (1992).

31. *Id.* at 320.

32. Andreas Hale, "Brock Lesnar's attorney blames foot cream, eye medication for failed UFC 200 drug test," Yahoo! Sports, October 14, 2016, https://sports.yahoo.com/news/brock-lesnars-attorney-blames-foot-cream-eye-medication-for-failed-ufc-200-drug-test-235712317.html.

33. Coral Barry, "Jon Jones refutes claims he used estrogen blockers to mask steroid use," *Metro UK,* July 19, 2016, http://metro.co.uk/2016/07/19/jon-jones-refutes-claims-

he-used-estrogen-blockers-to-mask-steroid-use-6017056/.

34. Avila, supra at n.19.

35. *Id.*

36. Order, February 14, 2019

37. Order, id at FN2

38. Order at p. 5

39. Mendoza v. Zirkle Fruit, Co., 301 F.3d 1163 (2002)

40. Knevelbaard Dairies v. Kraft Foods, Inc. 232 F.3d 979 (9th Cir. 2000)

41. Canyon County v. Syngenta Seeds, 519 F.3d 969 (9th Ci. 2008)

42. Order, Id p. 9

43. Email from Jim Guernsey to Bob Bennett dated May 26, 2014, attached as Exhibit A to the Nevada Athletic Commission Findings of Fact, Conclusions of Law, and Order In the Matter of Wanderlei Silva, dated November 24, 2014.

44. Nevada Athletic Commission, In the Matter of Wanderlei Silva, Findings of Fact, Conclusions of Law and Order, dated September 23, 2014.

45. Petitioner's Memorandum of Points and Authorities, *Wanderlei Silva v. Bob Bennett*, Nevada State Athletic Commission, District Court of Clark County, Nevada, filed January 16, 2015.

46. *Zuffa, LLC d/b/a Ultimate Fighting Championship v. Wanderlei Silva*, Clark County District Court, Case No. A-15–722258-C, filed July 28, 2015.

47. Motion to Dismiss Plaintiff's Complaint Under NRCP 12(b)(5) and Special Motion to Dismiss Under Nevada's Anti-Slapp Statutes, *Zuffa, LLC d/b/a Ultimate Fighting Championship v. Wanderlei Silva*, Clark County District Court, Case No. A-15–722258-C, October 2, 2015.

48. *Id.*

49. NRS 41.660, et seq.

50. Jacobs v. Adelson, 130 Nev. Adv. Op. 44.

51. Petitioner's Memorandum of Points and Authorities, *Wanderlei Silva v. Bob Bennett*; Nevada State Athletic Commission, District Court Clark County, Nevada, Case No. A-14–71–453-J, dated January 16, 1975.

52. Order re: Petition for Judicial Review, *Wanderlei Silva vs. Bob Bennett*; Nevada State Athletic Commission, District Court Clark County, Nevada, Case No. A-14–710453-J, dated January 15, 2015.

53. *Id.*

54. Notice of Appeal, *Wanderlei Silva vs.* *Bob Bennett*; Nevada State Athletic Commission, In the Supreme Court of the State of Nevada, No. 685058, dated August 20, 2015.

55. Appellant's Opening Brief, *Wanderlei Silva v. Bob Bennett*, Nevada State Athletic Commission, In the Supreme Court of the State of Nevada, Case No. 68058, dated September 11, 2015.

56. Shaun Al-Shatti, "Georges St-Pierre's lawyer calls UFC contract 'something out of the 1940s,' cautions UFC 'won't get away with it forever,'" MMAFighting.com, jasndd October 19, 2016, https://www.mmafighting.com/2016/10/19/13333778/georges-st-pierres-lawyer-calls-ufc-contract-something-out-of-the.

57. *Id.*

58. *Id.*

59. *Id.*

Chapter 10

1. *Monsanto Co. v. Spray-Rite Service Corp.*, 465 U.S. 752, 764 (1984).

2. *NCAA v. Board of Regents of Univ. of Oklahoma*, 468 U.S. 85, 109 (1984).

3. The United States Department of Justice web site, https://www.justice.gov/atr/competition-and-monopoly-single-firm-conduct-under-section-2-sherman-act-chapter-1.

4. https://www.justice.gov/atr/competition-and-monopoly-single-firm-conduct-under-section-2-sherman-act-chapter-1.

5. Defendant Zuffa, LLC's Consolidated Notice of Motion and Motion to Dismiss Plaintiffs' Complaints, p. 19, *Le, et al. v. Zuffa, LLC*, Case No.: 5:14-cv-05484 EJD, United States District Court of California—San Jose Division, February 27, 2015.

6. Order, *Le, et al. vs. Zuffa, LLC*, United States District Court of Nevada, October 19, 2016.

7. Non-Party Bellator Sport Worldwide, LLC's Notice of Motion and Motion to Quash or Modify Subpoenas, In re Subpoena of Bellator Sport Worldwide, LLC, U.S. District Court for the Central District of California, Case No.: 2:17-mc-0016, February 22, 2017.

8. *Id.*

9. Order on Bellator's Motion to Quash or Modify Subpoenas and Plaintiff's Motion to Compel Documents Responsive to Plaintiffs' Subpoena, Case No.: 2:15-cv-010405-RFB-PAL, June 13, 2017.

10. Nonparties Matt Hume and Group One Holdings PTE Ltd. Opposition to Motion to Compel, U.S. District Court of Washington, Case No. 2:17-mc-0074 RSL, August 4, 2017.

11. Plaintiffs' Motion to Compel Deposition and Production of Documents by Third Party Matt Hume and Motion for Sanctions, In re Subpoena of Matt Hume, U.S. District Court of Western Washington, Case No. 2:17-mc-0074 RSL, July 19, 2017.

12. Expert Report of Andrew Zimbalist in *Cung Le, et al. v. Zuffa, LLC*, Filed February 16, 2018.

13. Expert report of Hal Singer, Ph.D. in *Cung Le, et al.v. Zuffa, LLC*, Filed February 16, 2018.

14. Roger Blair ("Blair report"), expert report, February 16, 2018.

15. Blair report, p. 33.

16. Blair report, p. 32, ¶62.

17. Plaintiffs' Motion for Class Certification, p. 26, *Le, et al. v. Zuffa, LLC*, Case No.: 2:15-cv-01045-RFB-PAL, United States District Court for the District of Nevada, February 16, 2018.

18. *Id.* at p. 30–31.

19. *Id.* at p. 31.

20. Zuffa, LLC's Opposition to Plaintiffs' Motion for Class Certification, *Le, et al. v. Zuffa, LLC*, Case No.: 2:15-cv-01045-RFB-PAL, United States District Court for the District of Nevada, April 6, 2018.

21. *Id.*

22. Defendant Zuffa, LLC's Motion for Summary Judgment, at p. 16, *Le, et al. v. Zuffa, LLC*, Case No.: 2:15-cv-01045-RFB-PAL, United States District Court for the District of Nevada, July 30, 2018.

23. See *Golden Boy Promotions, LLC, et al. v. Alan Haymon, et al.*, Case No.: CV15-3378-JFW, January 26, 2017.

24. *Id.* at p. 16.

25. Plaintiffs' Opposition to Zuffa's Motion for Summary Judgment, *Le, et al. v. Zuffa, LLC, et al.*, Case No.: 2:15-cv-01045-RFB-PAL, United States District Court for the District of Nevada, September 21, 2018.

26. *Id.* at p. 24–25.

27. *Id.* at p. 30.

28. Deposition of Dana White, Volume 3 of 3 taking on August 10, 2017, p. 556, lines 20–24.

29. Deposition of Dana White, Volume 2, taken on August 9, 2017.

30. Plaintiffs' Opposition to Defendant Zuffa, LLC's Motion to Seal Plaintiffs' Opposition to Zuffa, LLC's Motion for Summary Judgment and Related Materials, *Le, et al. v. Zuffa, LLC*, Case No.: 2:15-cv-01045-RFB(PAL), August 13, 2013.

31. Plaintiffs' Opposition to Defendant Zuffa LLC's Motion to Seal Zuffa LLC's Motion for Summary Judgment and Related Materials, p. 6, *Le, et al. v. Zuffa, LLC*, Case No.: 2:15-cv-01045-RFB(PAL), United States District Court of Nevada, August 13, 2018.

32. *Id.* at 15.

33. Order re Sanctions, *Nevro Crop v. Boston Scientific Corporation, et al.*, Case No.: 16-cv-06830-VC, United States District Court of the Northern District of California, May 8, 2018.

34. Memorandum and Order, p. 4, *CAA Sports, LLC v. Ben Dogra*, Case No.: 4:18-cv-01887-SNLJ United States District Court Eastern District of Missouri, Eastern Division, December 20, 2018.

35. *Id.*

Chapter 11

1. Complaint, *MMAWC, LLC v. Shawn Wright, et al.*, Clark County District Court of Nevada. Case No.: A-15–724474-B, September 11, 2015.

2. *Id.* at p. 3.

3. Answer; Counterclaim; and Third-Party Complaint, *MMAWC, LLC v. Shawn Wright, et al.*, Clark County District Court of Nevada, October 6, 2015.

4. *Id.* at p. 8–9.

5. Complaint and Demand for Jury Trial, United States District Court of Nevada, *WSOF Asia v. MMAWC, LLC, et al.* Case No.: 2:15-cv-02065, October 26, 2015.

6. First Amended Complaint, United States District Court of Nevada, *MMAWC, LLC d/b/a World Series of Fighting vs. Shawn Wright, Vince Hesser, et. al.* Case No.: 2:15-cv-02065, October 29, 2015.

7. *Id.*

8. *Id.*

9. The lawsuit also included other violations of the Lanham Act and several other claims including Breach of Contract on the part of the defendants.

10. Dave Sheinin, "D.C. Group Led by Russ Ramsey set to Launch New Mixed Martial Arts League," *The Washington Post*, www.washingtonpost.com, April 19, 2017, https://www.washingtonpost.com/sports/boxing/

dc-group-led-by-russ-ramsey-set-to-launch-new-mixed-martial-arts-league/2017/04/18/68e01bda-2481–11e7-b503–9d616bd5a305_story.html?utm_term=.afa38996be29.

11. Complaint, *Zion Wood Obi Wan Trust, et al. v. MMAWC, LLC d/b/a World Series of Fighting, et al.*, District Court of Clark County, Nevada, Case No.: A-17–764118-C, November 3, 2017.

12. *Id.* at p. 6.

Chapter 12

1. Hearing on "Piracy of Live Sports Broadcasting Over the Internet" Before the United States House of Representatives Committee on the Judiciary Statement of Lorenzo J. Fertitta Chairman and Chief Executive Officer Zuffa, LLC / Ultimate Fighting Championship December 16, 2009, http://judiciary.house.gov/_files/hearings/pdf/Fertitta091216.pdf.

2. *Id.*

3. *Id.*

4. U.S. Copyright Act.

5. 17. U.S.C. sec 512(c)(3).

6. 17 U.S.C. 512(c)(1).

7. See *Harper & Row, Publishers, Inc., et al. v. Nation Enterprises, et al.* 471 U.S. 539 (1985).

8. *Campbell v. Acuff-Rose Music, Inc.*, 510 U.S. 569 (1994).

9. Opinion and Order, *David Adjmi v. DLT Entertainment, Ltd.*, 14-Civ. 568, United States District Court S.D.N.Y., March 31, 2015.

10. *Lenz v. Universal Music Corp.*, 801 F.3d 1126 (2015).

11. Mike Masnick, "UFC Makes the Awful Decision to Sue Some of Its Biggest Fans," Techdirt.com, March 22, 2012, https://www.techdirt.com/articles/20120320/10225718173/ufc-makes-awful-decision-to-sue-some-its-biggest-fans.shtml.

12. Jeremy Botter, "UFC Attorney Says Fans Who Stream UFC PPVs Are Not Actually Fans at All." Bleacher Report, March 15, 2012, https://bleacherreport.com/articles/1106577-ufc-attorney-says-fans-who-stream-ufc-ppvs-are-not-actually-fans-at-all.

13. http://www.ufc.com/news/zuffa-sues-justin-tv-copyright-infringement.

14. Complaint, *Zuffa, LLC v. Justin.tv*, United States District Court, District of Nevada, Case 2:11-cv-00114-RLH-VCF, January 21, 2011.

15. *Id.* at p. 13.

16. Motion to Dismiss Amended Complaint, *Zuffa, LLC v. Justin.tv, Inc.*, Case No. 2:11-cv09914-RLH-LRL, September 16, 2011.

17. Order, *Zuffa, LLC v. Justin.tv, Inc.*, Case No. 2:11-cv09914-RLH-LRL, March 8, 2012.

18. *Id.*

19. Brent Brookhouse, "UFC's DMCA copyright claim on St. Pierre vs. Diaz 'decimal controversy' video is questionable at best," BloodyElbow.com, March 28, 2013, https://www.bloodyelbow.com/2013/3/28/4156460/ufc-dcma-copyright-georges-st-pierre-gsp-nick-diaz-decimal-weigh-in.

20. See *Le v. Zuffa*, United States District Court of Nevada, Case No.: 2–15:-cv-01045-RFB-PAL.

21. https://support.google.com/youtube/answer/2807684.

22. Mike Masnick, "NASCAR Abuses DMCA To Try To Delete Fan Videos of Daytona Crash," Techdirt.com, February 25, 2013, https://www.techdirt.com/articles/20130224/22411222089/nascar-abuses-dmca-to-try-to-delete-fan-videos-daytona-crash.shtml.

23. Al Tompkins, "Daytona Crash Video Tests Fair Use, Copyright for Fans and Journalists," Poynter.org, February 24, 2013, https://www.poynter.org/news/daytona-crash-video-tests-fair-use-copyright-fans-and-journalists.

24. *National Basketball Association v. Motorola, Inc.*, 105 F.3d 841 (2nd Cir. 1997).

25. Ben Fowlkes and Danny Downes, "Why is the UFC going after its own fans on social media—again?" MMAJunkie.com, September 2, 2018, https://mmajunkie.com/2018/09/why-ufc-attacks-fans-for-copyright-social-media.

26. https://twitter.com/AmericanTop Team/status/1075034197155373057.

27. *Philip D. Murphy, Governor of New Jersey, et al. v. National Collegiate Athletic Association, et al.* 584 U.S. __ (2018).

Chapter 13

1. Complaint, *International Fight League v. Zuffa, LLC, et al.*, United States District Court S.D.N.Y., Civil Action 06 CV 0880, February 3, 2006. Notably, the UFC filed a lawsuit in Nevada one day earlier.

2. *Id.* at p. 14.

3. Complaint, *Zuffa, LLC v. International*

Fight League, Inc., et al., District Court of Clark County, Nevada, Case No.: A516841, February 2, 2006.

4. *Id.*

5. Reporter's Transcript of Proceedings, *Zuffa, LLC v. International Fight League, Inc., et al.,* Clark County District Court, Case No.: A516841.

6. *Id.* at p. 13.

7. Complaint, *Nobuyuki Sakakibara, et al. v. Pride FC Worldwide Holdings, LLC, et al.* Case 2:08-cv-00418-HDM-RJJ, April 2, 2008.

8. *Id.* at p. 9.

9. *Id.* at p. 11.

10. Spectrum Gaming Group, LLC, DSE Investigation Overview, Undated.

11. Plaintiff's Original Petition for Declaratory Judgment, *HDNet MMA 2008, LLC v. Zuffa, LLC,* In the District Court of Dallas Texas, February 13, 2008.

12. *Id.* at p. 2.

13. *Id.* at p. 3–4.

14. *Id.* at p. 4.

15. Plaintiff's Motion for Preliminary Injunction, *Zuffa, LLC v. Couture, et al.,* District Court of Clark County, Nevada, Case No.: A555208, February 1, 2008.

16. Opposition to Motion for Preliminary Injunction, Zuffa, LLC v. Couture, et al., District Court of Clark County, Nevada, Case No.: A555208, February 19, 2008.

17. Order Granting Preliminary Injunction, *Zuffa, LLC v. Couture, et al.,* District Court of Clark County, Nevada, Case No.: A555208, February 29, 2008.

Chapter 14

1. First Amended Complaint, *William Pegg vs. Connor McGregor, et al.,* District Court of Clark County, Nevada, Case No. A-17-753121-C, April 26, 2018.

2. Offer of Judgment, *William Pegg v. Conor McGregor, et al.* District Court of Clark County, Nevada, Case No. A-17-753121-C, dated April 10, 2018.

3. Notice of Removal by Defendant, *William Pegg v. Conor McGregor, et al.* District Court of Clark County, Nevada, Case No. A-17-753121-C, dated April 26, 2018.

4. Order, *William Pegg v. Conor McGregor, et al.* District Court of Clark County, Nevada, Case No. A-17-753121-C, dated August 22, 2018.

5. Supra at p. 2.

6. Motion for an Order Striking Defendant, Conor McGregor's Answer, *Pegg v. McGregor, et al.,* United States District Court for Nevada, Southern Division, October 19, 2018.

7. *Id.* at p. 8.

8. Order, *Pegg v. McGregor, et al.* United States District Court of Nevada, Case No.: 2:18-cv-000763-RFB-NJK, October 22, 2018.

9. *Id.* at p. 2.

10. Order, *Pegg v. McGregor, et al.,* United States District Court of Nevada, Case No. 2:18-cv-000763-RFB-NJK, Dkt. 43, dated October 29, 2018.

11. Verified Complaint, *Michael Chiesa v. Conor McGregor, et al.,* Supreme Court of the State of New York, County of Kings, Index No. 518314/2018, September 10, 2018.

12. Defendant Conor McGregor, et al. Memorandum of Law in Support of Their Motion to Dismiss., Michael Chiesa v. Conor McGregor, et al., Supreme Court of the State of New York, County of Kings, Index No. 518314–2018E, November 30, 2018.

13. Amended Verified Complaint, *Michael Chiesa vs. Conor McGregor, et al.,* Index No.: 518314–2018E, December 20, 2018.

14. New York State Executive Law §632-a.

15. Complaint for Wrongful Termination Based on Public Policy ("Light Complaint"), *Zachery Light v. Bellator Worldwide Sport,* BC 621583, Filed May 24, 2016.

16. Cross-Complaint of Bellator Sport Worldwide, LLC, Light Complaint filed in California Los Angeles Superior Court on July 12, 2016.

17. Light Complaint, supra at n. 15.

18. 18 U.S.C. sec 151(e) and 1514A(a).

19. California Business and Professional Code sec 17500.

Chapter 15

1. Korean MMA fighter indicted for taking bribes in match-fixing scam, August 14, 2017, The Korea Herald http://www.korea herald.com/view.php?ud=20170814000556.

Bibliography

Author's note: Due to the specificity and often technical nature of the sources used within the text, the bibliography is organized by chapter.

Chapter 1

References

Chemerinsky, Erwin. "Constitutional Law: Principles and Policies" (1997) Aspen Law & Business.
N.Y. Uncsol. Law §8905-a(2)-(3).

Cases and Court Filings

Jones v. Schneiderman, 974 F.Supp. 2d 322 (No. 11 Civ. 8215 KMW)(S.D.N.Y. 2012).
Zuffa, LLC v. Schneiderman, No. 15-CV-7624 (KMS), 2016 WL 311298 (S.D.N.Y. Jan. 26, 2016).

Chapter 2

References

Arbitration Award Pursuant to the UFC Arbitration Rules, *Jon Jones vs. United States Anti-Doping Agency* ("USADA") dated November 6, 2016.
In the Matter of an Arbitration Pursuant to The Ultimate Fighting Championship Anti-Doping Policy & The UFC Arbitration Rules re Felipe Olivieri, dated January 21, 2017.
In the Matter of an Arbitration Pursuant to The Ultimate Fighting Championship Anti-Doping Policy & The UFC Arbitration Rules re Francisco Rivera, dated January 19, 2018.
In the Matter of an Arbitration Pursuant to The Ultimate Fighting Championship Anti-Doping Policy & The UFC Arbitration Rules re Josh Barnett, dated March 23, 2018.
In the Matter of an Arbitration Pursuant to The Ultimate Fighting Championship Anti-Doping Policy & The UFC Arbitration Rules re Jon Jones, dated September 13, 2018.
Marrocco, Steven. MMAJunkie.com "Josh Barnett doesn't trust USADA and won't settle, expects four-year suspension." January 15, 2018, https://mmajunkie.com/2018/01/ufc-josh-barnett-usada-settlement-four-year-suspension.
"Nick Diaz Accepts Sanction for Violation of UFC Anti-Doping Policy." April 9, 2018, https://ufc.usada.org/nick-diaz-accepts-whereabouts-sanction/.

Al-Shatti, Shaun. "Cynthia Calvillo receives nine-month suspension, fine from Nevada Athletic Commission for marijuana failure." MMAFighting.com, March 13, 2018. https://www.mmafighting.com/2018/3/13/17117368/cynthia-calvillo-receives-nine-month-suspension-fine-from-nevada-athletic-commission-for-marijuana (last visited January 23, 2019).
UFC Anti-Doping Policy Rules re Arbitration at https://www.usada.org/wp-content/uploads/UFC-anti-doping-policy-EN.pdf (last visited January 23, 2019).

Chapter 3

References

"UFC Athlete, Carlos Diego Ferreira Accepts Doping Sanction." December 21, 2016, https://ufc.usada.org/carlos-digeo-ferreira-accepts-doping-sanction/.
"UFC Athlete, Romero, Accepts Sanction for Anti-Doping Policy Violation." April 4, 2016, https://ufc.usada.org/yoel-romero-accepts-sanction/.

Cases and Court Filings

Complaint for Damages, *Josh Barnett v. Bikor, L.L.C., et al.* Superior Court for the State of California for County of Los Angeles, Case No.: BC701422, April 9, 2018.
Complaint, *Good v. Gaspari Nutrition, Inc., et al.* Supreme Court of the State of New York County of New York, October 19, 2017.
Memorandum of Law in Support of Motion to Dismiss Due to Spoliation of Evidence, In re Lyman Good Dietary Supplements Litigation, Supreme Court of the State of New York County of New York, Case No.: 17-CV-8047, December 14, 2018.
Order, In re Lyman Good Dietary Supplements Litigation, Supreme Court of the State of New York County of New York, Case No.: 17-CV-8047, October 15, 2018.
Plaintiff's First Amended Petition, *Carlos Diego Ferreira Neves v. Zinpro Corporation, et al.* In the District Court of Hidalgo County, Texas 139th Judicial District, Cause No. C-1998–18-C, July 12, 2018.

Chapter 4

References

Appeal Acknowledgment Letter dated October 4, 2018 from Lucas K. Middlebrook to NLRB.
Declaration of Leslie Smith attached to Appeal Acknowledgment Letter dated October 4, 2018.
Leslie Smith Charging Letter Against Zuffa, LLC dated May 2, 2018.
Letter from United States National Labor Relations Board to Lucas K. Middlebrook, Esq. (attorney for Leslie Smith) dated November 27, 2018.
Middlebrooks, Lucas. Twitter.com. https://twitter.com/lkmiddleb/status/1012809097199177729.
NLRB Dismissal Letter to (Leslie Smith's attorney) Lucas K. Middlebrook, Esquire dated September 19, 2018.
NLRB web site. https://www.nlrb.gov/what-we-do/conduct-elections.
Samano, Simon. "Dana White: Yair Rodriguez released by UFC after refusing to fight Zabit Magomedsharipov." MMAJunkie.com. May 11, 2018, https://mmajunkie.com/2018/05/dana-white-yair-rodriguez-released-ufc.

Cases

FedEx Home Delivery v. NLRB 563 F3d 492 (DC 2009).
In re Velox Express, Inc. Case Number 15-CA-184—6, September 12, 2016.

Minnesota Timberwolves Basketball, LP, 365 NLRB No. 124 (2017).
Pa. Interscholastic Athletic Ass'n, 2017 BL 238231, 365 NLRB No. 10, July 11, 2017.

Chapter 5

References

Cruz, Jason. "NJ Court Grants Bellator MMA's Injunction; Rampage Off of UFC 186." MMA-Payout.com, April 7, 2015. http://mmapayout.com/2015/04/nj-court-grants-bellator-mmas-injunction-rampage-off-of-ufc-186/ (last visited January 28, 2019).
UFC Statement on Rampage Jackson, UFC.com, April 7, 2015.

Cases and Court Filings

Complaint and Jury Demand, *Bellator Sport Worldwide, LLC v. Eddie Alvarez, et al.* U.S. District Court for the State of New Jersey, Case 2:13-cv-00063-JLL-MAH, filed January 3, 2013.
Order, *Bellator Sport Worldwide, LLC v. Quinton "Rampage" Jackson.* Superior Court of New Jersey Appellate Division Docket No. F-001539–14, issued April 21, 2015.
Order, *Bellator Sport Worldwide, LLC v. Eddie Alvarez, et al.* U.S. District Court for the State of New Jersey, Case 2:13-cv-00063-JLL-MAH, signed by U.S. District Judge Jose L. Linares dated January 25, 2013.
Verified Answer, Affirmative Defenses and Counterclaim, *Bellator Sport Worldwide, LLC v. Eddie Alvarez, et al.* U.S. District Court for the State of New Jersey, Case 2:13-cv-00063-JLL-MAH, filed on January 15, 2013.
Verified Complaint, *Bellator Sport Worldwide, LLC v. Quinton "Rampage" Jackson,* Superior Court of New Jersey Chancery Division: Burlington County, Docket No.: C-025–15, March 2, 2015.

Chapter 6

References

Marrocco, Stephen. "Randy Couture Spent $500,000 Fighting UFC in Court Expects Tough Road for Georges St-Pierre." MMAJunkie.com, October 21, 2016. https://mmajunkie.com/2016/10/randy-couture-spent-500k-fighting-ufc-in-court-expects-tough-road-for-georges-st-pierre, (last visited February 1, 2019).

Cases and Court Filings

Appellant's Opening Brief, p. 6, *Ken Shamrock, Inc. v. Zuffa, LLC, et al.* In the Supreme Court of the State of Nevada, Case No. 55621, Filed November 5, 2010.
Appellant's Opening Brief, supra at n.7, p. 5, *Ken Shamrock, Inc. v. Zuffa, LLC, et al.* In the Supreme Court of the State of Nevada, Case No. 55621.
Complaint, *B.J. Penn v. Zuffa, LLC, et al.* Clark County District Court, Nevada, July 8, 2004.
Complaint, *Ken Shamrock, Inc. v. Zuffa, LLC, et al.* Eighth Judicial District Court Clark County, Case No.: A561085, April 15, 2008.
Complaint, *Zuffa, LLC v. Randy Couture,* Clark County District Court of Nevada, Case No.: A555208, January 14, 2008.
Declaration of B.J. Penn in support of Motion for Preliminary Injunction attached to Plaintiff's Motion.
Order of Affirmance, *Ken Shamrock, Inc. v. Zuffa, LLC, et al.* In the Supreme Court of the State of Nevada, Case No. 55621, November 18, 2011.

Plaintiff's Motion for Preliminary injunction, *B.J. Penn v. Zuffa, LLC, et al.* Clark County District Court, Nevada, August 31, 2004.

Zuffa, Letter to Randy Couture dated October 11, 2007. Attached to Zuffa's Motion for Preliminary Injunction.

Zuffa's Opposition to Plaintiff's Motion for Preliminary Injunction, at p. 8, *B.J. Penn v. Zuffa, LLC, et al.* September 13, 2004.

Chapter 7

References

Cruz, Jason. "Overeem paid in full for UFC 141." MMAPayout.com, January 4, 2012. http://mmapayout.com/2012/01/overeem-paid-in-full-for-ufc-141/.

Herbertson, Daniel. "Alistair Overeem Splits with Golden Glory, Possibly More to Follow." September 21, 2011. *MMA Fighting.* https://www.mmafighting.com/2011/09/21/alistair-overeem-splits-with-golden-glory-possibly-more-to-foll (last visited January 29, 2019).

"Overeem Cut from Strikeforce." MMAPayout.com, July 29, 2011. http://mmapayout.com/2011/07/overeem-cut-from-strikeforce/ (last visited January 29, 2019).

Smith, Michael David. "Marloes Coenen Among 3 Golden Glory Fighters Released." *MMA Fighting,* August 3, 2011. https://www.mmafighting.com/2011/08/03/marloes-coenen-among-3-golden-glory-fighters-released (Last visited January 29, 2019).

Williams, Alex. "Carry a Flag for Mixed Martial Arts." *New York Times,* September 22, 2010. https://www.nytimes.com/2010/09/23/fashion/23upclose.html.

Cases and Court Filings

Complaint, *Alistair Overeem v. Knockout Investments, et al.* Los Angeles Superior Court, Case No.: BC 473018, November 7, 2011.

Complaint for Breach of Contract, Etc., *Knock Out Investment, et al. v. Alistair Overeem, et al.* Clark County District Court, Case No.: A-11–653894-C.

In the Matter of the Arbitration of Contract Dispute Between Ronda Rousey and Fight Tribe Management, LLC dba Fight Tribe Management, Darin Harvey, California State Athletic Commission Decision of the Arbitrator, March 28, 2014.

Petitioner Fight Tribe Management, LLC's Notice of Petition and Petition to Compel Arbitration and to Appoint an Arbitrator, and Application to Seal Briefing, *Fight Tribe Management, LLC v. Ronda Rousey, et al.* Los Angeles Superior Court, Case No.: BS147674, March 7, 2014.

Chapter 8

References

Cruz, Jason. "Algieri situation presents problem with Ali Act." MMAPayout.com, April 14, 2016. http://mmapayout.com/2016/04/algieri-situation-presents-problem-with-ali-act/ (last visited January 29, 2019).

_____. "Is the Muhammad Ali Act helping protect fighters?" *The White Bronco.* May 2, 2016. http://thewhitebronco.com/2016/05/is-the-muhammad-ali-act-helping-protect-fighters/ (last visited January 29, 2019).

Federal Trade Commission web site on Muhammad Ali Act www.ftc.gov/enforcement/statutes/muhammed-ali-boxing-reform-act.

H.R.44—Muhammad Ali Expansion Act.

H.R. 1832 (106th)—Muhammad Ali Boxing Reform Act.

House Hearing on Mixed Martial Arts, December 8, 2016. https://www.c-span.org/video/
?419534-1/hearing-focuses-mixed-martial-arts-industry.

Marrocco, Stephen. "Randy Couture spent $500,000 fighting UFC in court, expects tough
road for Georges St-Pierre." MMAJunkie.com, October, 21, 2016. https://mmajunkie.
com/2016/10/randy-couture-spent-500k-fighting-ufc-in-court-expects-tough-road-for-
georges-st-pierre (last visited January 29, 2019).

Perspectives on Mixed Martial Arts, November 9, 2017. (U.S. House of Representatives.)
https://energycommerce.house.gov/hearings/perspectives-mixed-martial-arts/.

U.S. House of Representatives—Energy and Commerce Subcommittee on Digital Commerce
& Consumer Protection Hearing entitled "Perspectives on Mixed Martial Arts" Written
Statement of Randy Couture, November 9, 2017.

U.S. House of Representatives—Energy and Commerce Subcommittee on Commerce, Manufacturing & Trade Hearing: "Perspectives on Mixed Martial Arts" November 9, 2017,
Statement of Tracey Lesetar-Smith, Esq. on behalf of Bellator MMA.

U.S. House of Representatives—Energy and Commerce Subcommittee on Commerce, Manufacturing & Trade Hearing: "Perspectives on Mixed Martial Arts" November 9, 2017,
Letter from Jon Fitch, Professional MMA Fighter.

Chapter 9

References

Al-Shautti, Shaun. "Georges St-Pierre's lawyer calls UFC contract 'something out of the 1940s,'
cautions UFC 'won't get away with it forever.'" MMAFighting.com, October 19, 2016.
https://www.mmafighting.com/2016/10/19/13333778/georges-st-pierres-lawyer-calls-ufc-
contract-something-out-of-the (last visited January 29, 2019).

Appellant's Opening Brief, *Wanderlei Silva v. Bob Bennett*, Nevada State Athletic Commission,
In the Supreme Court of the State of Nevada, Case No. 68058, dated September 11, 2015.

Barry, Coral. "Jon Jones refutes claims he used estrogen blockers to mask steroid use." *Metro
UK*, July 19, 2016. http://metro.co.uk/2016/07/19/jon-jones-refutes-claims-he-used-
estrogen-blockers-to-mask-steroid-use-6017056/.

CBC Sports. "Bertuzzi receives conditional charge, probation," December 24, 2004, http://
www.cbc.ca/sports/hockey/bertuzzi-receives-conditional-discharge-probation-1.
477217.

CBC Sports. "In depth: The Bertuzzi Incident: A blow-by-blow account." March 11, 2004,
http://www.cbc.ca/sports/indepth/bertuzzi/timeline/.

CBC Sports Online. "A star player goes offside." February 15, 2005, http://www.cbc.ca/sports/
indepth/bertuzzi/.

Coppinger, Mike, "Brock Lesnar to retire from UFC" February 14, 2017, USA Today, https://
www.usatoday.com/story/sports/ufc/2017/02/14/brock-lesnar-retiring-from-ufc/
97922872/ (Last visited February 1, 2019).

Hale, Andreas, "Brock Lesnar's attorney blames foot cream, eye medication for failed UFC
200 drug test," Yahoo! Sports, October 14, 2016, https://sports.yahoo.com/news/brock-
lesnars-attorney-blames-foot-cream-eye-medication-for-failed-ufc-200-drug-test-
235712317.html.

Hunt, Mark. "If I die fighting, that's fine," PlayersVoice.com, July 4, 2017, https://www.
playersvoice.com.au/mark-hunt-if-i-die-fighting-thats-fine/#ZStRid030yzJccM8.97.

Klein, Jeff Z. "Bertuzzi Lawsuit Settled." *New York Times*, September 5, 2014, p. B12.

NRS 41.660, et seq.

Payne, Marissa. "WWE won't Punish Brock Lesnar for His Failed UFC Drug Tests Because
He Works Part-time." *Washington Post*, July 27, 2016. https://www.washingtonpost.com/
news/early-lead/wp/2016/07/27/wwe-wont-punish-brock-lesnar-for-his-failed-ufc-
drug-tests-because-he-works-part-time/?utm_term=.a7730de8ed2e (Last visited February 1, 2019).

"Reporter Says He Was Removed from UFC 199, 'Banned For Life' after Reporting Brock Lesnar Story." ESPN.com, June 5, 2016. http://www.espn.com/mma/story/_/id/15978217/reporter-says-was-removed-ufc-199-banned-life-reporting-brock-lesnar-story (last visited February 1, 2019).

USADA Athlete Test History database, accessed September 7, 2018 at https://www.usada.org/testing/results/athlete-test-history/.

UFC Anti-Doping Policy. https://ufc.usada.org/wp-content/uploads/UFC-anti-doping-policy-EN.pdf.

UFC Press Release. "UFC Athlete, Brock Lesnar, Receives Sanction for Anti-Doping Policy Violation," January 4, 2017, https://ufc.usada.org/brock-lesnar-receives-doping-sanction/ (last visited February 1, 2019).

"Williams Sought Millions but Pleased with Verdict." Associated Press, March 23, 2005.

Wolohan, John T. "Injured Ballplayer Strikes Out Before the Supreme Court of California." www.athleticbusiness.com, July 2006. https://www.athleticbusiness.com/injured-ballplayer-strikes-out-before-the-supreme-court-of-california.html.

Cases and Court Filings

Avila v. Citrus Community College District, 38 Cal. 4th 148 (2006).

Cheong v. Antablin, 16 Cal.4th 1063, 1075 (1997).

Guernsey, Jim. Email to Bob Bennett dated May 26, 2014, attached as Exhibit A to the Nevada Athletic Commission Findings of Fact, Conclusions of Law, and Order In the Matter of Wanderlei Silva, dated November 24, 2014.

Jacobs v. Adelson, 130 Nev. Adv. Op. 44 (2014).

Knight v. Jewett, 3 Cal 4th 296 (1992).

Motion to Dismiss Plaintiff's Complaint Under NRCP 12(b)(5) and Special Motion to Dismiss Under Nevada's Anti-Slapp Statutes. *Zuffa, LLC d/b/a Ultimate Fighting Championship v. Wanderlei Silva*, Clark County District Court, Case No. A-15–722258-C, October 2, 2015.

Nevada Athletic Commission. "In the Matter of Wanderlei Silva, Findings of Fact, Conclusions of Law and Order," dated September 23, 2014.

Notice of Appeal, *Wanderlei Silva vs. Bob Bennett*. Nevada State Athletic Commission, In the Supreme Court of the State of Nevada, No. 685058, dated August 20, 2015.

Order re: Petition for Judicial Review, *Wanderlei Silva vs. Bob Bennett*. Nevada State Athletic Commission, District Court Clark County, Nevada, Case No. A-14–710453-J, dated January 15, 2015.

Petitioner's Memorandum of Points and Authorities, *Wanderlei Silva v. Bob Bennett*. Nevada State Athletic Commission, District Court Clark County, Nevada, Case No. A-14–71-453-J, dated January 16, 2015.

Plaintiff Mark Hunt's First Amended Complaint ("Hunt FAC"), In the United States District Court for the District of Nevada, Case 2:17-cv-00085-JAD-CWH, June 1, 2017.

Statement of Claim. *Moore v. Bertuzzi* (Ont. Super. Ct. Feb. 14, 2006), *see also*, 61 Me. L. Rev. 205. Rewriting hockey's unwritten rules: MOORE V. BERTUZZI.

Zuffa, LLC d/b/a Ultimate Fighting Championship v. Wanderlei Silva. Clark County District Court, Case No. A-15–722258-C, filed July 28, 2015.

Chapter 10

References

Deposition of Dana White, Volume 2, taken on August 9, 2017.

Deposition of Dana White, Volume 3 of 3 taken on August 10, 2017.

Expert report of Roger Blair in *Cung Le, et al. v. Zuffa, LLC*, February 16, 2018.

Expert report of Hal Singer, Ph.D. in *Cung Le, et al. v. Zuffa, LLC*, Filed February 16, 2018.

Expert Report of Andrew Zimbalist in *Cung Le, et al. v. Zuffa, LLC*, Filed February 16, 2018.

United States Department of Justice web site, https://www.justice.gov/atr/competition-and-monopoly-single-firm-conduct-under-section-2-sherman-act-chapter-1.

Cases and Court Filings

Defendant Zuffa, LLC's Motion for Summary Judgment, at p. 16, *Le, et al. v. Zuffa, LLC*, Case No.: 2:15-cv-01045-RFB-PAL, United States District Court for the District of Nevada, July 30, 2018.

Defendant Zuffa, LLC's Consolidated Notice of Motion and Motion to Dismiss Plaintiffs' Complaints, p. 19, *Le, et al. v. Zuffa, LLC*. Case No. 5:14-cv-05484 EJD, United States District Court of California–San Jose Division, February 27, 2015.

Golden Boy Promotions, LLC, et al. v. Alan Haymon, et al. Case No.: CV15–3378-JFW, January 26, 2017.

Memorandum and Order, p. 4, *CAA Sports, LLC v. Ben Dogra*, Case No.: 4:18-cv-01887-SNLJ United States District Court Eastern District of Missouri, Eastern Division, December 20, 2018.

Monsanto Co. v. Spray-Rite Service Corp., 465 U.S. 752, 764 (1984).

NCAA v. Board of Regents of Univ. of Oklahoma, 468 U.S. 85, 109 (1984).

Non-Party Bellator Sport Worldwide, LLC's Notice of Motion and Motion to Quash or Modify Subpoenas, In re Subpoena of Bellator Sport Worldwide, LLC, U.S. District Court for the Central District of California, Case No.: 2:17-mc-0016, February 22, 2017.

Nonparties Matt Hume and Group One Holdings PTE Ltd. Opposition to Motion to Compel, U.S. District Court of Washington, Case No. 2:17-mc-0074 RSL, August 4, 2017.

Order on Bellator's Motion to Quash or Modify Subpoenas and Plaintiff's Motion to Compel Documents Responsive to Plaintiffs' Subpoena, Case No.: 2:15-cv-010405-RFB-PAL, June 13, 2017.

Order, *Le, et al. vs. Zuffa, LLC*, United States District Court of Nevada, October 19, 2016.

Order re Sanctions, *Nevro Crop v. Boston Scientific Corporation, et al.* Case No.: 16-cv-06830-VC, United States District Court of the Northern District of California, May 8, 2018.

Plaintiffs' Motion for Class Certification, p. 26, *Le, et al. v. Zuffa, LLC*, Case No.: 2:15-cv-01045-RFB-PAL, United States District Court for the District of Nevada, February 16, 2018.

Plaintiffs' Motion to Compel Deposition and Production of Documents by Third Party Matt Hume and Motion for Sanctions, In re Subpoena of Matt Hume, U.S. District Court of Western Washington, Case No. 2:17-mc-0074 RSL, July 19, 2017.

Plaintiffs' Opposition to Defendant Zuffa, LLC's Motion to Seal Plaintiffs' Opposition to Zuffa, LLC's Motion for Summary Judgment and Related Materials, *Le, et al. v. Zuffa, LLC*, Case No.: 2:15-cv-01045-RFB(PAL), August 13, 2013.

Plaintiffs' Opposition to Defendant Zuffa LLC's Motion to Seal Zuffa LLC's Motion for Summary Judgment and Related Materials, p. 6, *Le, et al. v. Zuffa, LLC*, Case No.: 2:15-cv-01045-RFB(PAL), United States District Court of Nevada, August 13, 2018.

Plaintiffs' Opposition to Zuffa's Motion for Summary Judgment, *Le, et al. v. Zuffa, LLC, et al.* Case No.: 2:15-cv-01045-RFB-PAL, United States District Court for the District of Nevada, September 21, 2018.

Zuffa, LLC's Opposition to Plaintiffs' Motion for Class Certification, *Le, et al. v. Zuffa, LLC*, Case No.: 2:15-cv-01045-RFB-PAL, United States District Court for the District of Nevada, April 6, 2018.

Chapter 11

References

Sheinin, Dave. "D.C. Group Led by Russ Ramsey Set to Launch New Mixed Martial Arts League." *The Washington Post*, April 19, 2017. www.washingtonpost.com, https://www.washingtonpost.com/sports/boxing/dc-group-led-by-russ-ramsey-set-to-launch-new-mixed-martial-arts-league/2017/04/18/68e01bda-2481-11e7-b503-9d616bd5a305_story.html?utm_term=.afa38996be29.

Cases and Court Filings

Answer; Counterclaim; and Third-Party Complaint, *MMAWC, LLC v. Shawn Wright, et al.* Clark County District Court of Nevada, October 6, 2015.

Complaint and Demand for Jury Trial, United States District Court of Nevada, *WSOF Asia v. MMAWC, LLC, et al.* Case No.: 2:15-cv-02065, October 26, 2015.

Complaint, *MMAWC, LLC v. Shawn Wright, et al.* Clark County District Court of Nevada Case No.: A-15-724474-B, September 11, 2015.

Complaint, *Zion Wood Obi Wan Trust, et al. v. MMAWC, LLC d/b/a World Series of Fighting, et al.* District Court of Clark County, Nevada, Case No.: A-17-764118-C, November 3, 2017.

First Amended Complaint, United States District Court of Nevada, *MMAWC, LLC d/b/a World Series of Fighting vs. Shawn Wright, Vince Hesser, et al.* Case No.: 2:15-cv-02065, October 29, 2015.

Chapter 12

References

Botter, Jeremy. "UFC Attorney Says Fans Who Stream UFC PPVs Are Not Actually Fans at All." *Bleacher Report*, March 15, 2012, https://bleacherreport.com/articles/1106577-ufc-attorney-says-fans-who-stream-ufc-ppvs-are-not-actually-fans-at-all (last visited February 1, 2019).

Brookhouse, Brent. "UFC's DMCA copyright claim on St. Pierre vs. Diaz 'Decimal Controversy' video is questionable at best." BloodyElbow.com, March 28, 2013. https://www.bloodyelbow.com/2013/3/28/4156460/ufc-dcma-copyright-georges-st-pierre-gsp-nick-diaz-decimal-weigh-in (last visited January 30, 2019).

Fowlkes, Ben, and Danny Downes, "Why Is the UFC Going After Its Own Fans on Social Media—Again?" MMAJunkie.com, September 2, 2018. https://mmajunkie.com/2018/09/why-ufc-attacks-fans-for-copyright-social-media

Hearing on "Piracy of Live Sports Broadcasting Over the Internet" Before the United States House of Representatives Committee on the Judiciary Statement of Lorenzo J. Fertitta, Chairman and Chief Executive Officer Zuffa, LLC / Ultimate Fighting Championship. December 16, 2009, http://judiciary.house.gov/_files/hearings/pdf/Fertitta091216.pdf.

Masnick, Mike. "NASCAR Abuses DMCA To Try To Delete Fan Videos of Daytona Crash." Techdirt.com, February 25, 2013. https://www.techdirt.com/articles/20130224/22411222089/nascar-abuses-dmca-to-try-to-delete-fan-videos-daytona-crash.shtml (Last visited February 1, 2019).

National Basketball Association v. Motorola, Inc., 105 F.3d 841 (2nd Cir. 1997).

17. U.S.C. sec 512(c)(3), 17 U.S.C. 512(c)(1)

_____. "UFC Makes the Awful Decision to Sue Some of Its Biggest Fans." Techdirt.com, March 22, 2012. https://www.techdirt.com/articles/20120320/10225718173/ufc-makes-awful-decision-to-sue-some-its-biggest-fans.shtml (Last visited February 1, 2019).

Tompkins, Al. "Daytona crash video tests fair use, copyright for fans and journalists." Poynter.org, February 24, 2013, https://www.poynter.org/news/daytona-crash-video-tests-fair-use-copyright-fans-and-journalists.

UFC. Files Copyright Infringement Lawsuit Against Justin.tv, January 22, 2011, www.torrentfreak.com, https://torrentfreak.com/ufc-files-copyright-infringement-lawsuit-against-justin-tv-110122/ (last visited January 30, 2019).

U.S. Copyright Act.

YouTube Answer page https://support.google.com/youtube/answer/2807684.

Cases and Court Filings

Campbell v. Acuff-Rose Music, Inc., 510 U.S. 569 (1994).

Complaint, *Zuffa, LLC v. Justin.tv,* United States District Court, District of Nevada, Case 2:11-cv-00114-RLH-VCF, January 21, 2011.

Harper & Row, Publishers, Inc., et al. v. Nation Enterprises, et al. 471 U.S. 539 (1985).

Le v. Zuffa, United States District Court of Nevada, Case No.: 2–15:-cv-01045-RFB-PAL.

Lenz v. Universal Music Corp., 801 F.3d 1126 (2015).

Motion to Dismiss Amended Complaint, *Zuffa, LLC v. Justin.tv, Inc.,* Case No. 2:11-cv09914-RLH-LRL, September 16, 2011.

Opinion and Order, *David Adjmi v. DLT Entertainment, Ltd.,* 14-Civ. 568, United States District Court S.D.N.Y., March 31, 2015.

Order, *Zuffa, LLC v. Justin.tv, Inc.,* Case No. 2:11-cv09914-RLH-LRL, March 8, 2012.

Philip D. Murphy, Governor of New Jersey, et al. v. National Collegiate Athletic Association, et al. 584 U.S. (2018).

Chapter 13

Cases and Court Filings

Complaint, *International Fight League v. Zuffa, LLC, et al.* United States District Court S.D.N.Y., Civil Action 06 CV 0880, February 3, 2006. Notably, the UFC filed a lawsuit in Nevada one day earlier.

Complaint, *Nobuyuki Sakakibara, et al. v. Pride FC Worldwide Holdings, LLC, et al.* Case 2:08-cv-00418-HDM-RJJ, April 2, 2008.

Complaint, *Zuffa, LLC v. International Fight League, Inc., et al.* District Court of Clark County, Nevada, Case No.: A516841, February 2, 2006.

Opposition to Motion for Preliminary Injunction, *Zuffa, LLC v. Couture, et al.* District Court of Clark County, Nevada, Case No.: A555208, February 19, 2008.

Order Granting Preliminary Injunction, *Zuffa, LLC v. Couture, et al.* District Court of Clark County, Nevada, Case No.: A555208, February 29, 2008.

Plaintiff's Motion for Preliminary Injunction, Zuffa, LLC v. Couture, et al. District Court of Clark County, Nevada, Case No.: A555208, February 1, 2008.

Plaintiff's Original Petition for Declaratory Judgment, HDNet MMA 2008, LLC v. Zuffa, LLC, In the District Court of Dallas Texas, February 13, 2008.

Reporter's Transcript of Proceedings, *Zuffa, LLC v. International Fight League, Inc., et al.* Clark County District Court, Case No.: A516841.

Spectrum Gaming Group, LLC, DSE Investigation Overview, Undated.

Chapter 14

References

New York State Executive Law §632-a.

Cases and Court Filings

Amended Verified Complaint, Michael Chiesa vs. Conor McGregor, et al. Index No.: 518314–2018E, December 20, 2018.

Complaint for Wrongful Termination Based on Public Policy ("Light Complaint"), Zachery Light v. Bellator Worldwide Sport, BC 621583, Filed May 24, 2016.

Cross-Complaint of Bellator Sport Worldwide, LLC, Light Complaint filed in California Los Angeles Superior Court on July 12, 2016.

Defendant Conor McGregor, et al. Memorandum of Law in Support of Their Motion to Dismiss., *Michael Chiesa v. Conor McGregor, et al.* Supreme Court of the State of New York, County of Kings, Index No. 518314–2018E, November 30, 2018.

First Amended Complaint, *William Pegg vs. Connor McGregor, et al.* District Court of Clark County, Nevada, Case No. A-17–753121-C, April 26, 2018.

Motion for an Order Striking Defendant, Conor McGregor's Answer, *Pegg v. McGregor, et al.* United States District Court for Nevada, Southern Division, October 19, 2018.

Notice of Removal by Defendant, *William Pegg v. Conor McGregor, et al.* District Court of Clark County, Nevada, Case No. A-17–753121-C, dated April 26, 2018.

Offer of Judgment, *William Pegg v. Conor McGregor, et al.* District Court of Clark County, Nevada, Case No. A-17–753121-C, dated April 10, 2018.

Order, *Pegg v. McGregor, et al.* United States District Court of Nevada, Case No.: 2:18-cv-000763-RFB-NJK, October 22, 2018.

Order, *Pegg v. McGregor, et al,* United States District Court of Nevada, Case No. 2:18-cv-000763-RFB-NJK, Dkt. 43, dated October 29, 2018.

Order, *William Pegg v. Conor McGregor, et al.* District Court of Clark County, Nevada, Case No. A-17–753121-C, dated August 22, 2018.

Verified Complaint, *Michael Chiesa v. Conor McGregor, et al.* Supreme Court of the State of New York, County of Kings, Index No. 518314/2018, September 10, 2018.

Chapter 15

References

"Korean MMA Fighter Indicted for Taking Bribes In Match-Fixing Scam." *The Korea Herald,* August 14, 2017. http://www.koreaherald.com/view.php?ud=20170814000556 (last visited January 30, 2019).

Index